MAKING
MONEY

MAKING
MONEY

An Insider's Perspective on Finance, Politics, and Canada's Central Bank

John Crow

wiley.com

John Wiley & Sons Canada, Ltd
22 Worcester Road
Etobicoke, Ontario
M9W 1L1

National Library of Canada Cataloguing in Publication

Crow, John W.
    Making money : an insider's perspective on finance, politics, and Canada's Central Bank / John W. Crow.

Includes index.
ISBN 0-470-83180-4

    1. Bank of Canada--History. 2. Monetary policy--Canada--History--20th century. I. Title.

HG1552.C76A3 2002   332.1'1'0971   C2002-904395-6

Production Credits
Cover & interior text design: Interrobang Graphic Design Inc.
Printer: Tri-Graphic Printing Ltd.

Printed in Canada
10 9 8 7 6 5 4 3 2 1

CONTENTS

୧୨

ACKNOWLEDGEMENTS

જી

Writing a book of this sort calls for more than a few solitary hours. But it was not done in a vacuum. In particular, Benjamin Friedman of Harvard University insisted to me years ago, brushing aside my protests, that there was something useful to produce along these lines.

Naturally, I owe a great deal over many years to all kinds of people at the Bank of Canada—more than I can even begin to catalogue here. Let me, then, limit myself to acknowledging their very recent help in testing and clarifying ideas while I have been writing up what I may have learned from them in the first place. Kevin Clinton supplied some valuable thoughts on the Bank's intellectual journey in the 1970s and 1980s that helped me to get going. Charles Freedman, Clyde Goodlet, and Serge Vachon generously combined to deliver a whole bunch of considered comments on the financial stability matters discussed in Chapter 4. Any errors that have stayed are not theirs. The same, more fully still, applies to John Murray, who patiently, diligently, and comprehensively supplied me with running commentary, chapter by chapter, as the book progressed—and cheerfully agreed or disagreed, always with his good reasons why, when and as he saw fit.

Outside the Bank, I am indebted to Grant Reuber for a thought-provoking read-through when the book was in its latter stages but not too late to change; to Jack Lawrence for his pointed comments on the fiscal chapter and his support generally; and also to Lily Fidelj, my assistant at Lawrence & Company Inc., who unstintingly helped me progress as fast and as accurately as I could from draft to draft.

When finally getting started, I feared that I would need to displace myself to Ottawa rather a lot if I was to make proper use of the Bank of Canada's excellent library. I made great use of it but was able to at a distance. This was thanks in part to the wonders of electronics but also to the readiness of the Bank's Toronto Agency to act as my mailbox. More particularly, it was because of the legendary efficiency of library staff—especially Lisette Lacroix, who proved time and again most prompt and ingenious at solving the riddles posed her in the interests of my narrative accuracy.

Finally, and with a brevity that belies its importance, my thanks go to my wife, Ruth, for her good-tempered encouragement and as well for her skill not only in deciphering my left-handed script, but also, as always, in making words say what I wanted them to.

FOREWORD

&

John Crow was governor of the Bank of Canada from 1987 to 1994, the period in which the inflation targeting approach to monetary policy was developed and first put in place in Canada, at a time when it was gaining ground around the world. So the reader naturally expects a book that focuses on, propounds, and defends inflation targeting.

Not at all. This is a far broader and more interesting book about central banking, one which not only expresses serious doubts about the Canadian approach to inflation targeting, but also discusses the choice of exchange rate regime, the role of the central bank as lender of last resort in the financial system, the interactions of fiscal and monetary policy, Canada's international role, and the future—including a brief reference to the possibility of dollarization in Canada.

And not only that. The adjective most often used to describe the art of central banking is "arcane." John Crow revels in demystifying the art, and in describing in straightforward terms complicated issues that others would prefer to complicate further. Crow shows a lively appreciation for the political context in which he and his predecessors had to operate, and a nice turn of phrase in describing some of the people he encountered while at the Bank of Canada. So the book is not only interesting, it is a very good read.

Making Money is of course written from the Canadian perspective—that of a medium-sized very open economy with an open capital account, living next to the world's most powerful economy and capital markets. That constrains Canada's policy choices. It also forces Canadians to reflect on international economic issues to a much greater extent than American economists have to. This is surely one of the reasons so many of the best international economists, including Robert Mundell, have been Canadian. This international perspective thoroughly informs the book and should enhance its interest for readers in all countries for which the international dimension of policy is critical—and that means virtually all countries.

Let me preview and comment on three themes: the choice of exchange rate regime; monetary-fiscal policy coordination; and the main theme of the book—inflation targeting, price stability, and the role of the central bank.

On the choice of exchange rate regime, Crow gives a convincing account of why Canada has so long operated with a flexible rate, and of the difficulties that the pegged rate between 1962 and 1970 caused for monetary policy. He remarks in passing that if the exchange rate is flexible, it is not surprising or unusual that it should move. He gives short shrift to the view that the competitive pressures that would have been brought to bear on Canadian industry if the exchange rate against the US dollar had been fixed would have led to significantly better productivity performance. He discusses the development, weaknesses, and later downplaying of the monetary conditions index as an indicator of monetary policy. He concludes that the central bank should seek to maintain the purchasing power of money in terms of goods rather than in terms of foreign exchange—that is, it should target the inflation rate (or price level) rather than the exchange rate.

Crow does not venture any grand thesis on monetary-fiscal policy coordination, discussed in Chapter 9. Rather he argues pragmatically that "this is difficult, slippery terrain that needs to be negotiated point by point." And he points out that "if you have a central bank that is in some sense independent, it is almost inevitably going to be at some stage a disappointment to a fiscal authority." The implicit view that emerges is that monetary policy should focus on its inflation or price level targets, avoid making any explicit deals on interest rate cuts in exchange for fiscal consolidation, and leave it to the fiscal authorities to manage fiscal policy. Most modern central bankers have reached a similar conclusion. Most feel free to press continuously for stronger fiscal policies, but Crow introduces a cautionary note when he says he avoided talking about the need for a stronger fiscal policy, lest he be interpreted as offering a deal to cut interest rates in exchange for fiscal tightening.

Readers will probably be most intrigued by Crow's dissatisfaction with Canada's present inflation targeting framework for monetary policy. He believes there is too much uncritical acceptance of inflation targets, certainly in Canada, and that it is important to choose the right numerical targets, and important that the targets be explained and justified. He also believes that the Canadian government has left its dominant role in the setting of inflation targets deliberately opaque.

Crow is uneasy with the view that inflation targets should ultimately be decided by the government. This is sometimes expressed as a recommendation that a central bank should not have goal independence, but should have instrument independence. He says that this reduces the central bank to a mere technical agency of the government, and that by leaving the ultimate choice of inflation target to the government, this allocation of responsibilities fails to deal with the inflationary bias of monetary policy that led in the first place to the need for central bank independence. Indeed, he appears to believe that the Bank of Canada is less independent now than it was before the inflation targeting regime was implemented, and certainly less independent than it should be. His views on this point are influenced by the 1961 conflict between the central bank and the government, which led to Governor Coyne's resignation and the institution a year later of a pegged exchange rate regime, and by his own discussions at the end of his term with Finance Minister Paul Martin.

The issue turns on how much power should be devolved to the central bank, and how precise its charge should be. In some places Crow seems to prefer that the central bank be mandated to secure "price stability" and that the interpretation of that mandate be left to the central bank. In others he argues that if the central bank has been given a price stability mandate, it should sign off on the choice of inflation target—in essence certifying that it agrees the target inflation range is consistent with the price stability mandate—even if the ultimate numerical targets are set by the government. The latter arrangement is in effect in place, since the governor can always resign if he dislikes the target—and that would be costly for the government. I believe that the democratic legitimacy of an independent central bank is a real issue, and that it is enhanced by giving the government the responsibility for the political choice of target inflation rate. It would be further enhanced by the government's accepting Crow's recommendation that it explain its choice of target and accept responsibility for the decision. In any case, I see no problem in the central bank being regarded as a technical agency of the government—that is just another way of saying that it has a well-defined mandate, albeit an exceptionally important one.

It is clear from the book that Crow regards the continuation of the 1 to 3 percent target inflation range in Canada as a mistake. At a minimum, he argues, the government should have explained in far more detail why it chose this range. But the reader can also discern that he would have preferred that the range be moved down a bit, closer to what he regards as an inflation range consistent with price stability.

A quiet note of pessimism underlies much of Chapter 11, "Financial Futures." "In the end," Crow says, "countries get the institutions they deserve and the monetary standard they deserve." And he warns that "in our globalized world, national currencies survive less by governmental fiat and more on their merits." This, he hopes, will lead the Canadian government to give the central bank genuine independence, including a charter to take price stability seriously.

Whether or not the reader agrees with this view, by the end of the book he or she will have been forced to wrestle with the basic issues of monetary policy in the modern world, by someone who has thought clearly and deeply about the issues, who expresses himself simply and cogently, and who makes an impressive case for his views.

Stanley Fischer

Vice Chairman, Citigroup, and President, Citigroup International
Formerly First Deputy Managing Director, IMF; Killian Professor
and Head of Department of Economics, MIT; and Chief Economist,
World Bank.

PREFACE

&

At the core of any central bank is a governmental licence to print money—an alchemy of such general wonder and fascination that there is no shortage of running commentary. Even in the calmest times, hardly a day goes by, in Canada or elsewhere, without media argument or exhortation of some kind. As for book-length examinations of these matters, this is hardly a first. Where it is unusual, and should be useful, is in the fact that it is commentary from someone who was on the inside of a central bank and actually did what most people talk about.

Does the Bank of Canada matter? Let me just note that what it does—through its impact on interest rates and the exchange rate, through money, through credit, and nowadays even through the stock market—has a profound impact on Canada's economy. So it is worth getting the story straight as to what the institution does, what it should be doing, and under what auspices it should be doing it.

While considerable space is devoted to the story of Canadian money, the Bank of Canada, and Canada's monetary policy, this book is not a narrative history; nor is it confined to Canadian experience. Rather, it is a memoir and an account from someone who spent 21 years there (from 1973 to 1994), occupied positions from researcher through to governor, and was deeply involved in all aspects of the Bank's policies. The experience of those 21 years figures centrally in what I have to say, but I have also reached back and forward in time in order to give a full account of the issues.

As for those issues, I conceived this as a series of linked personal accounts of the range of responsibilities that go into central banking and, in particular, into monetary policy. My hope has been to provide, through my perspective, a realistic picture that will inform Canadians and more generally those everywhere who are interested in the vital policy questions at the heart of central banking. This book portrays not only the life and institutional politics of an influential and involved central monetary institution, but also the main challenges any nation faces in pursuing a credible and worthwhile monetary policy in an open, and increasingly global, financial and economic environment.

PART I

୫୦୦

Domestic Bank

CHAPTER 1

ꙮ

A Question
of Purpose

What are central banks supposed to do? A clearly articulated, commonly accepted sense of purpose is to be prized in policy. This applies at least as much to central banking as to any other public activity. However, nailing down what central banks should be answerable for has from their very beginnings proved to be no simple task.

When the first central banks were set up, starting back in the seventeenth century, they were seen far more as special kinds of commercial banks and hardly at all as public policy institutions. They were special because they had been given franchises to act as the main banker of their governments. Also included in the deal would be privileges regarding the right to issue banknotes. In return, these well-connected bodies were expected to invest heavily in government debt. Not surprisingly, central banks became especially popular creatures to set up when government finances were burdened by the demands of war. At the same time, direct involvement of government in their affairs also tended to grow, even if the banks stayed privately owned.

In the more peaceful conditions that prevailed in the nineteenth century following the Napoleonic Wars, central banks, whatever their particular origins, inevitably came to concentrate on matters of broad national financial stability. While inflation was not an issue, since currencies were bound to gold under the generally unquestioned gold standard, the general stability of the financial system was not assured. And in those relatively freewheeling times, when governments were small and broad policies of national economic and financial management did not exist, central banks found themselves increasingly cast as experienced managers of the periodic financial crises that erupted. Besides acting as bankers for governments, they also increasingly did the same for commercial banks, from which it was a fairly short step to becoming lender of last resort to commercial banks when there was a run from bank deposits into the banknotes issued by the central bank. Taking on this backstopping role meant that a central bank also came under pressure to limit any commercial banking that it was undertaking for its own account, thereby becoming still more identified with government.

The other kind of crisis in which central banks became increasingly involved was one where the locus was external—showing up in a drain from a nation's gold reserves. To help staunch the outflow, a central bank could cut back on the credit it was supplying domestically. This would squeeze commercial banks' reserves, put some upward pressure on market interest rates, thereby encourage the inflow of interest-sensitive funds from abroad, and curb the decline in the gold stock. Such activities also led to a beginning of international financial cooperation through a growing network of arrangements among central banks to mitigate the impact of gold movements.

The upheavals from the 1914–18 war provoked further, much wider challenges. Gold reserves seemed increasingly to be poorly distributed among the various financial centres and generally insufficient in size. This was especially so as the 1920s wore on, with a weakened Europe and the emergence of the United States as a world economic and financial power and destination for international wealth. With the onset and international spread of financial and economic crises from the late 1920s (preceded by an extraordinary financial and economic boom in the United States), the gold standard collapsed starting with Britain's withdrawal in 1931, and national currencies came to float, even if awkwardly, against each other. Once countries severed their automatic currency link to gold, they were increasingly obliged to develop their own nationally oriented monetary frameworks, whether possessing central banks or not. Doing this in an activist way was further spurred by the economic hardships of the 1930s and the pressure for broad government policies—especially what came to be known as Keynesian policies to stimulate demand—to improve matters in any way such policies could. This brings us to Canada's situation.

In 1944, when Lord Keynes was in Ottawa for discussions regarding the settlement of British wartime debts, he also found the time to arrange a function marking the 250th anniversary of the Bank of England, of which he was a director. As might befit so many years of central banking history, the great man spoke for well over two hours—reportedly without notes—but probably did not spend much time at all on the Bank of England's beginnings. In contrast, the Bank of Canada was of extremely recent vintage, having been founded only 10 years earlier. Furthermore, what its creators thought it should do, and how they communicated that purpose through legislation, remains even today of more than archival interest.

Founding Thoughts

The idea of our own central bank had been in the Canadian air since at least the early 1920s, but it had not gathered momentum in either political or academic circles. No consensus existed among those with thoughts on such things as to why a central bank was needed, especially since the government already had powers under the *Finance Act* both to issue banknotes and to lend to banks. Adding to the uncertainty and doubt was the fact that the whole process and purpose of money creation was difficult to comprehend. And no group in Canada could discuss it from experience.

Nevertheless, in the early 1930s Prime Minister R.B. Bennett decided to move. His own thoughts on central banking seem to have been oriented more to matters of financial management than to broad economic policy. As he declared on one often-quoted occasion:

I made up my mind ... that this country was going to have
a central bank because there must be some financial institution that can, with authority, do business for the whole
of the Dominion with other nations of the world.[1]

What apparently concerned him in this regard was that in its international financial dealings, Canada did not have any mechanism
for settling payments balances directly with overseas countries but
had to do this indirectly through New York.

Still, no doubt his timing at least was influenced by the onset
of the Depression, and the ensuing debate certainly supplied views
as to how a central bank could improve economic conditions generally above and beyond any considerations as to how international payments might be better made. As Premier John Bracken of
Manitoba, for example, put it in his submission to the Royal Commission on Banking and Currency in Canada (the Macmillan commission), which had been established in 1933:

We believe that there should be provided machinery to
make possible a deliberate policy of publicly controlled
credit in Canada.... That body, a central bank, should guide
and regulate in matters of credit policies, and its first oblig-
ation should be to the public rather than private welfare.[2]

What exactly he meant, other than that he was thinking big, is difficult to say. Perhaps he hoped that the central bank should be
some kind of overarching chartered bank. In any event, note that
his emphasis was on the supply of credit, not on the regulation of
monetary expansion. This well reflected the mood of the times,
fuelled (especially in Western Canada) by then-popular Social Credit theories of financial management, as well as by deteriorating economic conditions across the nation and a widely held conviction
that chartered banks were too powerful and too niggardly in their
lending. The more things change...

[1] See, for example, Watts, 1993.
[2] Quoted in Fullerton, 1986.

The chair of the commission, the eminent British jurist Lord Macmillan, was known to be a proponent of a central bank when he was invited by the Canadian government to take on the task. Probably he already had a blueprint. The Bank of England, which also supplied staff to the commission, had been gathering experience for some time in helping to set up central banks in other parts of the Commonwealth. If he did have something in his pocket, and since he had the support and encouragement of the Canadian government, it is not so surprising that he was able to deliver a positive commission report in the remarkably short space of seven weeks after his arrival in Canada, in August 1933.

Even so, the commission's recommendation to proceed came through by only the slightest of margins—three to two. And of the three Canadians on the commission, two dissented. Both were chartered bankers, and their opposition reflected the broad concern of Canadian bankers regarding the powers that this new central bank might have over chartered bank activities, when they were basically content with the status quo. Still, the banking fraternity was not totally monolithic on the issue. An early proponent of a central bank, though not a member of the commission, was Graham Towers—later the first Governor (1934–55) but then a senior officer of the Royal Bank. With the commission's groundwork accomplished, legislation establishing the Bank of Canada was speedily passed and received royal assent in June 1934.

I shall deal with other important provisions of the *Bank of Canada Act*, particularly those relating to independence and accountability, in later chapters. Here, my focus is what it tells us about what the Bank of Canada should aim for through its broad powers of monetary control and expansion—in short, through monetary policy. These policy provisions are set out in the preamble, which manages to say a lot and rather little at the same time. Indeed, it says little precisely because it says so much, and in broad terms that have no simple definition. This was surely no accident. As Robert Bryce notes in his history of the Department of Finance, where he gives author's credit for the preamble to Clifford Clark, the deputy finance minister and a guiding spirit in the Bank's creation, it is "artfully worded." This art extends beyond the fact that the body is a single sentence of fully 80 words, without even a semicolon. But given the array of potential purposes that it aimed to convey, this syntactical seamlessness did not hurt.

> Whereas it is desirable to establish a central bank in Canada to regulate credit and currency in the best interests of the economic life of the nation, to control and protect the external value of the national monetary unit and to mitigate by its influence fluctuations in the general level of production, trade, prices and employment, so far as may be possible within the scope of monetary action, and generally to promote the economic and financial welfare of the Dominion.

The preamble was, in the best sense of the term, a diplomatic or political answer to an important, and at that time directly debatable, public policy question: What is Canada's central bank supposed to achieve? In that political sense, either by not answering the question or perhaps by giving a menu of general answers to the same question, it has proved its worth by surviving unchanged (except for the substitution of "Canada" for "the Dominion") up to the present time. But given the Bank of Canada's prominence in national economic and financial affairs, the simple question still deserves a more direct answer than is available in its statutes. That is one of the goals of this book.

While I do not believe that the preamble has turned out to be a sufficiently clear statement of central bank purpose, I gained a fuller appreciation of its considerable subtleties when taking its measure before parliamentary committees. Just as well then that I knew it by heart. Two clauses in particular could be relied on to attract parliamentarians' attention.

One was the injunction on the Bank to "control and protect the external value of the national monetary unit." Did this not imply, some would argue, that the Bank should take a view as to the appropriate value of the currency and, presumably, do something about it? Since in my time as governor the Canadian dollar was tending to appreciate, this line of argument was invariably focused on concern that the currency was too strong and that monetary policy should be applied, through lower interest rates, to bring it down. (In recent years, the more general concern has been its weakness rather than its strength against its US counterpart, though I have not heard anyone argue that interest rates should be raised to push it up.)

My broad response was to point out that since Canada had a long-established, government-mandated, floating exchange rate regime, the Bank would, at least for that reason, be ill-advised to take a strong view as to what the appropriate external value of the currency, in and of itself, should be. With only brief interruptions—during and immediately after World War II, and from 1962 to 1970—we had operated under a flexible exchange rate system since going off the gold standard right after Britain in 1931, and a floating exchange rate could almost by definition be expected to move around. So it would be a contradiction of declared policy for the Bank to try to hold it at any particular level. Rather, we would always have to look at the economic impact of the exchange rate in the broader context of our overall monetary policy stance— namely, whether we were trying to speed up or slow down spending in Canada by adding more or less bank liquidity to the financial system. As for the actual words that the preamble had used to describe what it wanted the Bank to do regarding the currency, I argued that the best way for monetary policy to "protect" its external value was through consistently protecting its internal value— that is, by avoiding inflation.

The second point that was often pressed related to our domestic responsibilities. Was the Bank living up to its requirement "to mitigate by its influence fluctuations in the general level of production, trade, prices, and employment"? There, I tended to emphasize the preamble's powerful qualifying clause, "so far as may be possible through the scope of monetary action," and tried to engage the changing cast of members of Parliament who were assigned to the House Committee on Finance in a discussion as to what that meant. My emphasis aimed to show that the real question to be dealt with was not whether all such fluctuations should be avoided, but rather what kinds of approaches to monetary policy would give the Bank the best chance of avoiding them, bearing in mind its particular influence and powers. It seemed to me that a policy aimed at sustaining inflation was more likely to encourage such fluctuations than to mitigate them, and that no country had become rich through inflationary policies. This view was evidently a source of controversy in committee hearings, but no one actually pressed for more inflation—just for lower interest rates. My position was that interest rates would come down, and stay down, once expectations of inflation had been brought down as well. It was the Bank of Canada's job to persuade people to expect less inflation by the actions it took to slow the pace of monetary expansion and by making sure they knew the Bank intended to do that.

Surprisingly, perhaps, the meaning of the preamble's first policy injunction, the call to "regulate credit and currency in the best interests of the economic life of the nation," never became a matter of inquiry or debate while I was governor. Possibly it had been so in much earlier years when Graham Towers was in charge. Then, it could have been exploited by those of a Social Credit persuasion, since at that time they had significant parliamentary representation. But by my term (1987–94), that particular clause was probably seen as too impossibly vague for a member of Parliament to get his or her teeth into and score a point or two. The possibility of temporary direct controls on credit was broached in the Finance Committee from time to time. But whatever their merits in particular situations, controls were not something the Bank of Canada had any authority to introduce, and I avoided being enthusiastic about them lest anyone thought that they could be more than a Band-Aid.

A Bitter Clash, But Not About Objectives

After the founding debate, general interest in the purposes of monetary policy stayed dormant for more than 20 years. Interest rates remained very low in the depressed conditions of the 1930s, and wartime brought direct financial controls of all kinds. But Canadian monetary policy began to be more active in the 1950s, as financial markets, and the market economy generally, became better established with the dismantling of the controls introduced in World War II.

Then, Bank of Canada actions came to be more regularly debated, and indeed turned incandescently controversial during the term of the second governor, James Coyne (1955–61). However, in the intense and complex dispute that erupted at the end of the 1950s between Coyne and the government of the day under Prime Minister John Diefenbaker together with Finance Minister Donald Fleming, the central issue soon became not what monetary policy was actually supposed to do and why, but rather the nature of the Bank's independence and accountability. How "independent" the Bank should be is surely linked to what it is expected to achieve, but I will hold questions of independence and accountability (and a fuller discussion of the Coyne Affair) for the next chapter. The matter of its purpose obviously has prior claim.

As Canadian Nobel laureate Robert Mundell made clear in classic economics articles published in the early 1960s, the relationships between monetary policy, fiscal policy (i.e., government budgetary policy), a floating exchange rate, and the structure of the balance of payments were not well understood when the Bank–government dispute gathered pressure in the 1950s and finally burst open in 1961. Consequently, the issue of what monetary policy could or should try to accomplish, particularly under the floating exchange rate regime that prevailed, was not addressed satisfactorily. The debate over monetary policy actions focused more on such side issues as the right definition of the money supply and whether the appropriate wording for the Bank's policy was "sound money" or "tight money," rather than on the sorts of goals that monetary policy should pursue. Even so, these side issues appeared to assume epic proportions.

However, one element in the controversy did relate to the purposes of the Bank of Canada and of monetary policy, and has remained a subject of debate. This was the question of how broadly the Bank should venture. Much ink was spilled over the vexed matters of how widely it should cast its net in terms of responsibility for various aspects of economic performance, and to what extent it should make pronouncements on broad national economic questions.

Despite the expansive language in the preamble—including its final, ringing summons to the Bank "generally to promote the economic and financial welfare of the Dominion"—in the early 1960s, many felt that the Bank of Canada under Governor Coyne had been ranging too far, giving the impression that monetary policy could rectify matters (such as the state of Canada's foreign indebtedness and the structure of its balance of payments) that they intuited were beyond its plausible grasp. By contrast, in more recent years the Bank has tended to be challenged for not ranging widely enough—for example, from one side (the right?) for not criticizing fiscal performance sufficiently roundly, and from another (the left?) for its focus on getting inflation down or on keeping it down. Latterly, it has been invited to take a strong position regarding the Canadian dollar's exchange rate. Many facets of these issues are discussed in later chapters. However, I will suggest here that perhaps the Bank has finally managed to get its music more right by sticking mainly to what it can most effectively do itself—that is, without relying greatly on the actions of others. Furthermore, in terms of what it can do itself, basically printing money faster or slower, less can often be more.

Fixing the Exchange Rate, and a Quieter Few Years for the Bank

Be all this as it may, and going back again to the early 1960s, any truly effective examination of the purposes and scope of monetary policy was chopped off in 1962, quite soon after James Coyne's departure and correspondingly early in the term of Louis Rasminsky (1961–73), by an overriding policy event—Canada's abandonment of its floating exchange rate. The government's pegging of the exchange rate, at 92.5 US cents per Canadian dollar, was a step born out of crisis. It started with an attempt by the minister of finance, Donald Fleming, to "talk down" the dollar, which turned into a currency rout. (As Mundell once archly put it, "the Minister of Finance tried to lower the dollar by announcing the intention of using the resources of the Bank of Canada to do so.") Drawing a line in the snow by pegging the currency, together with massive foreign currency borrowings from governments, central banks, and the International Monetary Fund (IMF), and eventually drastic budgetary action through expenditure cuts and tax increases, did serve to turn around the capital outflow that had been provoked by the massive loss of confidence—itself provoked by the government's own words and actions. But the point to focus on in the context of this chapter is that all the while that the exchange rate was fixed, monetary policy's overriding objective was pinned down in no uncertain terms. Simply put, the Bank's job now was not to manage Canadian monetary expansion, but rather to make sure that our fixed exchange rate against the US dollar was not threatened. In other words, interest rates would be determined by the need to protect the exchange rate rather than, for example, by the desirable course of spending and inflation in Canada. The preamble's "control and protect" was now in with a vengeance, and matters stayed that way until Canada floated again in 1970.

All the same, the rest of the 1960s saw much discussion of monetary and financial matters, in particular through the publication in 1964 of Canada's landmark Report of the Royal Commission on Banking and Finance (the Porter commission). This report was a response both to the dramatic institutional and financial happenings of the previous few years—the loss of a governor, the confidence crisis that led to the fixing of the currency—and to the more general tendency in a number of countries to take stock of the operations of their financial systems and policies. Particular note should be taken in this regard of the UK Radcliffe Report and the US Report of the Commission on Money and Credit.

The Porter commission report covered a wide range of concerns and brought down some far-reaching recommendations. It did review the purposes of monetary policy, as well as many other matters affecting the Bank of Canada. But in the circumstances of a fixed exchange rate and an economy where, as now, funds could be freely moved into and out of the country, the scope for monetary policy to have any domestic impact was in reality enormously circumscribed—even if most commentators at the time, official or otherwise, were either not aware of this or reluctant to admit it.

Furthermore, for most of the 1960s, the constraint on monetary policy went even beyond the fact that Canada had an exchange rate that was fixed. The already limited room for affecting domestic monetary conditions (interest rates and the supply of credit) independently of what was happening in the United States was further hemmed in by Canada's special financial dependency on its large neighbour. From 1963, in return for a partial exemption of Canadian borrowings from the Interest Equalization Tax, which put a special charge on foreign borrowings in the United States so as to protect the American balance of payments, Canada undertook not to increase its holdings of US dollars—effectively its international currency reserves.

Simply but not inaccurately put, under an exchange rate that was fixed, Canada could not really control its money supply or the trend of its inflation. These were, in the end, determined by whatever was done by our much larger trading and financial partner. But it could perhaps have tried to put a bit of temporary financial space between itself and rising inflation in the United States by limiting the pace of its domestic credit expansion, provided it was prepared to allow its international reserves to increase. However, with the international reserve limitation that had been imposed, it could not even try that, at least not very much and not in a very open way.

Floating the Currency Again

In May 1970, Canada again, as it had 20 years earlier, allowed its currency to float. Later in the book I will look at how Canadian monetary policy has developed since then. Here, I will only observe that at the time of their decision, the Canadian authorities contended that an important reason, perhaps *the* reason, for departing again from the International Monetary Fund rules calling for a pegged (even if occasionally adjustable) exchange rate was to regain control of Canadian monetary expansion. At the time, this was proceeding at a very rapid pace under the influence of massive inflows of foreign funds. The currency move was also, therefore, anti-inflationary in principle and a very powerful argument for floating. It was an argument that even the IMF, despite its rules, could appreciate. I know, because I was part of the IMF team visiting Ottawa (which had a lot to do with my eventually joining the Bank of Canada, in 1973). Still, the IMF's official position was that Canada should fix its exchange rate again, though at a new, higher parity. But Canada insisted on delaying its decision. By 1973, quite a few other countries were floating as well, and the decision whether to fix again had become academic.

With a floating Canadian dollar, monetary policy could now play a more purposeful role for the economy. But this change did not itself lead to any initiatives for a more focused definition of monetary policy objectives in regard to inflation, even though Canada's inflation performance deteriorated as the 1970s wore on, and without any improvement in growth or unemployment. In fact, it was quite the reverse. Where public opinion was on all this is difficult to say. My own feeling is that most people either believed that inflation was clearly a problem but that nothing much could be done about it, even by the central bank, or alternatively that whatever could be done was too difficult to expect anyone, including the central bank, actually to do it. Quite where matters were expected to finish up, and how this troublesome state of rising and uncertain inflation was supposed to help economic performance, was even less clear. Still, attitudes in the Bank concerning inflation certainly hardened over those years.

In 1982, Governor Gerald Bouey (1973–87) delivered the internationally prestigious Per Jacobsson Lecture at the IMF meetings in Toronto. Its title was "Finding a Place to Stand." While this may have reminded some of a catchy tune about Ontario written at the time of Canada's centennial, it also caught the basic issue facing Canadian monetary policy at that time: where and how to draw the line on inflation. In this vein, he stated that "monetary policy must therefore give high priority to the preservation of the value of money," and concluded that "economic performance over time will be better if monetary policy never loses sight of the goal of maintaining the value of money."

In January 1988 (one year after I took office), I delivered the Hanson Memorial Lecture at the University of Alberta, and took the process a step or two further. I began by emphasizing that it is hard to discuss the ways and means of monetary policy without establishing as clearly as possible the goals. I then went on to argue at length the case for "price stability" as the basic goal of monetary policy. I deliberately sidestepped defining what the term price stability meant in quantitative terms, but the thrust was clear and would become clearer still in the years that followed. I aimed to show, early in my term, that monetary policy would be taking the initiative in regard to long-term inflation performance and would anticipate being judged in that regard. Going by the strong reaction it received, particularly among professional economists, this was seen to be a real innovation. Some liked the innovation and some did not. Many were probably just intrigued, but no doubt also keen to see what, if anything, would happen next.

A Constitutional Interlude

Canada's constitutional situation, particularly with the emergence of the separatist movement in Quebec, had been a constant general concern from the early 1970s. The provincial election victory of the Parti Québécois in 1976 under the charismatic René Lévesque had had a clear negative impact on the Canadian dollar. However, the various initiatives on the constitutional side had no direct effect on the Bank until the early 1990s, when the Progressive Conservative government, under Brian Mulroney, attempted to deal directly with the constitutional issues through a new negotiated approach to provincial powers and various grievances.

In this vein, the early 1990s saw an intensive if inconclusive constitutional debate, the end of which was marked by the referendum in October 1992 that resulted in rejection of the intergovernmental

Charlottetown Accord on new federal–provincial arrangements. That was not surprising. What was surprising—not only, it turned out, to people at the Bank of Canada—was the fact that the purposes of monetary policy got caught up in that debate.

The immediate reason for involving us appeared to be provincial demands—especially from the West and from Quebec as one part of their wish lists—to have a direct say in the Bank's policies. In fact, in early 1991 the constitutional committee of the Quebec Liberal Party issued the Allaire report, which called for "a review of the structure and operation of the Bank of Canada." What particularly bothered the committee were the regional impacts of monetary policy, especially a policy that was anti-inflationary, where the report saw a need for mechanisms to ensure that "the needs of diverse regions were taken into account" when monetary policy was being decided. From one angle, this was a province-by-province, or "not in my backyard," prescription for how national monetary policy should be constructed. And it was a prescription that simply could not be met, given that Canada has a common currency and a common financial system. More generally, the theme of that report was to expand the special say of one province (Quebec) vis-à-vis the rest of Canada in any new constitutional arrangement, and going at the Bank of Canada was just one element on the Allaire agenda.

However, against this backdrop, and as part of its second (post-Meech Lake, pre-Charlottetown) try for constitutional renewal, the federal government did unveil in September 1991 its own proposals for changing the Bank's mandate. These proposals, contained in a document titled "Canadian Federalism and Economic Union," were one part of broader plans for fixing Canada's economic union, such as improving the internal market (officialese for interprovincial free trade in goods and services) and that even hardier perennial, improving coordination of fiscal policies. The particular proposal regarding a new central bank mandate also needs to be seen in the light of a series of federal suggestions regarding the Bank that were aimed, cautiously, at channelling more provincial input into monetary policy matters.

These suggestions regarding the Bank were not dramatic but were still quite extensive: regular semi-annual (instead of ad hoc) appearances of Bank officials before Parliament—first in the fall when "federal and provincial budgets are being prepared," and again in the spring; mandating the governor to meet with federal–provincial ministers of finance on a regular basis; nomination of Bank of Canada directors by the federal government "after consultation with provincial governments"; ratification of the governor's appointment by the Senate (recall the push at that time also for an enhanced provincial role in appointments to the Senate); and a greater public profile for Bank directors through their chairing of regional consultative panels, with the federal government undertaking to "solicit views of provincial and territorial governments with respect to membership of the regional panels."

The proposal regarding the mandate left room for manoeuvre and negotiation, but the thrust was clear. The essence of the government's proposal was to scrap or bypass the original preamble that had held for almost 60 years and bring in a mandate that would call upon the Bank, in the government's words, "to guide the pace of monetary expansion and credit conditions with the objective of achieving and preserving stability in the general level of prices in Canada."

In putting these ideas forward, it seemed quite clear that Ottawa was balancing two sets of concerns. On the one hand, its initiatives would go at least a modest way in accommodating provincial desires to share in the running of the Bank, although there was no knowing how far matters would move once public debate and/or federal–provincial negotiations started. On the other hand, the inevitable and surely damaging uncertainty as to how this experiment in sharing could affect policies might be headed off by a clear and constructive view as to what would be a suitable monetary policy mandate. The government's proposals provided such a view, and one with which it could be sure that the Bank would be happy.

While the general reception to all this detailed material on the central bank and its purposes was muted and uncertain, two sets of reactions were clear. First, a number of commentators cried foul. In their eyes, bringing in a more clear-cut specification of the Bank's mandate to replace the generalities and breadth of the preamble just when provinces were going to get the chance to have a direct effect on monetary policy was an infringement on provincial rights and opportunities. Indeed, what the federal government proposed was perceived by some constitutional and economic policy activists as in effect trying to block the good new things that provinces might be able to achieve if they got a foot inside the Bank's doors. That there was this desire to set up roadblocks was probably an accurate perception, given the fundamental uncertainties that meaningful provincial involvement in monetary decisions could generate. Second, and more broadly, most people polled could not see why it was at all necessary to inject detailed questions regarding one particular and not so well-understood institution into what were supposed to be constitutional discussions about really big issues. Furthermore, there was no real need to alter the constitution to bring about the changes that the government was proposing. Revising the *Bank of Canada Act* would have been sufficient for almost everything, and in many instances no change at all in legislation would be needed. All that would be required was just a political decision and a political consensus to act.

The Manley Report, and Fadeout

In the end, the second view prevailed: that the Bank had no business in the constitutions of the nation. But in the context of the Charlottetown process, there occurred an interesting initiative from the House Committee on Finance when it ordered hearings called "The Mandate and Governance of the Bank of Canada," which culminated in a published report of the same name, popularly known as the Manley report after its chair. In allowing John Manley to preside, parliamentarians were clearly trying to emphasize the non-partisan nature of the exercise and perhaps also the fact that this was really serious business. Mr. Manley, now Canada's deputy prime minister, minister of finance, and a few other things as well to occupy his time, was the finance critic of the Official Opposition, and he stood out as the most able tenant of that position during my term as governor. His group held extensive hearings over the fall of 1991 and into early 1992. Most of its witnesses were academic economists. The Bank of Canada gave extensive written and oral testimony, though remarkably, given where the constitutional proposals on the Bank had come from, there were no official appearances by Department of Finance staff or by the minister.

In the end, the group recommended no change in the Bank's mandate, notwithstanding its endorsement of a goal of price stability, stating that it "must be a central goal for the Bank." In its conclusions, the committee took the position that a mandate focused on price stability would simply be too narrow even if, as it conceded, this would aid accountability.

Not surprisingly, given the intellectual schizophrenia between the body of the report (probably left largely in the hands of staff) and its conclusions (where committee members were no doubt more heavily involved), the concluding reasoning becomes, to put it kindly, rather tortured. This is particularly so when the report argues—explicitly drawing on the testimony of Dr. Douglas Peters, then chief economist of the Toronto-Dominion Bank and later a Liberal junior minister—that "to clarify the Bank's responsibilities would be misleading ... leaving the impression that monetary policy would no longer require judgment and the Bank could be turned into a computer appropriately programmed."

This statement is itself worse than merely misleading, especially since monetary policy is inevitably based on a view of the future, with all the reasoned assessment of risks that this entails. A serious look at Canadian experience should be enough to show why this is so, but anyone who doubts this could also look at the awkward life of the European Central Bank over the past couple of years, even with its relatively precise mandate. And if "a computer appropriately programmed" could do it better, why not? On this, I shall give the last word to Alan Greenspan:

I wish there were a simple way to remove fallible human judgement from central bank policy making, as policy by "rule" would endeavour to do. It would make it a lot easier, especially for central bankers. Regrettably, there is no available option of that nature in the world that confronts us on a day-to-day basis.

There matters have stayed, at least as regards formal review of the Bank's monetary policy mandate. I will discuss later where all this leaves us, after considering how monetary policy actually developed, including the adoption of inflation targets. But in anticipation of that later discussion, I will leave here for the reader's consideration the following muscular sentences:

> High levels of economic growth and employment on a sustained basis are the primary objectives of monetary and fiscal policies. The best contribution that monetary policy can make to these objectives is to preserve confidence in the value of money by achieving and maintaining price stability.

These unusually clear phrases are the opening to the joint statement of the federal government and the Bank of Canada that was issued in December 1993 when new inflation targets were announced. The wording goes far beyond the position (namely, that a price stability focus is too narrow a goal) that characterized the all-party Manley report, and is the same in spirit as the previous government's proposals made in 1991. Really, who would have thought?

This declaration, especially the second sentence, is particularly striking because it was put out by a relatively new government (elected in October 1993) that when in opposition had been angrily and loudly critical of the monetary policy pursued and the person in charge. It did not have that luxury any more. But why such a statement, which would be an excellent point of departure for any central bank mandate, was made can only be properly appreciated in the context of the delicate political and financial market event of the day it was made—the announcement not just of new inflation targets, but also of the appointment of a new governor of the Bank of Canada.

A worthwhile question, also to be discussed later on, is to what extent these relatively clear words regarding the fundamental purposes of central banking and monetary policy can be taken seriously as commitment.

CHAPTER 2

∞

Putting the Bank in Its Place

In matters of institutional design, form should follow from the function desired. In practice, institutional developments everywhere tend to be more adaptive and circular than this precept would indicate. The Bank of Canada's experience has been no exception. Still, it remains true that the kind of central bank that Canada should have—the kind of responsibility, accountability, and governance structure it should get (the matters I want to discuss in this chapter)—ought to be based on the kind of role our society in its more reflective moments wants it to play. That is why the question of the Bank's mandate, or purpose, needed to be dealt with first.

Dealt with but not settled. Even allowing for the lags inevitable in institutional development, there has been a persistent reluctance to spell out the Bank's mandate in something concrete and to the point. This showed up clearly in the vacillating conclusions of the Manley report in 1992. It was evident again in 1993, when the first inflation targets were altered—brave initial words but no follow-through, and in fact, as I shall discuss later, on the substance it was something of a retreat. This hesitancy had also been apparent earlier in a more indirect but still illuminating manner when, in 1991, the government introduced its post-Meech Lake constitutional proposals. To be sure, those proposals did outline a constructive reworking of the preamble. But as previously noted, the real driver in this area was the need to accommodate provincial demands for a more direct say within the Bank's governing structure. It was only because of this pressure that the government felt it important also to affirm more directly than before what the Bank's monetary policy purpose really was. Once the constitutional pressure was off, any urge to proceed on the mandate evaporated as well.

One of the arguments that often came up when I was governor was that even with the admittedly loose mandate given by the preamble, the central bank was very clearly (and strongly, some would argue) focused on the integrity of money. So, it was contended by many, there was really no issue—the Bank was doing the right thing anyway. The Manley committee also latched onto this thesis when I appeared before it. My response, having had direct experience of what it takes to bring about solid confidence in our financial future, was that while there might not be a crisis, there was still an issue of clarity of purpose that deserved addressing. Furthermore, no good reason existed, barring the usual political preference to lead from behind, to wait for a crisis before addressing it.

But even if the official instinct is to have the Bank's professed policy purpose left pleasantly vague, underlying this is a consensus that a federal monetary institution with a certain separateness or independence is worth having—and even preserving. Why is that? The reason cannot be simply a matter of administrative convenience. Rather, it seems that people readily understand that it is worth having an institution that is directly concerned about the integrity of the nation's money and can also be trusted to do something about it. Newspapers, presumably reflecting their readership, fuss in almost a knee-jerk way about the Bank's "independence" when any issue arises (such as orchestrating the timing of Paul Martin's exit from the Cabinet in June 2002) in which the Bank appears to be sucked into decisions made by political Ottawa.

On a more official but still non-political plane, Canada's Porter commission of the early 1960s saw a measure of independence from political pressures as being desirable chiefly because it insulated the central bank from "the historical tendency of governments of all forms to develop the habit of inflating the currency." This insulation would make it harder for a government to push the Bank to create inflation through excessive monetary expansion.

Likewise, the Manley committee, almost 30 years later, was "convinced by the evidence that it would be undesirable to lessen the degree of independence of the Bank. A central bank too heavily influenced by politicians could well create a bias in favour of greater inflation...." Members of that committee, as politicians themselves, were certainly in a position to speak from authority, if not from direct experience of too heavy influence at the time.

I have to leave the mandate question there, having ventilated this unfinished business as far as I could from the inside and now from the outside as well. While unfinished, the situation could clearly be less favourable for good monetary policy than it is. Also, the fact that there is this widely shared, even if loosely defined, understanding of what the Bank is there for also provides a meaningful platform from which to probe questions about how it should be structured and governed. This means reviewing issues of responsibility and accountability, offering some thoughts on what can be meant by that much used but seldom explained term "central bank independence," and then taking a look at internal governance matters. Finally, I will go further afield and explore what experts have in mind when they talk, as they sometimes do, about the Bank's "political legitimacy."

Responsibility and Accountability

Early Skirmishes

Over the first quarter century of the Bank's life, questions were raised from time to time as to exactly how it related to government, especially if differences over monetary policy arose. But problems regarding accountability to the government of the day took some time to become a live issue. When they did, in the latter years of James Coyne's tenure, the impact was extreme and dramatic. A brief survey of earlier developments will help set the stage for what happened.

The question of accountability was certainly aired, though somewhat obliquely, right at the start. Prime Minister Bennett had

decided that the new Bank of Canada would be privately owned
(but with widely distributed shares), being persuaded that this was
the way to avert the dangers of government interference. Since the
opposition parties were supportive in principle of the creation of a
central bank, their parliamentary fire was directed mainly at the
specific issue of private ownership. However, this debate was fairly
speedily resolved later in the 1930s, when the new Liberal government brought in pieces of legislation progressively nationalizing
the Bank by making the minister of finance the sole shareholder.
This gave the minister (no doubt with help from the Prime Minister's Office) the power to appoint the 12 outside directors who
serve on the Bank's board along with the governor, senior deputy
governor, and deputy minister of finance.

Because the ownership issue received the initial attention it did,
the more basic question of the relationship of the Bank to the government of the day, above all its framework of accountability or any
lack thereof, did not get the billing it deserved. And when the question did arise, ministers were inclined to deny the possibility of any
conflict between what the central bank did and what the government wanted. A more refined but still not adequate argument was
that if at any time policies of the Bank were not in harmony with
the desires of government, government could secure the legislation
necessary to bring about harmony. The doctrine that seemed to
emerge from these early exchanges was that *Parliament* had given
the Bank responsibility for monetary policy, and this meant that
government did not need to accept responsibility for it, except to the
extent that it was prepared to seek legislative change. This was subtle all right, but not realistic because it conflicted with the generally accepted view as to what constituted responsible government.

In 1938, Graham Towers made a careful statement on the matter that brought the government more directly into the picture.

It becomes apparent, also, that the matter is of such great
national importance that it cannot be dealt with by a number of unco-ordinated agencies. Some one body must be
assigned the duty of exercising control, and have no other

interests which would clash with its responsibility for the regulation of currency and credit. This is the reason why there are central banks in operation in most countries. Instead of having central bank functions performed by a department of government, the governments have preferred to intrust these functions to specialized institutions. The laws under which they operate vary. But the banks all have one thing in common: their monetary policy must conform to the policy of their respective governments. No other conception of the situation is possible in this day and age, nor would any other state of affairs be desirable in view of the vital effect which monetary policy can have on the affairs of a country.

Strangely enough, the supreme control of government in matters of monetary policy does not lessen by one iota the responsibility of central bank executives and directors. If things go wrong, in a monetary sense, while they are in charge of the affairs of a central bank, they are in no position to pass the responsibility on to the government. For it must be assumed that the policies which have been followed are in substance policies which they endorsed and recommended. If they did not agree, they should have said so. And in those circumstances they would, no doubt, have been replaced by others who did not share their objection.[1]

In its reference to the fact that "it must be assumed that the policies which have been followed are in substance policies which they [central bank executives and directors] endorsed and recommended," this statement was fairly clear on the position that the Bank had a responsibility for creating policy as well as for carrying it out, but that there was a central place for government views as well. However, this formulation still left unclear the mechanism by which any disagreements got resolved. Much later, in 1954, Graham

---

[1] Quoted in Bryce, 1986.

Towers was a shade more explicit (bear in mind, though, that he was skating on ice that was in the government's domain) when he referred to "various ways and means by which directors and management can be got rid of."[2] Later still, at the time of the Coyne Affair, he observed in a public statement that "on various occasions when I was governor of the Bank of Canada, I publicly expressed the opinion that in the event of a disagreement between the Government and the bank on an important question of monetary policy, the governor should resign."[3]

Even so, until a dispute broke open, the tendency on the part of ministers (notably including Donald Fleming, Governor Coyne's nemesis) was to deny that they had any real authority over the Bank's actions, from which it followed that they had minimal responsibility. In their defence, it must be allowed that the specific arrangements then in place for exercising that authority were either unclear or impractical.

The Coyne Affair and Its Aftermath

As long as monetary policy remained uncontroversial, these inadequacies were of no great moment. But the issue was finally joined in the dramatic dispute over monetary policy, Bank of Canada accountability, and government responsibility that came to a boil at the beginning of the 1960s after simmering for some time, at least in Cabinet circles. It culminated in a bill declaring the governor's seat vacant, which was passed in the House on July 7, 1961, with all the speed the government could command. It then passed to the Senate, which extraordinarily, but fittingly in the circumstances, invited James Coyne to appear before it to argue his case.

By that stage, a crucial part of his case was that the government had not given an adequately reasoned explanation for its actions or a proper hearing. Admittedly, governments seldom give fully reasoned explanations for their actions, and even more rarely do they give hearings. But this instance was trickier. According to the *Bank*

---

[2] Fullerton, 1986.
[2] Ibid.

of Canada Act (and this has not changed), the governor, like the auditor general for example, serves "during good behaviour" and not "at pleasure." This distinction is extremely important when differences arise. It means that the government has a degree of direct accountability in that it must give solid reasons for its actions. This in turn implies a forum for assessing those reasons that is judicious and perhaps also judicial in nature. The Senate, admittedly in the hands of the Liberal opposition, took its time (relative at least to the instant spent on the matter in the House) in its oratorical deliberations on this situation. But once the upper house had turned the bill down, Governor Coyne resigned.

Apparently there was more than one thread of discord in this damaging and prolonged conflict. But the central issue was the lack of clarity as to how the government's ultimate responsibility for monetary policy could be exercised in a practical way, and the eventual political intolerability of this lack of clarity. So when Louis Rasminsky (then a deputy governor concentrating on the international side) was asked in mid-1961 whether he would accept appointment as governor, it seemed to him "impossible for anyone to function effectively in the role unless the respective responsibilities of the Government and the Bank for monetary policy were clarified once and for all."[4]

This he attempted to do by placing his views before the Bank's directors and before the government when they were considering his appointment. The views put forward were, he stated, based on two principles:

(1) in the ordinary course of events, the Bank has the responsibility for monetary policy, and

(2) if the Government disapproves of the monetary policy being carried out by the Bank it has the right and the responsibility to direct the Bank as to the policy which the Bank is to carry out.

---

[4] As he recalled in a letter in the Toronto *Globe and Mail* on October 3, 1975.

As regards the second principle, it is important to underline that in Louis Rasminsky's clearly expressed view at the time, this related to the existence of a "serious and persistent conflict." Accordingly, he further stated, if the government did in the end direct the Bank formally as to what to do regarding monetary policy, it would be the governor's duty "to resign and to make way for someone who took a different view."

This language regarding resignation was squarely in line with the position enunciated earlier by Graham Towers. So it is not surprising that Mr. Rasminsky had spelled out the likely consequences of a directive right from the start. But conspiracy theories are attractive. Therefore, perhaps I should not have been surprised to see in later years how persistent was the idea that the Bank had somehow slipped one by the government—first enunciating the principles under which a directive might come into effect, and then, only after these had been endorsed, letting it be known that a likely consequence would be that the governor would resign. Obviously, those with a view on these issues are perfectly entitled to object to the standard position that resignation is called for. This is something I want to discuss a little later. But it is totally incorrect to suggest that this stance regarding resignation was not set out in a clear and timely manner.

The "dual responsibility" views that Mr. Rasminsky expressed were accepted by the government, analyzed further by the Porter commission, and formalized through incorporation into the *Bank of Canada Act* in 1967. This part of the act—the provisions on consultation and the use of a government directive—merits citation in full:

(1) The Minister and the Governor shall consult regularly on monetary policy and on its relation to general economic policy.

(2) If, notwithstanding the consultations provided for in subsection (1), there should emerge a difference of opinion between the Minister and the Bank concerning the monetary policy to be followed, the Minister may, after consultation with the Governor and with the approval of the

Governor in Council, give to the Governor a written directive concerning monetary policy, in specific terms and
applicable for a specified period, and the Bank shall comply with that directive.

(3) A directive given under this section shall be published
forthwith in the *Canada Gazette* and shall be laid before Parliament within fifteen days after the giving thereof, or, if Parliament is not then sitting, on any of the first fifteen days
next thereafter that either House of Parliament is sitting.

Taking these provisions from the top, the first consideration to
note is that they specifically call for regular meetings between the
minister and the governor. This should at least forestall any policy
surprises. One of the difficulties that no doubt helped to create and
prolong misunderstandings in the period leading up to Governor
Coyne's resignation was that there was very little contact between
the Bank and the government—ships passing in the Ottawa night.
Bear in mind, however, that the deputy minister of finance was an
ex-officio member of the Bank's board and could, if the government had wished, have played a bigger role. No doubt the minister
of finance could also, if he had wished, have arranged for the governor to see him on a regular basis.

The desirability of regular meetings (during my tenure, every
week when feasible) was obvious. But what was the meaning of
"consult" in relation to the purpose of those meetings? Didn't this
mean that the governor should be taking instructions, House Committee on Finance members asked. Well, no. That should be clear
from Louis Rasminsky's initial formulation of the dual responsibility principles involved. Furthermore, if the term really did mean
taking instructions, there would have been no need for a directive
power, or for the careful conditions regarding how it was to be
used.

All the same, "consult" is a serious word. It implies substantive
exchanges over policy and the mutual consideration of alternatives.
My own position was always to go into those meetings, normally
one-on-one, with a view as to what needed to be done in the near

and longer term in the monetary policy area (and naturally how it should be done), and be ready to discuss all this with the minister. "Consult" obviously also means that governors are bound to consider ministers' views very seriously. However, what they cannot claim is that the Bank is pursuing a particular policy just because the minister wants it. What is necessary is that the governor should want it too.

While on the subject of consultation, I should also note that contact with Finance has never been limited to the minister or even the deputy minister. In my time, and I doubt that this has changed, there were frequent regular meetings with associate deputy ministers, assistant deputy ministers, and others. And if Finance officials were at all uncertain about what monetary policy was doing or where it was heading, my colleagues and I would go to considerable lengths to clarify matters. No surprises at that level either.

As regards expressions of views on monetary policy, the usual protocol was for officials to leave any expression of views to the minister. But that was not necessarily inappropriate. The important thing for us was that Finance officials should understand as clearly as possible what monetary policy was about, so that they would always be in a good position to brief the minister. Occasionally, a minister would bring staff with him to our meetings, but clearly such invitations were reserved for very special occasions dealing with particularly contentious or complicated pieces of business.

Good communication is terribly important. But what has rightly drawn most attention about these provisions, and not just because it is the most dramatic part, is the directive power. Spelling out that power has made absolutely clear that the government of the day takes ultimate responsibility for the monetary policy pursued because it now has a well-defined executive instrument for changing it. The way that instrument has to be exercised is also very transparent. Obviously, a directive must be reasonably specific, not a vague exhortation to do better, for example. However, the most important proviso is that any directive must be made public.

Given the way thinking has developed regarding openness in government, it may seem odd to many that this requirement for transparency, really quite advanced for its time, is also the part of the process that has been most heavily criticized. What upsets the critics, who would probably also be annoyed by the fact that the governor would most likely resign if one were issued, is that they think it means that the directive power cannot in fact be used. To quote one prominent critic, Professor Pierre Fortin, an economist at the University of Montreal, from his 1996 presidential address to the Canadian Economics Association:

> No sane minister of finance would ever dare start such a process, with the implication that, in practice, the Bank of Canada enjoys near-complete independence from the government, except once every seven years on the day a new governor is appointed.

Three comments are in order. First, it must be allowed that the intent of the directive provision was not to make it easy to use. It was believed by the Bank from the start that the motivation for a directive ought to be a difference that the government really cared about. In fact, the provision has never been applied, although I understand that there has been at least one occasion when, in the Bank's mind at any rate, the governor and the minister were into the further consultation referred to in subsection (2) above. Second, we can also surely take it for granted that the minister has thought through the issue, consulted widely, and secured considerable outside support for what would be a well-reasoned position. This doesn't sound like insanity. Quite the opposite, it puts a premium on what most people would think was fair good sense. My third point is that the idea of central bank independence is, as I hope to show in the next section, one that is a deal more subtle—and should be more principled—than the above citation would have us believe.

On the Bank's side, it seems certain that any issue giving rise to a directive would be one that the governor really cared about or there would have been no need for a directive. This reality, together with the fact that the directive would be made public, renders it virtually inevitable that he or she would resign. Furthermore, given the activity levels and fuss that I saw in late 1993, it does not appear that the appointment of a new governor in place of one whose term is expiring is quite as free from challenges for the government of the day as the view just cited suggests. Since the appointment process does not have to be rendered public, it does have the tactical political advantage of being more opaque than the directive provision. But the government still has to concern itself with having a policy and/or a governor (preferably both) that will stand examination. And of course, intense scrutiny will come in regard to how well the appointment, and what is said about the appointment, has satisfied the consensus that seems to exist for a measure of national monetary integrity—and some form of central bank independence to bolster it—above and beyond what the day's financial markets might think about it all.

That is presumably why the appointment of David Dodge, former deputy minister and former right hand of the minister of finance, as governor in 2001 to succeed Gordon Thiessen (1994–2001) came in for comment. Was he "independent" was the question that was most frequently asked by both the media and individuals. In this regard, it is telling and unfortunate that the policy independence of the Bank seems to the outside world to hinge more on the humour of the individual in charge than on the way the institution is structured and the responsibilities it is given. Popular emphasis on personality rather than on principles is no doubt inevitable, and in Mr. Dodge's case the popular saving point was that he had been known to disagree forcefully on occasion with his former boss, the minister of finance. That is just fine, but to my mind any approach to independence should be structured so as to encourage less weight on personality and more on principles, an issue that I want to take up in the next section. My point is not that personal characteristics, experience, and qualifications do not matter for the job of governor. It is simply that they should not be seen as determining the Bank of Canada's responsibility or independence.

What did the Manley committee think about all this? It certainly called many witnesses besides Bank of Canada management and directors. It also made clear that it had looked at a wide range of alternative models. But in the end, it opted for no change with regard to independence and accountability arrangements. It was "of the opinion that the existing relationship between the Bank and the Government of Canada strikes a good balance between independence and accountability." One might quibble at the contrast that it makes between independence and accountability, given that accountability arises as a consideration only because there is some measure of policy independence. Still, its "balanced" judgment is just about what one would expect from an all-party committee that wanted to stay out of trouble. Its standstill conclusions no doubt reflected the fact that notwithstanding the absence of an explicit, clear mandate, there was, as former federal minister Sinclair Stevens might have said (see Chapter 5), a consensual, "implicit," one. Furthermore, the network of specific arrangements in place, whether to do with independence, responsibility, or accountability, had not themselves given rise to any crisis—financial or otherwise. Crises have arisen, but for reasons quite apart from what Canadian monetary policy was trying to do. So why should the committee stir itself?

Independence for What?

There matters have stayed, at least on a formal level. But behind the formalities regarding who does what with monetary policy, the Canadian situation seems to be shifting further, although uncertainly as to where it will end up.

It will be recalled that the formal position to date has been that in the absence of a directive, the Bank's responsibility goes a very long way. The third recommendation of the Manley report pointed out that "monetary policy should continue to be formulated and conducted by the Bank of Canada, with the ultimate responsibility resting with the federal government." This recommendation again spelled out the Bank's responsibility for *formulating* policy as well as being charged with implementing it. As a more up-to-date example, Prime Minister Chrétien, in responding to a parliamentary question

in March 2001 regarding the sagging exchange value of the Canadian dollar, stated that "we have an independent monetary policy
that is decided by the Governor of the Bank of Canada...." This
seems to be pretty strong, unequivocal stuff, especially for someone
whose preferred position is to sit on the fence. Bear in mind,
though, that he was being scripted by his minister of finance so as
to disavow any governmental responsibility for our currency's
decline, and in this context Bank of Canada independence is no
more than a flag of convenience.

It is easy to see how, in the absence of precise instructions from
government, the Bank would have a fair latitude for deciding what
monetary policy should be, as well as how monetary policy goals
should be achieved. It is also likely to spend much more time
thinking the monetary policy issues through than anyone else in
Ottawa or elsewhere. But how "democratic" is this?

Some will no doubt be prepared to argue that it is undemocra-
tic because it lessens parliamentary authority. But to believe that,
you also have to believe that delegation of authority by government in a clearly specified and clearly revocable way is undemoc-
ratic. More broadly, the Bank's decision-making process is not conducted in a vacuum; if it is independent, it is independent within
government, not from government. Besides sharing its thoughts
with the public and with Parliament, the institution is, as we have
seen, also bound by statute to communicate views to the minister
of finance and to listen very hard. And in addition to the directive
power, there is also, as Professor Fortin could remind us, the ministerial power to approve or veto appointments of governors and
senior deputy governors, besides approving their salaries. On
another plane, there is also a basic public and parliamentary understanding as to what the Bank is really there for concerning the
nation's money. And that, evidently, is not merely to do the executive power's binding. The Bank may be headquartered in Ottawa,
but, apparently unlike the Business Development Bank, it has the
capacity to keep its distance from the Prime Minister's Office and
its operatives if it has a real mind to.

The question that I now want to examine, however, is whether or to what extent developments in the 1990s have altered or have genuine potential to alter the situation I have been describing.

There has in recent years been some evolution in academic thinking about central bank independence. Notable here has been the emergence of a commonly applied distinction between "goal independence" (responsibility for deciding on monetary policy objectives) and "instrument independence" (responsibility for the particular monetary policy actions required to achieve those objectives).

This distinction between goal and instrument was first drawn in the mid-1990s by Stanley Fischer, until recently first deputy managing director of the International Monetary Fund and before that an economics professor at the Massachusetts Institute of Technology. What he provided was a convenient and extremely popular way of organizing thinking about the nature of central bank independence. Less convincing, however, are the conclusions drawn from this distinction. The way the evidence was presented (bearing in mind that he was then addressing an academic audience) was that:

> The most important conclusion of the theoretical and empirical literature is that a central bank *should* have instrument independence but *should not* have goal independence.[5]

According to thinking along these lines, a central bank should have independence in deciding how to apply its instruments because of the inflationary bias in policy-making that otherwise arises, as the Manley committee also granted. Furthermore, as Fischer put it, "the evidence leaves little doubt that, on average, economic performance is better in more independent central banks."[6]

But are these "more independent" central banks goal independent, instrument independent, or both? From what I know about

---

[5] Fischer, 1995.
[6] Fischer, 1994.

central banks, those that are being generalized about here will likely have had important independence in both formulating policy and how they apply their monetary policy instruments. For one thing, goals may look as if they are firmly laid down by government (through legislation, for example) but may in fact be so imprecise or varied that the central bank has considerable scope in deciding *what* to accomplish as well as *how* to go about accomplishing it. In this latter sense, it can be argued that the Bank of Canada over the years has had significant goal independence because its legislative mandate has been lacking in focus and precision. By and large, goal independence, or the lack of it, seems to be a matter of degree rather than absolutes.

Indeed, the way matters are set up for central banks around the world with respect to goal and instrument independence allows a remarkably wide range of approaches. This suggests that however attractive the goal/instrument distinction is from the viewpoint of supplying a rationale grounded in economic theory, its real world basis is questionable. The "theoretical" reason why central banks should not have goal independence has to do with the possibility that they will not in the end be fully responsible in curbing inflation. So governments have to make sure that they are, by setting out firm, public, anti-inflationary guidelines. But in terms of what actually happens, this argument seems strained. Rare indeed is the government that has encouraged a central bank to be *more* anti-inflationary, while the reverse is very common. Furthermore, governments (and, I might add, legislatures) generally prefer less clarity rather than more. A few examples will illustrate these complexities.

In the United Kingdom, the Bank of England's chief responsibility under its new governing legislation—no doubt framed with one eye cocked toward common currency developments in Europe and the mandate of the European Central Bank—is the maintenance of "price stability." But so what? In actuality, the government of the day defines, year by year no less, what is meant by price stability. To date, this has been an inflation target of 2.5 per cent annually. At that rate, prices would double each generation, and to call this price stability seems to be stretching matters. "Inflation stability" would surely be a truer turn of phrase.

In one sense, it can be argued that the Bank of England does not have goal independence because it is legally constrained to pursue a policy of price stability. However, there is also quite another sense—a much more interesting and relevant one—in which it can be seen as lacking goal independence. This is because the government defines what price stability is and reserves the right to change that definition whenever it wants to. Obviously, the constraint on the British government is not the need to attach a serious meaning to "price stability." Rather, it is the fact that it now is responsible for setting a public inflation target, and, it follows, a target that is generally acceptable to public opinion.

I should also note that the independence that the Bank of England obtained as part of the recent legislative package was expressly instrument independence. Earlier, it did not even have that. The Chancellor of the Exchequer always had to agree to any change in its lending rates, and British monetary policy was at best mediocre—or more strongly perhaps, a jolly poor show. Now, a Bank of England committee sets its lending rates without reference to the chancellor but, possibly for greater objectivity (although the logic here is not at all clear), this committee is adorned with outside members as well as Bank of England insiders.

The set-up for the US Federal Reserve System supplies a quite different way of doing things. With the concept of separation of powers better established in the United States than in a parliamentary system, there is greater general acceptance of the idea that the Federal Reserve is in some general sense independent. But *how* is it independent? It may well be argued, as does Professor Alan Blinder (former vice-chairman of the Federal Reserve Board), for example, that "in a democracy, it seems not just appropriate but virtually obligatory that the political authorities set the goals—and then instruct the central bank to pursue them." Still, the formal goals for the Fed are sufficiently imprecise to allow it real scope in formulating policy, again subject to public opinion and any backlash, for whatever reasons including public opinion, from Congress or the administration. Neither of these bodies has shown any appetite for spelling out the Fed's mandate with more precision, although isolated tries have been made from time to time. Professor Blinder does not make clear whether his comment is a description of what happens for the United States or the expression of a desire to see the arrangements change. I would think the latter is a better fit.

The tortuous and confused journey of the *Humphrey-Hawkins Act*, finally passed and signed in 1977, provides a good example of what can occur in the US system. The initial legislative idea was twofold. Its aim was both to require the government to reduce unemployment to 3 per cent within four years of passage and to make government employment available to all who wished at the "prevailing wage" that already by law had to be paid on government construction contracts. Arthur Burns, then chairman of the Federal Reserve Board, clearly saw the dangers:

> Humphrey-Hawkins ... continues the old game of setting a target for the unemployment rate. You set one figure. I set another figure. If your figure is low, you are a friend of mankind; if mine is high, I am a servant of Wall Street.... I think that is not a profitable game....[7]

This was not the only problem. The *Humphrey-Hawkins Act* that finally passed after much internecine wrangling was somewhat different, and also had very much the look of having been produced with difficulty by a committee even larger than for the initial formulation. Its goals were many, varied, and sometimes craftily worded: reduce unemployment to 4 per cent by 1983; put price stability on the same level of importance as full employment; establish a goal of zero inflation by 1988; reduce federal spending to the lowest level consistent with national needs (this provision deserves the gold medal for cunning drafting if the objective is to turn out an honourable but ultimately meaningless phrase); and have the Federal Reserve chairman testify before Congress twice a year.

Nowadays, the legislation is known only for the fact that it was, until it finally lapsed recently, the umbrella under which the chairman testifies. And the Federal Reserve carries on (with its requirement to testify now incorporated into the *American Homeownership*

---

[7] Quoted in DeLong, 1996.

and Economic Opportunity Act of 2000)—with the broad implicit mandate to worry about inflation without of course "forgetting" the real economy—but in more recent years with a clearer focus from the Fed on inflation and with less sniping from the White House, to the economy's evident benefit.

My final example is the newly minted European Central Bank (ECB). By statute, and reflecting the earlier provisions for the Bundesbank, it is enjoined as its primary objective to maintain price stability, just (it so happens though not purely by coincidence) as is now the Bank of England. The important difference is that it is the ECB that defines price stability. Its target in this regard is not more than 2 per cent inflation. So presumably, most of the time, inflation will be less. There are some technical questions about defining an inflation target this way as opposed to having a band and/or a point. But what must be allowed is that the number chosen does less linguistic violence to the term "price stability" than does the figure currently handed down annually by the Chancellor of the Exchequer.

Interestingly enough, however, while the ECB does have this highly significant degree of goal independence (perhaps reflecting the absence of a true European political counterweight), its independence on the operational, or instrument, side is somewhat less clear-cut. The Maastricht Treaty embodies the time-honoured principle that responsibility for the exchange rate *system* (e.g., deciding whether or not to fix) belongs to the Council of Ministers, and therefore not to the ECB. This is non-controversial. What is more problematic is the further statutory provision that the council can give "general orientations" to the ECB regarding exchange rate policy. Those orientations are, admittedly, supposed to be without prejudice to the ECB's price stability objective, but they could cause it trouble in meeting its goals. No such orientation has so far been issued. Still, what is clear is that this provision has encouraged national politicians from time to time to try to inject exchange rate considerations into the discussion of monetary policy for the Eurozone. Given the predilection in European circles (which I do not share) to think that there can be an exchange rate policy that is somehow separable from the goals of financial policy in general and monetary policy in particular, this provision has the potential to be a continual source of tension, particularly as Eurozone ministers of finance as a group attempt to increase their authority.

In Canada, independence for the Bank of Canada seems reasonably clear with regard to the operations side. For one thing, Canadian governments generally do not get themselves lured into the trap of saying very much about the exchange rate.[8] Canadian politicians certainly steer clear of the term "exchange rate policy," and rightly so. The same goes for the United Kingdom. Furthermore, as I observed earlier, our minister of finance generally refrains from discussing monetary policy actions publicly (if he did not, he would have a bunch of hornets from the media descend upon him), although he could in principle use the directive power to intervene in operational matters, in addition to matters concerning strategy or goals. But where the Canadian ground seems to have shifted is in regard to broad policy formulation and the Bank's latitude for setting goals.

The inflation targets that now exist and are discussed in more detail later in this book have from the start been formally "agreed" with the federal government. Indeed, the original proposal for inflation targets came from the government, and I knew very well at the time that in engaging in this exercise, the Bank was undertaking something with long-term implications as to how and where initiatives over basic decisions for monetary policy were going to be taken. It is telling that while the monetary aggregate targets that existed in the late 1970s and early 1980s had not been announced in the budget or in any joint statement but rather had been set forth by the Bank alone, inflation targets have been the subject of joint announcements from the start.

---

[8] In March 2002, John Manley, perhaps feeling out his new deputy prime minister wings, did get caught pronouncing on the currency in what was interpreted as a negative way. My view is that ministers are allowed one mistake of this kind, and if they are smart, they do not make it again.

The existence of these targets adds an important concreteness to the regular consultations that are called for under the *Bank of Canada Act*, and in the right policy direction. That is all to the good. But there are deeper issues. In the periodic business of agreeing to reset the targets, the minister demonstrably has the upper hand. So it is a fair question to what extent this hand will be pressed to produce more, rather than less, inflationary outcomes.

The good news is that like directives, the targets do have to be announced publicly, so there is that element of transparency. What is less favourable is that the hand that the government has played to date in setting targets has been biased toward propping inflation up. Even if this is not quite what the economic literature referred to above tells us is going to happen, it is a recognizable fact.

What more might be done? I deduce from other experiences as well as from Canada's that merely referring to price stability in the mandate does not get us very far. Like the term "non-inflationary growth," which has been rolled out so many times in G-7 communiqués, it has become virtually devoid of serious meaning. What would be progress would be to think more of inflation targets as an integral constituent of long-run monetary policy rather than as something that happens to be "agreed" from time to time. This would require progress in the governmental mindset toward something more in keeping with the direct responsibility the government has now acquired. To do this would also require more substantive discussion and analysis from authoritative official circles and obviously, given who has the last word in this area, not merely from the Bank of Canada. Canadian ministers of finance have yet to face up squarely to the responsibilities they have now acquired for deciding monetary policy strategy.

It does not seem very likely that any improvement along these lines will be made, especially if the incentives all have to be found domestically. But as I shall show later, there is an international side to the argument that reinforces the likelihood for a more principled approach—provided, that is, that we want to keep a Canadian money of any kind in a world of increasingly competitive currencies. I return to these larger issues in my final chapter.

Governance

Given the ground covered so far, my focus in this section is a relatively narrow one—what in the private sector would be termed as
corporate governance. I am going to address mainly the role of the
Bank of Canada's board—in particular, the part played by the 12
outside directors.

One of the misunderstandings from outside observers that frequently cropped up when I was in Ottawa was a tendency to liken
the Bank's board to the board of governors of the US Federal
Reserve. They are very different. Fed governors serve full-time in
Washington and meet regularly in full session. They are appointed
in essentially the same way as the chairman and vice-chairman—
that is, by the administration with the consent of the Senate. They
have particular fields assigned to them, such as international relations in the case of Henry Wallich (previously a professor of economics at Yale) and Wayne Angell (subsequently chief economist at
the US investment and brokerage house, Bear Stearns), who often
represented the Fed at the Bank for International Settlements in
Basel during my years as governor. They also vote regularly on
monetary policy issues. In contrast, in Canada directors are
appointed by the government for relatively short (but renewable)
terms of three years, and according to the *Bank of Canada Act* are to
be from "various occupations." This means that they do not necessarily have particular expertise in matters relating to monetary policy. Furthermore, like regular corporate outside directors, they serve
part-time, operating through board meetings and the various board
committees, and in this way bring their varied experiences to bear
on the Bank's affairs.

Like directors in the private sector, Bank directors (who, by the
way, cannot be directors, employees, or shareholders of a financial
institution that is a client of the Bank of Canada) have a particular
responsibility for the way the Bank is managed. They also concern
themselves with the quality of the Bank's staff. Since it is the outside directors who actually appoint the governor and senior deputy
governor (subject, as already noted, to ministerial veto), they

should concern themselves particularly with the quality of potential successors to these positions. This is unlike the situation in most Crown corporations, for which the relevant minister hands down the choice. The view I took when governor was that while top management positions obviously could not and should not be reserved for Bank insiders, it was important for the quality of the institution to be able to recruit and retain people who could potentially fill those positions. Directors agreed with this view.

The *Bank of Canada Act* does not specifically exclude directors from taking a stand relating to monetary policy. But given their part-time status, they would not be in a strong position to do so. Still, they must have an oversight role in this regard, particularly regarding the "good behaviour" proviso that the governor is subject to under legislation. In principle, one can conceive of a situation in which a governor might just welcome a ministerial directive in order to override some decision taken by a board majority. In this case, the governor would be unlikely to resign, although the whole situation would clearly need further explanation and disentangling. The reader can also note that the directive that the minister may hand down is addressed directly to the governor (that is, does not cover the board as a whole), but is also one with which "the *Bank* [my emphasis] shall comply." Whether directors would be likely to resign if the governor did seems an open question, the answer to which would depend on the circumstances.

The one time when this was clearly put to a test was, of course, when James Coyne was forced out in mid-1961. Directors were certainly caught up in the maelstrom and had some difficult decisions to make. Just one, George Crosbie from Newfoundland, resigned along with the governor. Not surprisingly, Bank directors who stayed were the object of media criticism. However, apart from any views directors may have formed as to which side of the dispute was right, an appropriate broad reason *not* to resign (at least not on the spot) would have been in order to ensure an appropriate transition in the Bank's leadership.

The fact that directors are directly appointed by the government was underlined by a newsworthy dispute in the summer of

2002 over which faction of the government party (Mr. Chrétien's or Mr. Martin's) would get to choose a director from Quebec. Still, while many directors have had political backgrounds or connections, from my experience they tend to leave partisan considerations at the door—although we once had an avowed Quebec sovereignist on board (not *management's* bright idea), which created a certain polite but clearly visible tension. The fact that many directors were politically plugged in seemed to me a distinct benefit. People at the Bank tend to avoid political situations. My view was that directors could act as a shield or as a link in relation to the political world, depending on the circumstances, and I was grateful for the advice and/or interventions that they undertook.

I saw the pattern of interactions regarding Bank governance as being essentially triangular in nature, the three points being the directors, the minister of finance and his officials, and the governor and Bank staff. From each point, lines of communication went out to the others. On some matters, such as appointments of governors, directors would deal directly with the minister's office, although most of the time their communication would be with the Bank's management. The same options applied, as circumstances warranted, for the minister and for Bank management.

Directors were not expected to be responsible for monetary policy in the formal sense in which I have been using the term "responsible" in this chapter. But they were kept very well informed about what was happening and what the issues were, so as to be able to form judgments about the quality of what the Bank was doing. For example, although I could not discuss with them the negotiations that were taking place in late 1990 and early 1991 in regard to the initial inflation targets (because the matter was confidential until announced in the budget speech), once matters were wrapped up, we held a special advance meeting of the board to put them in the picture.

In general, the management had to be forthcoming on monetary policy matters but very careful about market information. The reason was not that directors would pass on that information—they were, of course, bound by the same commitment to "fidelity and secrecy" as was Bank management. But they were not limited in the same way as Bank staff in regard to their own investments or other business activities. For this reason at least, it was better for them not to be in receipt of certain kinds of market-sensitive information, and virtually all directors understood this. I do not believe that this hampered them in performing their essential oversight tasks, including those for monetary policy.

It is not for me to say how worthwhile directors have found the Bank board experience. But from my viewpoint it was always stimulating to deal with people from different backgrounds as we journeyed together across an event-filled monetary policy landscape with an institution that was continually in the news. Not many dull moments in the Bank, including at the board level. Guylaine Saucier, a board member in the late 1980s (and later chair of the Canadian Broadcasting Corporation), once told me that her time there had been one of the most interesting that she had enjoyed in her considerable corporate experience. That is very good, because directors certainly did not do it for the money. The pay was very modest by private corporate standards, as I now know. But then again, there was no need for directors to worry about such issues as earnings management. Audits were as easy as pie, and for the auditing firms fortunate enough to get the governmental mandate, they were money for old rope.

Political Legitimacy

Lastly in regard to the board, it is useful to comment here on a particular aspect—regional representation. The regional question has been a persistent issue for the Bank in regard to what is perceived to be the institution's political legitimacy, my final topic for this chapter.

While the *Bank of Canada Act* requires that directors hail from "various occupations," there is nothing in the legislation that requires them to be, for example, from "various regions of the country." But the longstanding practice of the government has been to appoint directors on a regional basis—two each from Quebec and

Ontario, and one from each of the other provinces. This way, the Bank gets the benefit of a wide-ranging Canadian representation, both in terms of occupation (in my time, from labour leader to rancher to industrialist, with quite a few lawyers in between) and in terms of geographical distribution. The issue that cropped up continually outside, however, was that if it was so desirable to have regional representation, why not let the provinces themselves provide it?

There seem to have been two issues here. One was the Bank's responsiveness to the particular concerns of different regions, and the other its responsiveness to the outside in general—that it did not listen hard enough. Both these issues got a full hearing before the Manley committee. Sometimes the point was put in rather stark terms, as when Professor Fortin was cited in the committee's report as warmly observing that there was a perception that the Bank "is being run by a non-representative, unresponsive, monolithic and self-perpetuating clique of bureaucrats." That being said and recorded, while questions regarding the Bank's mandate are well within the competence of economists, it may be that such professionals are not so well qualified to pronounce on matters of accountability and political legitimacy. That is to say, the committee might have obtained more subtle and rewarding, if less quotable, advice on these sorts of questions if it had chosen to listen to more political scientists rather than relying so much on macroeconomists.

The committee got a wide variety of views from the witnesses it did summon, but in the end it opted for very little change. It stated that it felt that the concerns of witnesses regarding the concentration of decision-making power in the hands of the governor (though note that Professor Fortin said that the problem was a "clique"—something like the Bank's recently instituted governing council, perhaps?) and the lack of regional input into such decision making had merit. However, Manley and company were not convinced that the extent of the problem was very great. The committee thought that minor changes could rectify these apparent flaws. Accordingly, it recommended that the practice of regional balance for directors be enshrined in law and that some directors also be chosen for their expertise in monetary policy. These were indeed minor changes.

As regards expertise, there had from time to time been board directors with more than the average degree of familiarity with monetary policy issues. Gail Cook-Bennett, an economist by training, is a good example from my time, and there were others earlier. The Bank encouraged the minister to appoint such people whenever possible. But it should be noted that however refined their experience, under the Manley committee recommendations, directors would still have remained part-time.

The other side of the coin was regional representation. Here at least, all the Manley witnesses agreed that whatever the issues were, they should not be taken to imply that there could be a regionally differentiated monetary policy. While there had been occasional calls over the years for such differentiation, the fact is that it is not possible to have different monetary conditions (for example, different interest rate levels) in different parts of the country. Canada has sophisticated financial markets linked through a common currency. Accordingly, such differences would be eliminated in nothing flat by flows of funds from one region to another to offset any emerging differences in the cost of funds. For a while, I felt it necessary to include a paragraph that would point this out in virtually every speech I gave.

All the same, if pressed I would have had to allow that it was conceivable that even if monetary conditions were right for the nation as a whole, they might not be right for any single region or province. In other words, there might be no region or province that was actually at the national average in terms of economic conditions—a head in the refrigerator, feet in the oven kind of thing. The only systematic "cure" for that problem would have been different currencies and different central banks in different parts of the country—although cyclically responsive budgetary transfers from the federal government, such as unemployment insurance, could be a significant, if partial, offset. I did not get the impression that anyone really wanted to take the regional differentiation argument onto the separate currency plane—except, that is, in Quebec. More on this in a later chapter.

Some of the interest in somehow regionalizing monetary policy seemed also to be reinforced by the fact that the United States has an elaborate system of reserve districts and reserve banks under the Federal Reserve System. This interest would also be stimulated by the fact that Federal Reserve governors have to meet certain criteria (exceedingly flexible in reality) with regard to regional origin. But whatever the initial motivations for such a system, there is now no basis for a view that the United States has regional monetary policies in any meaningful sense, or any strong perception that governors or even reserve bank presidents vote regionally. Gerald Corrigan, now with Goldman Sachs but then president of the Federal Reserve Bank of New York, once underlined for me that the particular virtue of their system lay in the fact that the whole regional framework, with its network of local directors, local committees, and so on, provided the Federal Reserve with an invaluable base of grassroots, opinion-leader, support across the country. Evidently, this network develops a sense of ownership in regard to the Fed, and this must surely be important in bolstering the Federal Reserve's political legitimacy when the going gets tough.

No doubt there are steps, essentially cosmetic but perhaps worthwhile anyway, that can be taken to deflect the kinds of legitimacy criticisms aired at the Manley hearings. The Bank has moved in this direction in recent years in a number of ways. But it would certainly be a challenge, and expensive, to replicate a Fed-type regional bank system for the Bank of Canada, especially since the Bank is not a supervisor of financial institutions, and since we do not have many different banks distributed across the country that require a supervising hand, as the United States still has.

Underlying all this is a more deep-seated, even constitutional, issue: provincial versus federal accountability from the institution. As an organ of a federal institution, it is hardly surprising that the Manley committee would tiptoe around such a matter. But it keeps coming up, especially when constitutional issues gain prominence. One obvious problem is to gauge what would become of the *federal* directive power if there were full-fledged *provincial* representatives on the Bank of Canada's board. Another similar set of issues would arise if provinces felt that they were entitled to a say in determining inflation targets. My only answer to the conundrums posed by the possibility of many masters—like the federal government's when it made its post-Meech proposals in 1991—is that this would be yet another excellent reason for bearing down on the Bank of Canada's mandate, and increasing its precision in a constructive way.

As a final point on perceptions of legitimacy, the Bank has surely gained points from being viewed as a public institution that was highly professional and non-partisan. Furthermore, as competent central banks go, I must say that I thought it was, to use that overworked Toronto adjective, world-class. Some Canadians may have recognized this, and that would have helped its political legitimacy also.

CHAPTER 3

A Place
to Work

Operating a central bank involves more lines of work than the broad issues of monetary management, interest rates, and exchange rates that have been touched upon so far. As the banker for chartered banks (and directly or indirectly for financial institutions generally) and the supplier of banknotes, as well as the government's debt manager, the Bank of Canada has had some other significant businesses to run. In fact, the part of its staff occupied in those kinds of operations has been larger than that involved in monetary policy matters. So here I want to look at some of the issues and events in those areas, starting with the Bank's staffing in general.

Getting and Keeping Central Bankers

With a nod toward its independent status, the Bank's employees, even if concentrated in Ottawa, do not come under the Public Service Commission and all the wide range of rules and regulations that it brings in its train. Its staff is not unionized, although there was a union for a few years in the Bank's Montreal agency. But of course, as a medium-sized bureaucracy it has its own set of staff rules and internal relationship issues to manage. Ultimately, it is very much influenced by the climate in which it operates—the Ottawa public service—in terms of staff pay, benefits, and the like.

In the early 1990s, the House Committee on Finance decided to have an inquiry into the Bank's salary policies. This was led by its

chairman, Don Blenkarn, a parliamentarian of some colour—
indeed, at times so full of hue as to be almost iridescent. His eager
interest had been sparked by headlines in the *Ottawa Citizen*. These,
in turn, had been generated by a reporter taking the Bank's salary
bill for two successive years, calculating the percentage change, and
then dividing it by the percentage change in the staff from one year
to the next—all material available in the Bank's annual report. This
provided an average increase in the wage bill per head and, as the
professionally indignant *Citizen* saw it, a smoking gun. So I then
was called before the committee, and was happy to bring with me
a detailed reconciliation of these crude numbers (which did not
adjust for such things as changes in the mix of staff) with what had
actually been happening in pay policy for individuals at the Bank.
Perhaps I should not have been surprised, but it seemed remarkable
how quickly the chairman lost interest in my presentation when he
perceived how little there was to answer for. Still, I absolutely insisted on plowing through the full answer for the record.

Before lunch, and raising the stakes (or perhaps merely striking
back), the committee also asked for the Bank's detailed operating
budget. This meant a lively noon debate back at the Bank as to
whether we should comply. Louise Vaillancourt-Châtillon, then
the Bank's corporate secretary, provided a forceful view (her views
were always agreeably clear) that we should decline. I returned after
lunch prepared to do so on the grounds that the matter at least
required further consideration on our part, and it certainly would
need to be presented to the Bank's board for its consideration—
where I would argue for declining. My basic concern was not over
supplying the budget itself. We were careful managers, although I
knew that this was not adequate protection if politicians were on a
pseudo-righteous warpath. Rather, my concern was over the implications for a future role of the Finance Committee in the Bank's
management. Where would this end? Much ado about nothing. In
the afternoon, the committee did not return to its fishing expedi-
tion at all. Perhaps it had reflected further on the matter during
lunch, or had even plain forgotten about it. And all's well that ends
well, I must say.

By and large, the quality of the Bank's staff reflects that of the federal public service. After all, it recruits from the same gene pool. But given the Bank's more compact operation (in my time, slightly over 2,000 people, now appreciably fewer after the major and timely reorganization led by Gordon Thiessen), it ought to be more cohesive than the public service generally and with a greater sense of identification with the institution. At the very least, people knew each other better across the body as a whole.

This seemed to show up to particularly good effect in our success in bringing about a more truly bilingual institution. In the 1970s, it became particularly apparent to William Lawson—the Bank's more than able senior deputy governor (1973–84) and in effect its chief operating officer—that our efforts to encourage a bilingual operation needed more focus. So toward the end of the decade, he set up a triumvirate to make sure the institution got what he was looking for. This trio was led by Deputy Governor Douglas Humphreys, who spent most of his time overseeing the Bank's securities market operations, with Serge Vachon, who advised on financial stability matters (see the next chapter) and was also the chair of the Canadian Payments Association, and myself as sidekicks. Its main challenge, simply put, was to get anglophones to the point where they could operate in French, since most francophones could already manage in English. We also wanted to encourage francophones to use French in the workplace and not to feel uncomfortable about doing so.

Ensuring that language training was better focused on where it would add most value was one avenue. The other was to generate a clearer understanding that being able to operate in both English and French did matter for one's career prospects. Because of the Bank's compactness, we were able to avoid the general Ottawa approach of designating certain positions as "bilingual" in and of themselves. Our view was that *all* supervisors should be bilingual, and we would be working systematically toward that goal. To that end, we would be seeing to it that each unit had its critical mass of bilingual capability, which would then generate momentum of its own as French became more readily used. We were able to make great strides. Our language advisor, Martin Samuels, played an important and imaginative role in keeping up the momentum and particularly the enthusiasm for self-learning. We were able to carry the staff with us in a cooperative and enlightened effort that had exceptional payoff for its *esprit de corps*.

The Bank has always recruited widely for professional staff, though not usually as far afield as it did in my case. I was invited in from Washington, D.C., after making the Bank's acquaintance through regular visits to Ottawa from 1970 on behalf of the International Monetary Fund to talk about exchange rates—in particular, about when Canada was going to fix its exchange rate again. I joined the staff on the same day that Gerald Bouey became governor. In later years, having had to make the recruiting pitch myself, I was aware that the Bank's reputation stood it in wide, good stead. That was important because people certainly have not joined for the money. There may have been a time relatively early on when, as Bank lore has it, its professionals were paid well, at least by Ottawa standards, but in more recent years this has been less true and perhaps not at all. The Bank's capacity to attract good people has depended more upon the interest and relevance of the work it could supply and on the likelihood that there were also good people to work with. And people did not lose out later when they recorded Bank of Canada employment on their resumés. In fact, quite the opposite, judging by the turnover, which was onward and upward generally, and certainly for more money, whether the move was to elsewhere in Ottawa, to the financial services industry, or to international financial institutions. In case the reader is wondering, I should note that I took a pay cut when I moved from the IMF to the Bank, valuing highly the change of scene and the chance to do policy in one place rather than just to advise on it in one country after another. But I would not recommend this as a general Bank hiring strategy.

It is a fair question whether the nation would be better served from an efficiency standpoint by relocating the Bank to Canada's main financial centre—Toronto. But that would be daunting from the distributional viewpoint of Canadian politics, whatever the efficiency considerations. And there have also been important advantages to the federal public sector in having the Bank where it is. What would the rest of Ottawa have done without the Bank of Canada as a staffing pool? While recently there has been a significant senior transfer into the Bank from the outside, particularly and quite unusually from the Department of Finance, the basic pattern over the years has been for the Bank to supply human resources to the rest of Ottawa—including several who eventually became deputy ministers of finance.

Of course, turnover had its important good points: fresh faces, fresh ideas, renewal in general. But at times this became difficult to manage. I still recall vividly when, during my time as chief of the Research Department in the late 1970s, we lost virtually the whole middle management of the department in one summer. Fortunately, we had good people coming up who then got their chance, even if it was sooner than we (and perhaps they) had anticipated. Leo de Bever was one of those who ably filled the gap and also revamped our forecasting methodology, until he moved on as well, to economic consulting in Toronto and then to the Ontario Teachers' Pension organization. What this turnover meant was that one could seriously offer new recruits the chances of quite rapid advancement. Maybe the starting pay was not so brilliant, but the potential rise could look attractively steep and quick if the recruits were as good as they thought they were. The trick in this process was to retain a core of reasonably good senior people who could supply leadership. Somehow we seemed able to do that, though at times it was close.

Before turning to the Bank's more operational areas—debt management, banknotes, and the functioning of agencies across the country—it is worth noting the Bank's involvement with the government's Business Development Bank of Canada (BDC). Our association went back a long way. The BDC started as the Industrial Development Bank and was set up back in 1944 to be an arm of the Bank of Canada. At that time, the prevailing view was that there might be a market "gap" in the supply of credit to small businesses, and that this justified the creation of an official lending mechanism.

Whether such a gap actually exists is far more questionable now than it was then, and even then it was debatable. Gordon Thiessen wrote his doctoral thesis on this very subject and came away far from convinced.

In the early 1970s, the federal government took over the institution to run it as a Crown corporation. But given the historical links, the Bank stayed involved through the governor's role as a member of the BDC board. Although that presence might have been useful when, for example, the institution was securing Eurodollar financing, it became less and less relevant. The BDC's activities were diversifying rapidly as it shifted from focusing on any credit gap to being cast as the government's instrument in a broad array of activities with small business—some systematic, some rather ad hoc, and some at the very least debatable from the viewpoint of the institution's plausible mandate. So in the early 1990s, choosing the moment when Guy Lavigueur retired and François Beaudoin took over as president, I resigned from the board. The controversial recent history of the BDC, particularly the alleged pressure to make "political" loans in Quebec, has to my mind only confirmed the wisdom of that decision.

Looking back, perhaps the most concrete contribution that I made to the affairs of the BDC (apart from helping in the nomination of François Beaudoin as president) was at the time of the "strip club" affair that made headlines in 1989. Among the small businesses that BDC had helped to start were a great many motels and small hotels. Some of these establishments were hiring strippers to boost bar revenues, and when this came to public attention it created a flurry in the media and consequently in Ottawa. BDC management overreacted and proposed a new set of financing codes more suited to the stricter sort of religious foundation than to the Canadian business environment. My view, supported by Georgina Wyman, on the board as deputy minister of Supply and Services and also familiar with how such things went in Ottawa, was that all the attention was a nine-day wonder. We were able to persuade management to calm down and consider necessary changes in a more measured and realistic way.

Managing Debt Management

The whole debt operation changed greatly while I was at the Bank, as we started moving from a paper-based, labour-intensive system to computers. The early years were particularly difficult, as we tried to keep a lid on the overall budget while running what were in effect two debt management systems in parallel: the old manual one and the emerging electronic platform. When, we wondered, would the savings from computers ever start showing up? They did eventually, but it took a long time and the transition was expensive. It was small consolation that we were not the only ones in that particular boat.

One basic step, taken soon after I became governor, was to settle on the approach to take in relation to the budding Canadian Depository for Securities (CDS). This outfit had been established some years before by a forward-looking group of financial institutions as a means of making transactions in the Canadian securities market—stocks, bonds, and treasury bills—more efficient and secure. In essence, with everyone plugged into the depository, there was no need to process and lug around the debt documents themselves, with all the risks and delays that this entailed. A "book" or electronic transfer within the depository, made in the same way as payments from one account to another at an automated teller machine, would be all that was needed.

The unique issue facing the Bank—both as fiscal agent for the government and as the institution in Ottawa most knowledgeable about the nuts and bolts of financial markets—was where to put government debt. Should it be set up as an account in the depository? If not, should anything else be done? One school of thought in the Bank was that it was not appropriate to move the debt on to the CDS. After all, this was a private facility, and in some sense the authorities would be ceding control over how the debt was coped with at this rather basic, fairly clerical level. There were also precedents elsewhere for separate government debt depositories.

In the end, this go-it-alone view did not prevail for two reasons. In the first place, it would have worked against the general Canadian interest in having an effective depository in our country. By bulking up the CDS through the addition of the very large (too large from any other point of view) government debt book, the Bank made the depository solution far more effective for everyone. Indeed, it was questionable whether the CDS would have had the heft and momentum to succeed if government debt had not been included. Second, there was a great deal to be said for a private sector-driven exercise. Leaving the initiative to the private sector would improve the incentives. It was the best way of ensuring that the efficiencies that private institutions sought would be forthcoming at a pace that they themselves considered worth financing. The same could not be said for initiatives from Ottawa, whether the Bank of Canada was in charge or not.

However, a private sector answer did call for a formal supervisory framework. We had to have assurance and in turn provide assurance to the minister of finance that the government's debt in the depository had proper accounting and internal controls. This supervisory role was taken on by the Superintendent of Financial Institutions, and the way it was done was by having the CDS become, for these purposes, a federally incorporated trust company.

Quite a few years of work with the CDS, including much work by a Bank task force, were required before the project reached fruition. Dealing with bonds was relatively straightforward, but for treasury bills the arrangements had to be much more elaborate, given the fact that they moved around so much more—often on a day-to-day basis as they were used as collateral for large (billions of dollars) and varying short-term borrowings by financial institutions as they managed their day-to-day liquidity needs. But now the CDS is up and running, with no more than the usual hiccups. Typically for Canada, one of those hiccups has been how to deal with the Government of Quebec's demands as to how the new body would operate with regard to that province—in particular, how sizable its physical presence would have to be in Montreal. The bigger the better, was the province's determined view.

Trimming and Designing Banknotes

When economists talk about the Bank of Canada "printing money," they are using a concrete metaphor for the fact that the Bank, as a central bank, has special powers that allow it to decide how much liquidity to supply to the Canadian financial system—overwhelmingly in the form of additions to chartered bank reserves. But of course, the Bank does also really print money in the form of bank notes. The actual printing is done by private firms, which I view as an advantage, having seen the productivity and labour management problems some other central banks have had with their own industrial operations in the form of captive banknote printing shops. Even so, this banknote work involves the Bank in a lot of planning and painstaking control, especially in regard to currency design, distribution, redemption, and destruction of (over)used notes. Banknotes may be small change for the Canadian financial system in general, but these millions of pieces of special coloured paper represent a big processing activity for the Bank of Canada, and one that has to be conducted with extraordinary security.

Before the Bank of Canada was set up, the issuance of banknotes was shared between the banks and the Ministry of Finance—in the latter case, dominion notes. The right to issue notes was transferred to the Bank from its start in 1934, but with an extended period of transition for the chartered banks—presumably because they were giving up a profit centre in the form of the interest-free liabilities issued.

In pre-loonie days, the thinking at the Bank as regards its profit and loss statement (or, as it is put officially, its "balance of revenue") was that we were making money on dollar bills as long as the rate of interest on treasury bills was above 6 per cent—not that this was any incentive to keep interest rates up. The calculation was as follows: a physical dollar bill lasted in circulation for about a year before it became so worn that it had to be replaced; its all-in cost of reproduction was about six cents (or 6 per cent of one dollar); and the proceeds of this dollar would be invested, most likely in Government of Canada treasury bills. From all this, it followed that we would be in the black on this denomination if rates stayed above 6 per cent annually. Obviously the "profit" (technically known as seigniorage) for the Bank is greater on bills of larger denomination. The percentage cost for each denomination goes down as the face value of the note goes up, since the cost of production does not change very much, and in addition, higher denomination notes have a circulation life longer than one year.

Since the Bank, after paying its operating expenses, turns its profits over to the government, the latter has a pecuniary interest in the banknote business. But the government is also in charge of issuing money through the Royal Canadian Mint, the official producer of coins, so it has currency choices in looking at ways to maximize its revenue. And the profit calculations are different for the Mint. A coin costs considerably more to produce than a note, but to all practical intents it never has to be taken in and replaced. Once a coin leaves the Mint it stays outside, except on those rare occasions when it is presented back as being mutilated. Therefore, provided the initial cost of, say, a dollar coin is less than a dollar (which it is), a clear upfront profit is available regardless of the going rate of interest. In the late 1980s, the government saw that the profit on a dollar coin was greater than it was on a paper note.

The Mint was keen to expand its business. It had clearly had its eye for the longest time on a dollar coin, and beyond. The Bank had no particular problem with this, but it pointed out to a parliamentary committee and to the government that the costs and benefits to society of different kinds of monies were not to be found just in the pockets of the public sector. The conveniences or inconveniences for the private sector also needed to be taken into account, besides any budgetary gain to the government and empire building by the Mint.

When these other factors were looked at, it seemed that the private sector had, overall, a preference for banknotes over coins. Desire for larger denomination coins came from just two sources—

the vending machine sector and transit companies—but not from the public at large or from financial institutions. Both these latter groups found coins, because of their heavy bulk, more difficult to handle than banknotes. It was indeed telling that when new coins had been introduced elsewhere—as they had in the United Kingdom (the pound coin) and the United States (the Susan B. Anthony dollar)—they had not caught on with the general public. We deduced from this that the public would accept the coin only if the dollar bill were withdrawn from circulation. So that was done, and soon after, a two-dollar coin was issued as well.

One further complication. There existed, and no doubt still exists, a group in North America (mainly in the United States, but also with a following in Canada) that was convinced that one of these fine days, the government will destroy wealth by refusing to honour its currency. Argentina, it must be allowed, has just supplied an innovative way of doing this by restoring its local, more inflationary peso. But the basic scenario in the past, across a range of countries, has been some kind of currency reform—out with the old currency and in with a completely new set. Starting afresh with a new currency has usually been billed as a token of the authorities' determination from then on to be strict about inflation, but also at times as a device to eliminate ill-gotten gains (from, for example, black marketeering) cached away in the form of banknotes. To avoid this charge, the Bank, while ceasing to issue or reissue dollar bills after June 1989 and two-dollar notes after February 1996, was also at pains to ensure that these bills stayed legal tender—as they still are today if you can find them.

Let me end this section on two less portentous notes—first on the market for coins, and second on banknote design. As regards coins, while the Mint does not generally take them back, coins do tend to disappear from circulation over time, and for economic reasons.

On one occasion, the Bank had visitors from the central bank of Zaire. Among the various interesting things they had to tell us (not many of which we were likely to imitate) was that in their country, there were no coins in circulation. Our questioning revealed that this was because of inflation. If prices rise sufficiently rapidly, the metal value of coins soon comes to exceed the face value. Then—as has happened here particularly strikingly with quarters containing silver, but much more radically in Zaire—coins are extracted from circulation to be melted down for their metal. But what is the particular problem with that (besides the inconvenience factor), above and beyond the fact that it is a symptom of endemic inflation? The government will still have made its seigniorage profit on the coins when they were first minted, and the coins' disappearance would be no direct loss to the *public* purse. The particular trouble for a mint comes when the authorities feel that they still have to continue to issue a certain coin (such as the penny in Canada) that may cost more to produce than it can be issued for. It would be difficult to drop the penny, given that we all want proper change and certainly not a penny less after we pay our GSTs and PSTs. The Zairians apparently had no such preoccupation. Perhaps they did not collect taxes, except through inflation, that is.

As for banknote design, discretion requires me to skip the sensitive territory of banknote security and limit myself to presentation—also sensitive, but in a very different way from counterfeiting. Legally, the minister of finance is responsible for banknote design and is, of course, carefully briefed and consulted as the Bank staff and management work through what is bound to be the long, painstaking process of introducing a new design. In fact, the Bank of Canada steps up to take on whatever problems or criticisms the design choices stir up, as they invariably do.

As an illustration—birds. Most Canadians will recall that the last complete redesign of our notes displayed various Canadian birds on the reverse side. The two-dollar bill, traditionally ochre-red in colour, was a natural for the robin redbreast. But while the colour was perfect, the technically correct name, "American robin," was an issue. "American" on a Canadian banknote? No way. So the bird was labelled just "robin." But curiously enough, there was less sensitivity about the nomenclature in French, where the unambiguously correct term, "merle d'Amérique," was applied. As for the five-dollar bill, the problem there was that the obvious contender, the blue jay, had to be ruled out as unlikely to play well outside of Toronto. So it carried a belted kingfisher by default.

Despite such precautions, the bird series could not escape criticism, not just retail but also wholesale. An angry citizen wrote to Governor Bouey to complain that no birds at all, whatever their name or colour, should figure on our currency. It seemed that the complainant's spouse was phobic about birds, and that this phobia extended even to pictures of birds. The letter concluded indignantly, "How could you be so thoughtless!" Anyone knowing Gerald Bouey would appreciate that "thoughtless," in whatever sense, was just about the last label one could apply. In any event, Canadians now can register that the newest notes will not be showcasing birds, although one must also allow that the first one released, the 10-dollar bill, does have on its reverse, but in the background, a pair of doves. A peace offering?

Rethinking Agencies

When the Bank of Canada was set up, it inherited, by virtue of its assigned functions as banknote issuer and government debt manager, a series of note and bond distribution points across the country that had come under Canada's receiver general. (This office is now best known as the one to which we send our income tax cheques.) These points in turn became the Bank of Canada's agencies for similar distribution functions. As the physical distribution function has shrunk because of debt computerization and the substitution of coins for notes, so has the need for such points. But the agencies have also fulfilled a role as a symbol of the Bank's (and perhaps even, at times, the federal government's) presence and contact across the nation.

I can well recall that when discussing our budget with the Bank's directors, coming as they did from various regions, we used to get a rather dusty response when we suggested that the institution could generate major efficiency savings by shutting down many of these agency buildings. They saw it a bit like the Mounties offering to save money by cutting out their popular musical ride spectacle. One thoughtful director said that he understood perfectly the rationale for closing agencies, but as he saw it, if the agency in his province were closed he would be obliged to resign. This ended the internal debate. Agencies have now been cut way back, but only after the major Ottawa budget slashing of 1995, which provided important political cover. Of course, the musical ride continues.

In a similar vein, the Bank's management tended to have difficulty persuading directors that the best site for the banknote operations of an agency was not, as it seemed to be in the past, close to the financial district. The point we made was that they were in reality quasi-industrial operations processing large amounts of paper, and were therefore best operated on one level rather than in an office tower over several floors. It was also helpful for distribution purposes to be close to good truck routes. This issue had to be confronted when the Bank came seriously to consider replacing its superannuated operation in Montreal, situated in unacceptably cramped quarters on Place Victoria in the centre of town. Reflecting the symbolic importance of signalling a federal presence in the middle of town, especially in that town, one of our directors was moved to opine that if you had to have an industrial operation located in the financial district, he could not think of a better business than one that manufactured money! In the end, however, one of our Quebec directors, Nancy Orr-Gaucher, and I were pleased to inaugurate a state-of-the-art Bank of Canada agency outside the city core. In time, the Toronto agency followed suit and moved from its old downtown location on University Avenue to a site several kilometres away.

A similar story about central bank size, but in a broader context, is now being played out in Europe among the countries that have adopted the euro as their common currency. The establishment of the European Central Bank in Frankfurt has diminished enormously the monetary policy roles of the individual national central banks. But they are having great difficulty reconciling the size of their establishments to this diminution of responsibilities. To make matters worse, quite a few can be fairly reckoned to have been grossly overstaffed even before the currency changeover. The usual suspects—entrenched job security, local sentiment favouring the hometown boy, and such—are clearly playing a role in the dogged defence of maintaining the size of these grand old institutions.

However, the latest point at issue is more substantive: the role of European central banks—generally far bigger establishments than the Bank of Canada (whether absolutely or per head of population)—in supervising financial institutions, and whether that role should last. This has never been an issue for the Bank of Canada for the simple historical reason that it has never been a bank supervisor. Of course, the mere fact that the Bank of Canada does not do supervision does not mean that a central bank should not be involved, or at least that there are not real issues in this area. Indeed, those issues underlie much of what I discuss in the next chapter.

CHAPTER 4

Financial Stability: Doing What a Central Bank Can

As I see it, the proper responsibility of the central bank—assuring the financial well-being of society—requires an intimate involvement in financial supervision and regulation. In fact, I have long believed that it is only the central bank among the various regulatory bodies which share responsibility in this area, that can represent the perspective of the financial system as a whole. This should be the central organizing principle behind any comprehensive reform of financial regulation and supervision....

I hasten to add that I did not say this. It wasn't even said in Canada. This is Henry Kaufman, the long-time and highly respected expositor of US financial markets, writing in 1994. At about that time, the Federal Reserve was fending off an attempt by the US Treasury to consolidate banking examination into one agency—in principle, a worthy attempt to avoid duplication and expense. But this also meant cutting back the Fed's supervisory involvement, and Mr. Kaufman saw good public policy reasons why this should not be allowed to happen.

The Fed won that round—the jury being Congress—and it won ostensibly on the argument that in order to do its monetary policy

job properly, it needed to continue to have direct, leading involvement in US banking supervision, at least as regards those banks
that had important dealings in international financial markets. It
also won because of another, generally unstated but widely appreciated, view of matters: that the Federal Reserve had considerable
financial market know-how at its disposal which would not be
equivalently on tap at other agencies and that its absence could be
damaging to effective supervision—especially in a crisis, when an
authoritative but deft hand would be needed. Behind this view was
a further one: that the Fed's know-how could not be, or would not
be, used effectively by other agencies if the Fed itself did not have
some direct authority.

The way supervision of financial institutions is handled around
the world varies quite a lot. And it continues to change. Historically, the largest single common denominator in the mix has been
that central banks have played a key, direct role in supervising
banks. However, as I pointed out at the close of the previous chapter, this has never been the case in Canada. The supervisory function, originally through the Office of the Inspector General of
Banks, was established in 1924 upon a serious bank failure, the
Home Bank, and about a decade before the Bank of Canada began
operations. Certainly, Graham Towers thought that bank supervision should be moved to his shop, but he found his match in Clifford Clark and supervision stayed, as before, under the wing of the
Department of Finance.

While the Bank is far from being a supernumerary in dealing
with issues relating to stability of the Canadian financial system,
given its lack of supervisory authority, its actions are at one remove
and somewhat episodic. Furthermore, with the presence of other,
full-time players—the Office of the Superintendent of Financial
Institutions, the Canada Deposit Insurance Corporation, and,
always somewhere, the minister of finance and his officials—the
way the Bank manages its involvement is appreciably more complex than when it goes about its monetary policy business.

Does this matter? I cannot think of any clear instance where
excluding the Bank from supervision has harmed its capacity to

conduct monetary policy. But I would argue on the evidence that its expertise and familiarity with financial markets can make a valuable contribution to the supervision of Canadian financial institutions, and certainly to financial stability overall, provided its capabilities and experience can be properly brought to bear.

The crucial question, as it also appears to be in the United States, is whether these attributes can be brought to bear effectively if the Bank does not engage directly in supervision. Alternatively, one might ask whether the Bank could be an effective supervisor, or at least more effective than the incumbent agency (until the late 1980s, the Office of the Inspector General of Banks and since then its successor, the Office of the Superintendent of Financial Institutions). Both these questions became real issues through the events leading up to the collapse in 1985 of two Western Canadian banks— the Canadian Commercial Bank (CCB) and the Northland—and the subsequent public commission of inquiry led by Supreme Court Justice Willard Estey.

The Collapse, the Estey Inquiry, and the Changes

For a great many decades, Canada had no history of overt bank failures—just as well, because we did not have that many banks to begin with, certainly not compared to the United States. Until the events of 1985, there had not been a bank collapse since the Home Bank in 1923, which is not to say that there had been no difficulties in the banking industry, with some burials (as discreetly as possible) from time to time. So when these twin failures came, they created a real stir. The CCB and the Northland may have accounted for only 1 per cent of the total assets of our banking system, but this still represented some $4 billion of messy financial claims and obligations to be sorted out by receivers, courts, and government agencies.

This is not the place to narrate the whole painful episode, lasting some six months from start to finish, even if one excludes the subsequent legal manoeuvrings over liability and indemnification.

The basic story can be found in Justice Estey's official report, a volume of over 600 pages released in late 1986. Here, the point to be stressed is that the news of imminent failure that was brought by the CCB to Ottawa in the spring of 1985 came as a complete surprise to the inspector general and also, it seems, to the CCB's auditors. As Estey put it, and not too strongly, it was a "startling message."

Furthermore, while there was an initial official declaration of solvency by the supervisory authorities (in the absence of good knowledge, what else could they say?), it took them quite some time to establish with confidence the actual financial condition of those banks (soon after the CCB news, the Northland Bank also began to experience difficulty retaining deposits) and to advise Minister of Finance Michael Wilson, in September 1985 to close them. And all the while that the jury was out on the weighty matter of whether the two banks had any capital left—that is, they were deemed sound until proven insolvent—the Bank of Canada poured in extraordinary liquidity support at one end (making direct advances to both institutions as required), while funds on deposit with them drained away at the other. This help, received in the form of Bank of Canada advances, meant that the banks did not have to sell assets at knock-down prices to cover the erosion of deposits. This support mounted rapidly over the summer of 1985 and reached close to $2 billion by September. Spillovers of loss of confidence onto other smaller banks called for additional liquidity assistance, and total bank advances peaked at over $5 billion in March 1986. At that point, these loans took up fully a quarter of the Bank of Canada's balance sheet.

To manage this expansion in one component of its assets without ballooning its liabilities, the monetary base, the Bank in effect sold off equivalently large amounts of the treasury bills it was holding. Doing this left its balance sheet at about the same size as it would have been if it had not made any emergency bank advances at all. We could not be sure that this operation would go so smoothly, especially if broader confidence regarding Canada had taken a knock on account of this domestic financial problem, but it did. Fortunately, the general economic and financial situation at that time was relatively calm, so the operation proceeded as if the funds withdrawn from these smaller banks had been transferred directly into the additional treasury bills that were now on the market.

Although it was not the supervisor, the Bank was thrown into the centre of this fray from the moment that the news of the CCB's impending collapse hit Ottawa in March. Indeed, many people, including parliamentarians, assumed initially that the Bank, rather than the Inspector General of Banks, was the supervisor. However, Justice Estey summed up nicely the rather more complicated and uncertain position that the Bank was in when he observed:

> The Governor of the Bank of Canada was seen as the leader of the banking system. Naturally, therefore, he was looked to for leadership in this time of crisis. Indeed, it was taken for granted by all participants that the Governor of the Bank of Canada was the appropriate person to preside over the 22 and 24 March meetings to determine the fate of the CCB. Unfortunately, the Bank of Canada is not clothed with the necessary statutory powers or staff to select the appropriate program in such circumstances and to guide its performance.

Not surprisingly in the light of these and broader considerations, at one stage Justice Estey and his staff investigated the possibility of the Bank of Canada taking over the bank supervisory function. I must say that I and some others at the Bank were intrigued by the thought. There was no doubt that once it got going on this, the Bank would do a decent job. Besides the quality of the staff it could bring to bear, it would be able to contribute directly a wide range of market intelligence and knowledge, both as regards particular institutions and more generally. Furthermore, from the standpoint of properly aligning incentives, there was something to be said for combining the supervisory and liquidity lending functions under one roof. If they were housed together, this could promote earlier supervisory intervention and prompter corrective action, as the Americans would later put it when they got around to an overhaul of their own regulatory and supervisory arrangements in the early 1990s. The Bank of Canada was unlikely to drag its heels in getting a good read on a bank's difficulties, since its mind would be concentrated by the fact that it could be on the hook for large liquidity advances if confidence evaporated. Justice Estey again phrased the general issue well when he asked:

> How can one build into the present system the incentive and the will to intervene in a timely fashion so as to reduce to a minimum the risks to depositors and investors, and the cost to the community associated with the liquidation of a bank?

Other heads prevailed. Notwithstanding Justice Estey's promotion of the idea, neither the banks nor the minister of finance were in favour of the Bank's taking over supervision. Still, if we ourselves had been more receptive, Justice Estey would probably have pursued the thought more vigorously. But Governor Bouey did not provide any encouragement either. One consideration that he had noted in his testimony, as had William Kennett, the Inspector General of Banks, was the possibility of conflict between the Bank's monetary policy role and the supervisory function. That is, we might conceivably be persuaded to follow an inappropriately expansionary policy in order to take pressure off a financial institution—in other words, print money to save a failing bank. Another challenge that could have been raised but was not was that by becoming a supervisor and potentially having to close down financial institutions, the Bank would be courting political unpopularity (there are bound to be recriminations when a financial institution is closed down), which could hamper its role in monetary policy—not that monetary policy was a popularity contest.

But these are secondary points. More broadly persuasive was the fact that Governor Bouey could see that the financial system was becoming increasingly complex, with the roles of different kinds of institutions increasingly intertwined, and that it therefore made less and less sense to have single-purpose supervisors—for example, just for banking. The governor alluded to this issue in his testimony but expanded on it more forcefully within the Bank to those of us who were inclined to give the idea of supervision by the central bank a whirl. He pointed out that no one could think seriously that the Bank of Canada should, for example, get into the business of supervising insurance. His clinching argument was that we might as well forget the idea because political Ottawa would never accept our engaging in banking supervision, since in its eyes at least, that would make the Bank too powerful. Furthermore, the Bank's statutory independence, and its tendency to think for itself, might not have sat too well with government in this regard. In Canada, the decision to liquidate a financial institution has always been, as Justice Estey was at pains to emphasize, an explicitly political one.

It is also worth recording that this kind of exchange at the Bank had its counterpart at the Federal Reserve. No so long ago, Governor Laurence Meyer, commenting on the move in some countries (such as Australia and the United Kingdom) to a single regulator for all financial institutions, observed:

> Adding a powerful single regulator to a powerful and independent central bank would create an entity with significant authority outside the day-to-day direct purview of government, so governments have opted to combine the regulators and strip the supervisory and regulatory power from the central bank.

At the same time, Meyer noted that governments "have continued to make their central banks responsible for financial stability." So the question that comes up again is whether this financial stability responsibility can be discharged adequately if the central bank is not well plugged in to supervision and the information that supervision can generate.

The Canadian government decided, post-Estey, to combine federal deposit taking and insurance supervision under one roof by establishing the Office of the Superintendent of Financial Institutions (OSFI). This move provided a convenient burial place for the Office of the Inspector General of Banks (OIGB) and the basis for a

fresh start in banking supervision. More importantly, it also provided the basis for synergies in the financial supervisory effort overall. All the same, this organizational change did not address in any
direct way Justice Estey's main concern, which was the absence of
proper incentive mechanisms—or as he put it, a "will to act"—on
the part of supervisors.

His diagnosis was that it was not simply absence of information
that held supervisors back from doing what they needed to do, but
something more fundamental. Neither was it clear that new
arrangements (referred to in more detail a little later) to increase
the flow of information among interested parties in Ottawa would
do the trick. Discouraged in his efforts to entice the Bank of Canada into the ring, Justice Estey's actual recommendation was to
house the OIGB as part of the federal government's Canada Deposit
Insurance Corporation (CDIC). This body, located in Ottawa, provides basic insurance for household deposits at most Canadian
financial institutions (credit union deposits, insured by provinces,
are the large exception). Since 1986 it has a mixed board—partly
federal officials, partly private sector—but operates clearly as a government agency. The fact that CDIC, like the Bank of Canada,
would have a direct financial interest in what was done in relation
to an ailing financial institution, because of the financial liabilities
it could incur obviously could also encourage the will to act—the
willingness to pull the trigger promptly on an ailing financial institution and minimize the losses.

Subsequent tussles between OSFI and CDIC, which I observed
from close quarters as an ex officio director of CDIC, were more
over this issue of timely action than anything else, as one federal
trust company after another exited the scene in various ways and
calls were made on CDIC to cough up funds to smooth their depar-
tures. As for non-federal trust companies, there OSFI was off the
hook, since only CDIC dealt directly with provincial financial institutions. As Ronald McKinlay, then chairman of CDIC, would cheerfully volunteer about the other Ottawa institutions represented
around the table, we might be federal in scope, but CDIC was, after
all, "national"—that is, federal *and* provincial in scope.

Still, even in the federal sphere, there was room for a better exchange of information and, hopefully, cooperation. Some who were less pessimistic than Justice Estey may have thought that this would be sufficient to improve incentives. To that end, the federal government, among its various responses to the conclusions of the inquiry, established an Ottawa umbrella group known as the Financial Institutions Supervisory Committee (FISC).

&c.

The Bank and what it knows cannot be ignored in supervisory decisions regarding financial institutions. As the body in Ottawa that is best informed about what is happening in financial markets generally, and often in particular financial institutions as well, it is in a position to make well-informed judgments on the state of confidence and the degree of risk to the financial sector as a whole, and from there to the economy. I hesitate to say that the Bank's judgments are bound to be right, but I would argue that its views on these matters should be given great weight.

In this regard, the declared purpose of FISC—chaired by the Superintendent of Financial Institutions and including CDIC, the Department of Finance, and the Bank[1]—has been to ensure that pertinent information, including of course any news from the Bank of Canada, is shared for the general benefit of the supervisory function. This is sound in principle, but in practice it works only as well as the chair wants it to. In my time at the Bank, OSFI was reluctant to engage in meaningful sharing of information. It seemed that important people felt that somehow their authority, or even their supervisory role, could be threatened by the existence of such a consultative body. This being said, I understand that matters have improved in more recent years, which shows that the conflicts that OSFI has in chairing this process, given that its own operations and competence will need to be assessed if the process is to be serious, are at least not terminal.

---

[1] With the addition also of the Financial Consumer Agency of Canada since 2001.

Settling Accounts

One area in which Bank of Canada involvement in financial system matters has remained fairly intensive and quite likely has increased, judging by the volume of material that pours forth, has been on the payments and settlements side of financial transactions. It has to be that way. As the liquidity backstop for the financial system and the only institution that can print money, the Bank is unavoidably involved in seeing to it that such systems work the way they are supposed to—that is, safely, hopefully efficiently, and certainly unhesitatingly.

At the simplest level, paying cash on the nail for a good or service, there are no settlement problems at all. Delivery and payment come at the same moment. But once payments are channelled through financial institutions, and especially once the transactions get very large (billions of dollars a day for securities, for example), questions as to how or when a payment gets settled and becomes final assume a huge importance. Essentially, it is a question of ensuring that if the financial intermediaries (basically banks) stumble, they do not infect the general system through the channel of clearing and settlement arrangements, thereby producing financial chaos and general outcry. This is because the common response of financial institutions to uncertainty is to stop payment first and verify later, as they rush to protect themselves in case another institution goes under. Even a relatively small institution that falls under a cloud can cause a chilling effect. The object of good design of clearing and settlement systems is to remove that chill, so that clearing and settlement of payments can continue.

The Bank has always had a role in payments issues, but the stakes and the complexity increased greatly in the 1980s as the financial system, nationally and internationally, became increasingly electronic and fast-paced.

A basic step taken soon after I became governor, detailed in the previous chapter, was to settle on the approach Ottawa should take in relation to the budding Canadian Depository for Securities (CDS). At the same time, we also started, under Deputy Governor Charles

Freedman's immediate leadership, on the far more complex set of issues involved in modernizing and risk-proofing Canada's major financial clearing and settlement systems to face the new environment. This has involved considerable resources, not only in staff dedicated to thinking through the difficult technical issues, but also in liaising and negotiating with a wide range of interested parties in both the public and private sectors in Canada and abroad.

Central to payments systems issues are the thorny questions of risk: how the risk is to be measured, who shoulders it, and in what proportion. In the private sector, the tendency is, naturally enough, to view these systems as smooth operations, always working in the way they were designed to. But the question that constantly preoccupied the Bank was what would happen if things went wrong. In particular, what was the likely outcome if an institution in the payments network failed? The hopeful private sector assumption (again, naturally enough) is that the public sector, in particular the Bank of Canada as the ultimate supplier of liquidity, would pick up the payments pieces—and also, no doubt, finish up with the bills.

Because the system is effectively a public utility, in the end the public sector will, one way or another, have to backstop it. But that certainly does not mean that the set-up has to be constructed in such a way that Ottawa (i.e., the taxpayer) is bound to be left holding any payments-system losses coming from the failure of particular institutions. Getting parties to agree on fair shares of risk relating to any debts left in the system if there was a failure was a complex and arduous process. At times, the Bank's hand was made even more difficult to play, vis-à-vis the large banks in particular, because of the public policy and/or political interest in including as many different institutions as possible within the inner circle of the payments system. Delicately put, this difficulty arose because not all such politically attractive financial institutions had top risk profiles. This, understandably, made the large banks edgy and gave them a difficult-to-counter bargaining chip.

These various tensions led to complicated and lengthy negotiations with financial institutions, especially of course the large banks. Both sides were keen to move forward, but both were also concerned to protect what they regarded as important. For the banks, a key goal was to minimize their costs in providing risk collateral. For the Bank of Canada (consulting, of course, with the Department of Finance and OSFI), the main aim was to ensure that systemic risk concerns were addressed thoroughly, including a fair distribution of the costs of failures—i.e., one that involved the private sector picking up at least part of any bill.

At times, discussions ground to a halt. To my mind, an important breakthrough came when I was at the annual meeting of the International Monetary Fund in Washington in September 1992 and had occasion to sit next to John Cleghorn, then number two at the Royal Bank. He raised the matter, and I readily agreed that the issues had to be dealt with at a higher level among our institutions (especially, I thought, on the banks' side, where the lines of communication were no doubt longer than at the Bank of Canada) if the log-jam was to be broken. And that is what happened, through a meeting that we jointly set up of senior bankers and the Bank of Canada in October at the Bank's headquarters. Another banker who particularly impressed us at that meeting as having the understanding and vision to move matters forward at this crucial time was Tony Comper, now head of the Bank of Montreal but then his bank's number two.

Systemic Issues and Liquidity Crises

In financial emergencies, diagnoses have to be made quickly and actions taken on the basis of limited information. This must be true of all crises, but a particular hallmark of the financial world is the rapidity with which a problem can spread and possibly become systemic.

The general phenomenon of financial contagion or even panic is hardly new, although rapidly changing financial technologies and relationships seem continually to provide new ways for it to arise. Enforcing a "bank holiday" is one sweeping way to provide space for reflection and response in the face of a real or apprehended crisis, as in the United States in 1933 when the banks were closed for several days by presidential proclamation and were only allowed to reopen after inspection. (How much inspection was actually done before they reopened is another question.) Intervening in the affairs of a particular institution in difficulty so as to ward off a disorderly grab at assets by creditors and thus facilitate an orderly payment and wind-down is another way—as practised by the Federal Reserve Bank of New York in the case of the US brokerage house and investment bank Drexel Burnham Lambert in 1990. Marshalling the interests, and therefore resources, of financial institutions in the same line of business to effect a rescue (often euphemistically called a merger) is a third approach. If necessary, the potential acquirer can be spurred on by a financial sweetener— here, funds managed by the deposit insurer always come to mind. In such cases, the argument presented is that a deposit insurance dowry at this earlier stage would cost that agency less than it would have to disburse if there were a full-blown liquidation. This kind of calculation is inevitably open to a lot of interpretation.

In this latter situation, the crucial public policy consideration has to be a view that the open bankruptcy of the institution in question would indeed have unacceptably widespread, or systemic, consequences. Otherwise, why put in public funds or undertake other heroic measures? On the other hand, it can also be argued that allowing the institution to go under will encourage others to be more careful in the future, limiting moral hazard. This is a dilemma well known to insurers, whether public or private, and relates to the problem that availability of some kind of guarantee will induce people or institutions to take on bigger risks—to the detriment of the insurer and, in this case, of society in general.

As a broader illustration of this point, not for nothing was the willingness of private investors to pump funds into high-yielding Russian government debt in 1998 known as a "moral hazard play." The pump was primed precisely by the perception, justifiable on the basis of the track record to that point, that Western governments would do whatever was necessary to avoid a Russian default. And to extend the point further, when Russia did default on its ruble debt (officially termed a "restructuring") in August of that

year, there was a dramatic reappraisal of risk positions not just for
Russia but the world over—for Hong Kong, Brazil, and a highly lev-
ered, presumed state-of-the-art, US hedge fund, Long Term Capital
Management, to cite a few of the more prominent instances. The
Canadian dollar also sagged sharply for a while. Clearly, there was
contagion on a global scale that might conceivably have snow-
balled into something more serious still. That is why the Federal
Reserve eased and also intervened in resolving the particular crisis
that overwhelmed Long Term Capital Management and threatened
to seize up bond markets as well.

But back to emergencies *within* Canada, and back to the Canadian Commercial Bank. Upon the revelation to Ottawa in the
spring of 1985 that the CCB was about to collapse, the Bank argued
to federal officials and the large banks that it was worth putting
together a rescue package to make the patient whole. It emphasized
the serious repercussions of a bank failure at home and abroad.
Even though the CCB was small as Canadian banks went, a sudden
failure like this could shock the marketplace and cast doubt on
Canadian financial institutions generally.

Whether the shock would have been contagious and systemic
enough to warrant the truly strenuous efforts made in late March
(including an all-night vigil) to put together a rescue package will
never be known with certainty. But what is known is that the chartered banks solicited for support were reluctant and grudging contributors. This is not so surprising, since they were being asked to
supply shareholders' money to a competitor. More broadly, however, they were also inclined to question whether their own institutions would be so seriously affected as to warrant their making a
contribution. The fact that they did participate was as clear an
example as one is likely to see of moral suasion on the part of the
Bank, on this occasion together with the Department of Finance.
Still, moral suasion is something that has had less and less currency over time, as markets become more competitive and clublike
understandings erode.

But of course the CCB did fail, as did the Northland Bank. Furthermore, as already noted, some other smaller Canadian banks

were caught up in the aftershock and eventually absorbed by larger and more resilient rivals. I recall Gerald Bouey arguing—and his view prevailed at the Bank and in Ottawa—that even though the initial rescue operation did not succeed, it was still worthwhile in that it did buy time. The fact that the debacle took place in a relatively gradual and somewhat controlled way might have helped to mitigate the impact on confidence overall—a series of small, partly anticipated earthquakes rather than one large one that could possibly have had a big impact precisely because it came out of the blue. Governor Bouey and I were also aware that however unlikely this overall danger appeared to other Canadian banks, on other occasions some of our larger banks had themselves been the object of bouts of market nervousness. But anxious moments of this kind were not to be discussed except in hushed tones and in the most narrow of circles.

During my time as governor, the clearest manifestation of a general confidence and/or liquidity crisis affecting Canadian institutions came in late 1987. The dramatic October 19 sell-off in the US stock market that brought a one-day drop of more than 20 per cent in the Dow Jones Index was strongly echoed in Canada, where the TSE 300 fell 11 per cent, as well as in other countries. The Hong Kong exchange was shut down for the rest of the week—quite a market holiday, almost a coma.

The sudden slump in the stock market presented two dimensions for the Bank to worry about: first, its abruptness; and second, the magnitude of the loss in values and the effect on general economic expectations and behaviour. The latter aspect was macroeconomic in nature. We could and did attempt to assess the effects on consumption, investment, and so on through our models, and thereby think about the effect on monetary policy settings in the weeks and months ahead. My own overlay was that it was easy to exaggerate the likely impact across the economy and that the Bank would be well advised to take a skeptical view of forecasts of a general economic slowdown.

Our more immediate concern was the across-the-board steepness of the changes in equity prices and the chance that this alone would have an adverse impact on the Canadian financial system. Such an impact could spread well beyond the stock market into the banking system generally, from there to payments and credit, and out to the economy. This could not be measured in the Bank's models, but as we saw quotes spiral down through the day on October 19, we saw those risks becoming increasingly real. The particular concern that preoccupied us was the possible financial market repercussion from a surge in failed trades. In other words, stock market purchases that were entered into at a pre-crash price would now be highly disadvantageous to the purchaser. Given the lag in settlement, the purchaser might then be disposed to walk away from the commitment, leaving the selling institution holding the bag. Enough of this, and there would be a real crisis of confidence and shrinkage of credit. When financial institutions pull in horns and are unwilling to extend credit to each other, this is known as financial gridlock. Then, as in an extreme traffic jam, some kind of police officer is needed to untangle the mess and get things started again.

The Bank had no surefire way of assessing how likely such an adverse outcome might be. Neither did the relevant supervisors. But we did have the ability to affect the supply of liquidity overall, and our judgment was that the day's events were likely to have a major impact on the demand for liquidity in Canadian financial markets generally, as participants tried to come to terms with their exposures. Accordingly, later that afternoon the Bank's senior management got together and decided that this was an occasion to inject unprecedentedly large amounts of overnight funds (commonly known in the Bank as "cash") into the system. This step was followed early next day by two sets of phone calls.

One set, at about 8:00 a.m., was to the most senior officers of our large chartered banks I could find at that unbankerly hour, to tell them that we had put an exceptionally large amount of overnight liquidity into the system—hundreds of millions of dollars more than usual—and that if this injection was not enough to make a difference as the day passed, we would not hesitate to put in more. Our purpose was to ensure that Canadian securities market creditors, effectively the banks, would not move to tighten up on any securities dealer because of general liquidity concerns. Rather, any decision of that kind would revolve around considerations more specific to the financial condition of the business in question. Such individual credit decisions were clearly up to each bank, since it was their capital they were risking. But we thought that knowing that conditions in the Canadian money market would be distinctly easier would have a bearing on their stance. At least they would be more inclined to take their time in deciding whether to change it.

I had called Gerald Corrigan, president of the Federal Reserve Bank of New York, even earlier that morning. The Fed had given no indication to that point of what its reaction might be, but it seemed worthwhile to let its officers know what we had done. If that encouraged them to move as well, so much the better. Among its various beneficial effects, their action would provide some protection for our currency. In any event, the Federal Reserve also moved to expand liquidity and made a general announcement to that effect in the course of the morning.

The operation was a success overall, but the seismic shift in stock market valuations did exact a toll. Notable in the pantheon of Canadian casualties was Wood Gundy, a venerable prop of the Canadian investment dealer community, which had made an ill-advised bet with the firm's capital. As on earlier occasions, it had participated in an international offering of stock brought about by a major British privatization—this time British Petroleum. Earlier privatizations had proven a bonanza for underwriters, and it had enthusiastically extrapolated this string—not allowing for the kind of risk that hit the markets in mid-October. One could argue that this was bad luck, but few other Canadian participants were lulled into the sense of security over underwriting exposure that overcame Wood Gundy, and led to its crippling losses.

The Canadian government became remarkably exercised over Wood Gundy's difficulties and tried to get concessions out of the British. The Americans pushed the same way. I was asked to write a letter to the governor of the Bank of England and felt it politic to do so, but the government didn't regard my letter as strong enough.

That was fine by me. What I said was as strong as the circumstances warranted, and those circumstances were hardly reason for reopening the underwriting contract that Wood Gundy and others had signed. Governments pressed further, and the British, led by Nigel Lawson, budged a little but not much. Obviously, it's a nice business if you can privatize the underwriting gains but socialize the losses, but this was hardly fair and was also, again, morally hazardous. Furthermore, the problem was not systemic, even if Wood Gundy was taken over soon after by a large Canadian bank.

Following these events, I recall that one of our directors made a special point of congratulating the Bank on what it had done to buoy up liquidity. It must have seemed an agreeable change from the standard line, where management was continually harping on the need to remain vigilant, tighten up or whatever, to combat inflation pressures. Still, by the end of 1987, with the market crisis clearly over and the economy remaining subject to inflation pressures, we were vigilantly beginning to tighten liquidity again.

The Last Resort

It is well known that in economics there is no free lunch, though, as a wag once observed, some lunches ought to be cheaper than others. The power of the Bank to create ultimate liquidity is certainly extraordinary, but that does not mean that it is economically unconstrained or problem-free. While Bank lending will make a real difference when used at the right time (which also means in appropriate circumstances), just like any insurance policy it comes with some qualifications, and even exclusions, that are worth exploring. It is particularly useful to look at the distinction between lending operations related to individual institutions, as in 1985–86, and those in which the action is broader or market-based, as in October 1987.

Starting with individuals, the Bank fussed a great deal over getting assurance from the Inspector General of Banks that a particular institution was solvent—first the CCB and then others. We wanted to know whether the bank's assets on a going concern basis (i.e., not fire sale) were worth more than its liabilities, so that there was some capital left in the business. Assessing a bank's solvency position is not a simple matter. Calculating the market value of the core of the asset base—commercial loans—is art as well as science. All the same, determining solvency was the inspector general's job and, as was repeatedly stressed before Justice Estey, it was only on the basis of solvency that the Bank was ready to lend. If the bank in question was not solvent, extending it credit would not help, barring a time-delayed miracle of resurrection. Additional debt would only put off, not reverse, the inevitable. What the institution needed was more capital. Providing more capital was the general idea (however imperfect it proved to be in practice) behind the CCB support package hastily put together in March 1985.

Even if a bank has to be judged to be solvent to receive Bank of Canada credit, that does not mean that the Bank lends without security. In fact, under its legislation it is required to take security for its advances. Furthermore, the Bank has always understood that taking security means having a margin of safety that appears broadly adequate in terms of the quality of the collateral it acquires. So, for example, in the case of the two Western banks, the dollar amount of collateral assigned to the Bank (essentially the bulk of the loan portfolio) was much larger than the advances actually supplied. Happily, the value of those portfolios, when they were realized, turned out to be enough to cover the principal of the advances. But in one case, it was somewhat short in terms of the interest that was supposed to be received.

Indeed, an awkwardness that the Bank faced in the summer of 1985 was that its advances, particularly to the Canadian Commercial Bank, were climbing so rapidly that there was some question whether the value of the collateral taken would be enough to cover them in the event of failure. But there was not much else left to take by way of additional protection. Quite what to do next was never resolved, but this predicament did give additional urgency to the fundamental issue of that time—whether the CCB and the Northland Bank really were solvent. Ottawa agencies were ready to believe that they were insolvent in the sense that they had no capital left.

However, all the while that the Bank was making advances to them, they could pay their bills, which was unfortunately the way the relevant legislation defined solvency. After the inspector general had got on with making further inspection of the books, he finally judged in September that the two banks were not "viable"—upon which carefully orchestrated news the Bank of Canada stopped making advances, with the result that cash ran out for both institutions and they were closed.

A broader awkwardness arose from the hard reality that other things remaining equal, taking security is a zero-sum game. In other words, the more collateral the Bank took, the less protection was left for depositors or other lenders, or for CDIC for that matter. Not surprisingly, and perhaps for this particular reason and/or because they themselves had serious doubts whether the two banks were solvent, over the summer of 1985 commercial banks were reluctant to extend credit to these small cousins in difficulty. Appeals to any considerations of banking system solidarity—again, moral suasion—were not warmly received. Since Bank of Canada support came as a last resort when other possible financing fell short, this lending must have been a help to the two banks. Otherwise, they would already have been out of business. But because of any discouragement to other lenders through its taking of security, not as much Bank financial help may have been forthcoming as the sum total of our advances would suggest.

We had ample chance to recognize the difficulties our lending potentially made for other lenders, since they told us so in no uncertain terms. Still, the policy case for our taking security (apart from the simple fact that we were legally obliged to) was very defensible. We were employing public funds in the interests of private institutions precisely as a lender of *last* resort. In other words, we were there, and stayed there, because private creditors or depositors had, for whatever reasons, chosen not to be. Furthermore, the fact that we took security would mean, as it undoubtedly did in the spring of 1985, that our lending would be ample and unhesitating.

Still, it was interesting that no one put back to us the point that the Canada Deposit Insurance Corporation, also a public body and also in the financial stability business, did have the power to make loans to financial institutions that were not secured by a claim on the assets of the borrower, and has in fact done so on occasion. CDIC funds were also used to provide part of the initial $255-million CCB support package—money that was not retrieved. One element that is arguably different about CDIC is that it collects its funds through a direct levy on insured deposits. In that sense, the resources available to it are less "public" in nature than those available from the Bank of Canada. But even if this is somehow taken to justify lending without security, chartered bankers will be quick to point out that it raises other questions of principle—namely, whether it is fair to tax bank depositors, borrowers, and shareholders when they are not represented in the corridors of CDIC decision-making power. While there are private sector appointees on the board of CDIC, they are not there to represent deposit-taking institutions as such. This representation issue was particularly alive in the early 1990s, when CDIC funds were being used intensively in regard to a string of failing trust companies—also something that did not go down well with banks, since it was bank deposits that provided the bulk of CDIC's tax base. Since then, as CDIC activity has fallen away and as it has repaid its earlier borrowings from the federal treasury, levies on insured deposits have dropped and the argument has become less urgent.

The private sector dimension of CDIC has occasionally been still more prominent. It is only from this angle that the institution, though effectively an agent of the Crown, could have made the decision to mount a legal attack on the validity of the security that the Bank had taken against its CCB and Northland advances. But this is only surmise. Although I was an ex officio director of CDIC, I naturally did not take part in the board's discussions of what CDIC should do regarding the Bank of Canada and why. What I do know is that there was lingering resentment within the bowels of CDIC over the fact that, except for being dunned for $75 million for the CCB support package, its involvement in the deliberations that took place in the spring of 1985 was marginal. I am unsure why its involvement was not more central, but that it was not does seem in retrospect an oversight, at least as a general principle of public policy.

Let me turn now from the case of individual institutions to the issue of more general liquidity support. Open-market-type operations, through which the Bank puts out money in exchange for government securities, obviously do not raise the same kinds of questions regarding security and the solvency of particular institutions. But that does not mean that they are issue-free. The basic problem is one of confidence. Pumping out lots of cash in short order, as in the stock market crisis of October 1987, might be poorly received by markets globally. Then, not only would the currency fall, but interest rates might also lurch in the wrong direction. In 1987, we hoped to avoid this by explaining as clearly as possible that the liquidity expansion did not represent a shift in monetary policy. Rather, it was addressing a particular but potentially widespread increase in the demand for liquidity by Canadian financial institutions. And this is how financial markets perceived it, especially since other central banks were tending to do the same thing.

But the operation did raise other questions. Why, for example, would the Bank not lend directly to investment dealers in potential distress? One answer, accurate but too narrow, is that the Bank of Canada's statutes did not allow it to lend to institutions other than members of the Canadian Payments Association. This emphasized that the focus had to be on preserving the payments system, and not on helping out individual institutions. A broader answer is that giving the Bank this power would be the thin end of the wedge. Where would this lending in response to credit problems stop? And what pressures would be exerted on the Bank not to stop? Better that private financial institutions figure out particular credit problems rather than the central bank, which has no authoritative oversight role over investment dealers or anyone else in the private financial sector—except, now, over aspects to do with major clearing and settlement systems.

The statutes for the Federal Reserve allow it wider discretion than the Bank of Canada has generally had over whom to lend to. That being said, the Fed is notably reluctant to use those more expansive powers, no doubt for the same broad reasons as I have just put forward. Some might argue that this kind of broad liquidity action is not lending of last resort at all, but rather a variant of monetary policy. I am inclined to disagree, although there can be some overlap. What was undertaken in October 1987 was liquidity expansion of an emergency nature to make credit easier to come by for a range of institutions in the financial system. In the same vein, I would also argue that the Fed's easing in the fall of 1998 in response to the Russian default crisis was not so much a monetary policy move as one connected to credit turmoil and a rapid escalation in aversion to risk, which itself posed systemic financial dangers.

One way in which the distinction I am making between monetary policy actions and last resort operations might be substantive in a Canadian context relates to the scope for a ministerial directive. I recall getting an evening call from my good friend Hyman Calof, then the top legal officer at the Department of Finance. He wanted my thoughts on whether the minister of finance might be able to direct the Bank to make special advances to banks. Apparently Barbara McDougall, then the minister of state for finance, was about to testify before a parliamentary committee, and Hy wanted to be ready for every possible line of questioning. My quick answer was that lending of last resort was not monetary policy, so the directive power, which refers specifically to monetary policy, could hardly apply. He seemed to have no problem with that answer, but I do not believe that the subject ever came up—then or since.

The next two chapters are devoted to international questions, including the various implications of a currency board and of dollarization. One aspect is worth touching upon here, however. Proponents don't flag the issue, but one outcome of a move toward a currency board or dollarization would be severe limitation on the Bank's ability to undertake lender of last resort operations of any kind for Canadian financial institutions, the simple reason being that it cannot create US dollars. Still, alternative ways of going about such operations might be found. One way could be through establishing foreign bank lines of contingency credit, as Argentina did when it had a currency board arrangement. There has also been considerable discussion about the possibility of the IMF acting as lender of last resort to currency-board countries in distress. Funding might also be available from the Federal Reserve Bank of New York, with which the Bank of Canada already has a long-standing mutual credit facility. But canvassing these possibilities raises another question. If there were a continuing need for external liquidity backing of this kind (and the amounts available would have to be many tens of billions of dollars to be worthwhile), then there would inevitably be more external oversight of Canadian financial supervision. To satisfy this oversight, would Canada throw in an additional, foreign, seat at our Financial Institutions Supervisory Committee in Ottawa? Who knows?

Global Bank

CHAPTER 5

ଚଚ

Trying to Be Diplomatic

Some countries are clubbable almost by reflex, while others, such as Switzerland, take on memberships with anxiety and hesitation. Canada is among the former—an enthusiastic joiner of international institutions of all kinds. We never see one we don't like, and there are hundreds waiting to be liked. No doubt it is always an advantage, other things being equal, to be on the inside for the more select gatherings. But other things are not necessarily equal. Perhaps our leaders get a better feel about what is going on, so there are fewer surprises. But it does not follow that we have much influence over what there is to be surprised about, and being a member of a club means that there are dues to pay. These may at times be onerous. The few countries that have real influence over a serious club's agenda are naturally concerned at least as much about national interests as they are about more broadly based ones. Their national interests will not necessarily be the same as Canada's.

Notwithstanding Prime Minister Bennett's earlier-cited rationale for having a central bank—to act as an international financial agent for the nation—the Bank has tended to keep international issues very much in their place. (Indeed, I had it on good authority from the late George Watts, the Bank's first historian, that Graham Towers did not think too much of Bennett's reasoning here.) Given the natural primacy of domestic priorities and the Bank's considerable role in domestic monetary policy, this has always been the logical focus for our resources. Furthermore, the minister of finance has traditionally been the nation's immediate spokesperson on international financial matters, and he does things his way, giving a lot of weight to political as well as economic considerations.

With this reality, any tussles during my tenure over who was entitled to do what were not so much between the Bank and Finance as between Finance and the Department of Foreign Affairs, which obviously also has a legitimate (if somewhat unfocused) interest in the international financial domain. The Bank tried to avoid being caught up in these turf tussles, such as who should sit on which committee of the Paris-based Organisation for Economic Co-operation and Development (OECD). We preferred to get on with business in areas in which our expertise had real value and the questions were important to the economy and to monetary policy. Senior management tended to leave decisions on the research agenda to our deputy governor on the international side, William White, now chief economist at the Bank for International Settlements (BIS) in Basel, Switzerland, and to John Murray, then chief of the Bank's International Department. One of their important tasks was to analyze and explain the exchange rate. That included the difficult job of forecasting it.

It follows from this that in such broad international financial arenas as the G-7 process or the many-faceted dealings with the International Monetary Fund, the Bank's role has been much more as advisor to the minister than as a separate player—and certainly not at centre stage for photo opportunities.

G-7 Operations

In February 1987, days after I became governor, there took place in Paris the well-remembered meeting of ministers of finance and central bank governors that gave rise to the Louvre Accord. This accord can be seen as a kind of bookend. Its counterpart was the so-called Plaza Agreement of late 1985, which had the express purpose of trying to halt and perhaps reverse the remarkable appreciation of the US dollar over the early 1980s. That appreciation was initially sparked by the simultaneous pursuit of an expansionary fiscal policy (President Reagan) and a tight monetary policy (Paul Volcker) in the United States, but it gradually took on a more extrapolative and speculative cast. The specific international angle in Plaza had been to endorse a plan for joint intervention *against* the US dollar. US trading partners had one strong incentive to sign on to an agreement to push up their currencies—namely, to forestall a further upsurge in the US protectionism that had been provoked by a high dollar.

For the world as a whole, the crucial difference between Plaza and Louvre was that while the first agreement was aimed at pushing the US dollar down, the second was designed to prop it up after its decline threatened to become a rout. But through official Canadian eyes, the big difference was that we were not present at Plaza (a G-5 effort by Germany, France, Japan, the United Kingdom, and, above all, the United States), but were there in full complement for Louvre. Canada had managed, along with Italy, to gain entry to the G-5 heads of government summit before Louvre, turning it into G-7. But we had only just succeeded in being included in the parallel but pickier meetings of ministers of finance and governors—again along with Italy. Accordingly, the Canadian delegation—Finance Minister Michael Wilson, Deputy Minister Stanley Hartt, and I—turned up at four o'clock on a Sunday morning in late February at a military airport near Paris, to be met with impeccable protocol by our ambassador, Lucien Bouchard.

Our plan was to retire to a hotel for a few hours of sleep before the meeting started in mid-morning. But then the fun started. We soon learned that the other inductees—the Italians—had already gone back to Rome. They had somehow found out when they turned up the night before that the G-5 had dined together that evening *and* that the dinner meeting had included a substantive discussion and agreement about exchange rates. (My guess is that someone had taken mischievous delight in making sure that they found out.) Michael Wilson decided not to take umbrage but to press on regardless. This was surely the sensible thing to do, since most governments cannot really tell others whom they should meet with or expect to get much return from a show of annoyance.

An immediate consequence of staying was that we were invited to meet with our French hosts that morning before the start of the meeting. They put forward the suggestion that we consider entering into some kind of multilateral agreement whereby all parties would commit to exchange rate targets against the US dollar (and, implicitly, against each other as well). But the proposition was somewhat vague.

A much more basic problem than vagueness was that whatever the specific commitment we made on our currency's level, we would also be committing our monetary policy to defend it. Given that the US economy is over 10 times as big as ours and looms so large, this could have huge implications and complications for a policy addressing Canadian priorities (even if that policy had in any event to keep a close eye on what was happening across the border) but hardly any for the United States. In particular, if it came to currency intervention, who would be calling the shots, and in whose interest? This question was hardly worth posing, since it certainly would not be Canada. As the one whose policy ox had most potential to be gored, I was quick to advance to our French counterparts all the difficulties with our participation. These they accepted with great equanimity, in part no doubt because the Italians had already excused themselves and quite likely also because our hosts did not care greatly whether we joined in. After all, they were G-5 and we were not. They had already done their important business. And what was the Canadian dollar to them? They would be far more interested, for example, in what target rate was agreed to by Germany. Indeed, "interested" would be an understatement.

The eventual meeting later that day in the Louvre offices of the French Treasury was pretty much a non-event, with some participants gazing out the window at the splendid surroundings, making it even clearer to us that the real work had been done the night before. What I remember most clearly was the mini-debate about how to refer to the meeting in the press release—as G-6 or G-7? No one had the gall to suggest G-6½, as an indirect homage to Fellini's brilliant film *8½* and thereby to our absent Italian friends. But, Canada favoured G-7, so G-7 it was.

Our decision not to jump into the various exchange rate target ranges that had been agreed upon among the five countries (and not intended to be revealed, although some of the participants could not avoid dropping broad hints the moment they left the meeting) proved to be wise on tactical as well as strategic grounds. That agreement took its first knock as early as April 1987, when it had to be rejigged to take account of what had happened to the Japanese yen in the weeks immediately following the accord. The Bank of Japan had been doing its easing job a bit too enthusiastically, and the yen had fallen much more than contemplated. However, the accord received its *coup de grâce* in the fall over what US Treasury secretary James Baker saw as Germany's failure to live up to its bargain. In his view, this bargain included a looser German monetary policy. But the Bundesbank really was independent and did not choose to loosen at that time. That well-publicized incident of evident international financial discord was seen by many commentators, with reason, as the immediate trigger for the US stock market plunge of October.

From this time on, G-7 financial exercises would be engaged much more in other issues. One particularly thorny question when I was attending (and no doubt after) was trying to cope with the unravelling Russian financial situation. Another was that of the newly independent Ukraine. Here, Canada seemed to acquire a special interest, no doubt because of the many Canadians of Ukrainian origin. Exchange rates were still on the table, especially the yen/US dollar relationship. But the kinds of jawboning and attempts at multilateral exchange rate stage managing that were an earlier feature of international economic and financial cooperation were no longer evident.

That was surely a relief for the central banks around the table—certainly for the Bank of Canada. As already noted, our chief worry had been the extent to which exchange rate agreements cobbled together to achieve something for the US dollar would result in constraints on Canadian monetary policy doing the right thing for domestic purposes, since the priority would become defending a particular exchange rate rather than the course of overall demand, or inflation, in Canada. But central banks in general would also have nagging concerns about the whole process of multilateral monetary policy coordination, exchange rate-driven or not. Since the arrangements, and therefore the agenda, are kept very firmly in the hands of finance ministries, there is always the risk of being presented with deals cooked in their kitchen that may not be consistent with the basic goals of monetary policy. And then, how can you digest them, or even better, avoid eating them at all?

The commanding irony at the time was that while the United States was by far the most strenuous proponent of activist policy coordination, it could not make much of a contribution through domestic policies. In particular, it could not deliver by reducing its own budgetary deficit, since this was in the hands of Congress, not the administration.

The constructive evolution of the G-7 process toward more caution in regard to the fruitful possibilities for detailed economic policy coordination, and indeed to exchange rate management in general, was led by the United States under the leadership of Robert Rubin and then Lawrence Summers. Furthermore, whereas in the 1980s US policy regarding its exchange rate had lurched convulsively from one side of the boat to the other, more recently it has consistently taken a "strong dollar" stance.

Canadians advocating a strong dollar policy here should be aware that this does not mean that the US authorities will do anything in particular to push their currency up or even to hold it up. What it *does* mean is clearly accepting the universe—the fact that the United States has until recently been such a magnet for inflows of capital from almost everywhere else that its exchange rate simply had to be on the strong side. Admittedly, this kind of universe is easier to accept, and an easier place from which to fend off calls for protection, when the unemployment rate is low. Certainly, US joblessness has been lower in recent years than in the mid-1980s. All the same, protectionism has put in a reappearance there in 2002, as it did in that earlier period.

On another level, US policy-makers also recognize that the converse of a strong dollar policy—encouraging the view that you actually like to see your currency sink—imparts an upward bias to what internationally minded investors expect in the way of US dollar interest returns. This in turn adds an upward bias to domestic interest rates, something US policy-makers think they can do without. Some in Ottawa could learn from this.

My final topic in this section, the free trade agreement with the United States that was negotiated in the late 1980s, is not G-7 material as such. But given that the G-7 process itself has been dominated by our generally friendly giant to the south, adding some considerations around that agreement fits quite nicely.

In principle, freeing up trade is about increasing and sharing prosperity through the greater exchange of competitive goods and services. The exchange rate in this context is merely a financial adjustment mechanism. But the real world is messier, and it is not surprising that the question of what to do about the US–Canada exchange rate was put on the free trade negotiating table—by the Americans.

The Bank was not particularly close to those negotiations (after all, they were not supposed to be about exchange rates or interest rates), but at one point in the fall of 1987, I was consulted with some urgency because the US Treasury wanted to introduce an arrangement that would see to it that our currency was somehow kept up—thereby, supposedly, precluding the possibility that Canada would somehow engineer a depreciation to gain a trade advantage in the US market. I did not believe that it would be right or practical to try to use policy, least of all monetary policy, to move the Canadian dollar around to gain a pseudo-competitive advantage. But I could also see that such an exchange-fixing arrangement involved the same general problems as the proposition the French had brought to us before Louvre—that is, Canada would incur all the policy obligations and all the potential inconsistencies with domestic monetary objectives. My position was that we should always be very happy to discuss with our US counterparts our monetary policy and where it was going. Why not? And if we did, I conjectured, we could expect the Fed to explain its strategy to us. That would also be fun. But we should not be expected to commit on the exchange rate.

In indirect support of our position, we were able to supply to Canada's negotiators—by this stage led from Finance—a statement by a prominent representative of the US Chamber of Commerce to the effect that Canada had *not* used the exchange rate as a competitive weapon. Most of our dollar's slide to that point could be explained by the higher rate of inflation in Canada since the early 1970s. In that sense, a weaker Canadian dollar had not been "competitive," even if it was a currency performance we could hardly celebrate.

The upshot was that this initiative from the US side was fairly quickly withdrawn. My own take is that the US Treasury negotiators were not particularly concerned to get a side deal but felt it was worth a try. It was probably inspired by the US labour lobby, which, like Canada's, is instinctively hostile to freer trade, seeing it as an export of jobs. No doubt the Americans were curious to see how we would react to such a proposal. They had nothing to lose by putting it forward, especially if they took, as trade negotiators are obliged to in order to satisfy domestic producer constituencies, a mercantilist approach to these matters—that is, promote *your* exports, but give ground grudgingly on theirs.

Ironically enough, at about this time a widespread suspicion arose in Canadian quarters that our dollar was being pushed up as a kind of concession to the Americans over free trade. That long-serving Progressive Conservative politician Sinclair Stevens kept calling out from the wings that there had to be an "implicit" deal on the exchange rate, since he could find no evidence of an explicit one. In fact, the Canadian dollar was tending to strengthen during the free trade negotiations, but for reasons unconnected with those dealings (rising commodity prices, an anti-inflationary monetary policy). These developments in themselves might well have made the US side less aggressive in the actual bargaining than it would otherwise have been, and perhaps some Canadian negotiators recognized this. But there was no exchange rate deal of any kind—new or old, fair or unfair, explicit or implicit.

Other Relationships

International Monetary Fund

In earlier times, the Bank had played a significant part in Canada's dealings with the International Monetary Fund (IMF), particularly through Louis Rasminsky, who had made an important contribution in chairing the drafting committee for the Fund's articles of agreement at its founding. He then served for many years as Canada's executive director at the Fund until he became Bank governor. But in later years, the Bank's role gradually diminished as Finance took more of the Canadian space available, including filling the Canadian executive director position, which in the 1960s and 1970s had alternated with the Bank of Canada. As far as I was concerned, this did not matter too much because it had no implications for Bank of Canada policy. Also, we still retained strong, direct links into the IMF. Furthermore, I knew full well that the flow of advice on IMF matters that the Bank supplied to the executive director's office was superior in quality, which made Canadian executive directors grateful.

We would meet with IMF missions whenever they came to Ottawa on their regular policy consultations (roughly once a year). This was a particularly interesting occasion for me—not just because I had made the same trips from Washington many years earlier, but also because our IMF interlocutors were both focused and informed, showing an appropriate dose of friendly skepticism about what we were up to. Even if they did not tell us anything we did not know already, it was always worthwhile to see how they put together the whole economic policy story and their views in a few tight pages. They compared favourably with their counterparts from the Organization for Economic Co-operation and Development (OECD), who would undertake a similar kind of surveillance exercise but with less analytical sharpness or policy challenge. I should note, however, that at the end of the OECD process, a member country goes through a lively and searching examination by representatives of a couple of other member countries. The review conducted by the IMF's large executive board is more likely to consist of one set speech after another.

Basel and G-10

When it came to the Bank for International Settlements (BIS), we were much more on our own ground. The BIS, based in Basel, Switzerland, has had many lives—starting off as the vehicle through which German reparation payments were channelled after World War I, but since then finding other useful housekeeping roles as international financial relations have evolved. The focus was very much on central banking matters. In this vein, the BIS has housed the regular meetings of the G-10 central bank governors.

The G-10 organization of ministers of finance and central bank governors (the G-7 countries plus Belgium, the Netherlands, and Sweden, as well as the more recent addition of Switzerland but with no further increase in the number sign for the group) had originally been set up to provide a line of credit for the IMF additional to the resources available to it through national gold and currency quota subscriptions. But while that role has been largely transformed and widened to include more participants, the narrower G-10 grouping has also lived on. Its life is much more vital among central banks than it is for ministries of finance, where its activities have largely consisted of going through the motions of a report before each IMF meeting, with only occasional forays into something more demanding.

The G-10 central bank governors, besides getting together several times a year to discuss their immediate business, also have spearheaded important work on international payments systems (especially after the hugely messy failure of the small Herstatt Bank in Germany in 1974, which left behind an astonishingly large pile of unsettled transactions and unanticipated losses on account of the business gaps between banking time zones) and, more broadly, on the regulation and supervision of commercial banks operating internationally. The Basel Committee on Banking Supervision, operating under the aegis of the G-10 central bank governors, had become a central contributor to the continuing efforts to provide an effective supervisory framework to deal with the never-ending stream of issues arising out of the cross-country operations of financial institutions. Of course, since not all central banks are responsible, even partially, for banking supervision, in a number of cases, including Canada's, non-central bank officials (in our case, the Superintendent of Financial Institutions) have become part of the Basel Committee alongside their country's central bankers.

In my time, the most significant activities coming out of the G-10 governors' ruminations were the various arrangements for bridge financing of debtor nations starting in the 1980s and the seminal Basel Accord on bank capital standards that was reached in 1988.

The bridge financing exercise turned out to be a messy, highly artificial business, and one that would not go away for quite a few years. The typical issue that kept being presented was the case of a country (from Brazil to Hungary) that was seeking IMF credits but was in arrears in repaying earlier loans from the IMF. Since the IMF at that point did not lend to anyone in arrears (matters have been relaxed a bit in this regard since the financial crises of the 1990s), it was necessary to arrange for a door-opening bridge loan to pay off those arrears and thus pave the way for the IMF funds. That credit, when consummated, would be used in part to pay down the bridge loan.

And what was the assurance that all this would happen in the way planned? That tended to be a bit vague, not least because we were dealing with a sovereign country and no recognized legal procedures exist for obliging a country to pay or work out a deal with creditors. Initially, there were attempts to engineer some kind of security (for example, oil export receipts deposited at the Federal Reserve Bank of New York) against these financings, but this proved increasingly impractical. In practice, the funds for the bridge were provided by the BIS, with the general guarantee of various central banks in various proportions, but with no tangible security.

What bothered many of us about the whole operation was that while these were essentially international exercises in financial diplomacy under the responsibility of governments, not the central banks themselves, we were being asked to assume commitments that did not meet standard banking criteria. This was uncomfortable, even if each time we got an assurance of government support for the operation. And even if the commitments had been bankable, there was still a case for getting government assurances, because some of the nation's international reserves were being put at risk in a rather direct way. In sum, the governance was problematic. For this reason, the Bank of Canada made a point of including a reference to these operations in each of its annual financial statements, as well as always issuing a press release at the time that they occurred. Fortunately, none of the operations collapsed, although one or two had to be extended so that they could succeed. By the end of the 1980s, as the debt crisis simmered down, the need for such exercises began to taper off. Understandably, the Bank's own efforts to find adequate answers to these awkward governance questions also lapsed.

Similarly, the Bank of Canada, like other central banks, got involved from time to time in international efforts to manage the refinancing of billions of dollars of credit that commercial banks of many industrial countries, including Canada, had extended to developing countries in the 1970s. These refinancings were a constant feature of the 1980s, starting from Mexico's announcement at the 1982 IMF annual meetings in Toronto that it could not pay, and followed closely by Brazil. Such multi-country, multi-bank refinancings were in principle voluntary, and we certainly did not try to instruct our banks on what to do. For one thing, we did not have the authority. For another, being perceived as expressing a view as to what a bank should do (a form of moral suasion) could put the Bank in an awkward position—namely, being seen as attempting to influence the business judgments of a privately owned institution, but without having money in the business.

Nevertheless, I was always available, as Gerald Bouey had been earlier, to "explain" to any Canadian banker who needed an explanation in his pocket just how banks' involvements in the refinancing effort mattered for the international financial system. Such conversations at crucial negotiating moments, besides showing a continuing friendly concern as to how matters were coming out, seemed to be important from the standpoint of the bank executives involved. No doubt they were happy to tell their boards that such a conversation had occurred—a kind of verbal comfort letter perhaps. Sometimes I felt like a peacemaker between the heads of Canadian banks who were at loggerheads over these issues, and also over who was entitled to lead the Canadian banks' participation on a given occasion. I would alternate in talking to one and the other, in the apparent absence of a direct conversation between them—thus doing my bit for international financial cooperation, but now back on the home front.

Of more far-reaching international significance was the 1988 Basel Accord. It formed the basis for an effort that continues to this day (and doubtless will continue to eternity) to attune commercial banks' capital backing to the magnitudes and kinds of financial risks that they incur.

The basic reason for the adoption of minimum capital requirements on an international basis was a general desire on the part of central bankers, whether formally supervisors or not, to stop the rot in banks' capital cushions. The post-war years had witnessed a sustained and pronounced erosion in the amounts of capital that commercial banks found they could live with in conducting their business. But our perception, and that of others, was that this erosion did not reflect any lessening in the actual risks incurred. Indeed, as banks became more international in scope and entered new lines of financial service business, their overall risk profile probably increased under the spur of increased competition. It was not possible to tell precisely what would be an adequate provision of capital. Still, we were concerned that banks were tending to assume that they could afford to be very light on capital and reserves because they had a semi-official central bank financial safety net beneath them—clearly a moral hazard.

Another reason for seeking consistency in minimum capital requirements was that banking systems in different countries seemed to rely on different proportions of capital to carry on their business. One thorny reason for this stemmed from the fact that countries had different standards of government safety netting for their banks. Since capital is costly to sustain, this meant that the more protected systems were more competitive on that score than others. This problem seemed at that time to apply particularly to Japanese banks—a special source of concern to the United States, given the rapidly increasing Japanese penetration of its financial market. At the limit—where banks were to all practical intents nationalized, as was then largely the case for France, for example— it could be claimed as a point of logic that those institutions did not need any assigned capital at all, any more than did central banks. (For example, the Bank of Canada has capital and reserves of only $30 million against total liabilities of some $40 billion.) The difference is that this relative absence of capital is not an issue for central banks because they do not compete with privately funded institutions for business.

The reader can readily imagine how complicated it was to arrive at a capital ratio framework that commanded common assent. Indeed, the whole multilateral Basel exercise had been triggered in the first place when US Fed chairman Paul Volcker and Bank of England governor Robin Leigh-Pemberton (now Lord Kingsdown) quietly informed the rest of us in 1986 that, being frustrated over general foot-dragging in recognizing the issue, they had reached a deal of their own. I am sure that some further intensive bilateral, trilateral, or even broader discussions also took place, no doubt resulting in some national alliances and side deals.

The exercise was further complicated by two contentious issues: what risk weighting to apply to different kinds of bank assets; and how to decide what was authentic bank capital, given the increasing sophistication of hybrid instruments (part debt-part capital) that banks might issue. There seemed to be no limit to the inventiveness of investment bankers' try-on schemes for banking clients looking for eligible capital, and the Basel Committee had to squash quite a few at the start.

When the time finally came to settle these issues, perhaps by majority vote if necessary, I felt for Jacques de Larosière, then governor of the Banque de France. He was clearly under enormous pressure from his government to negotiate special clauses in favour of the French banking system, which was able to be rather skimpy on capital funds because of direct governmental involvement. He had our sympathy, but the general problem was that from a competitive standpoint, we needed a fairly level playing field in regard to capital and therefore could not cut the French much slack. If we had, using the excuse that French banks at the time were not so competitively efficient generally, the precedent would have undermined other countries' efforts to solidify their own banks' solvency positions.

These tough issues had to be thrashed out around a table confined to the G-10 governors. This put me in a slightly tricky position as a non-supervisory central banker. But the Superintendent of Financial Institutions, Michael Mackenzie, and I kept in touch on these matters, and we both were of a mind that strong international capital rules, with as few escape hatches as possible, were decidedly the way to go—for other countries' banks as well as ours.

Since 1988, matters have become more sophisticated. The original Basel Capital Accord was, as we all knew then, a pretty blunt instrument that only made an initial stab at one dimension of risk—credit risk. But it was a start from which to tackle other kinds of risk—principally market risk (risk of losses in securities trading, for example) and operational risk (risk of losses from poorly functioning systems or people, or from external events). It has stood the test of time as a platform from which to build a more sophisticated and comprehensive view of banking risk worldwide, given how international banks have become. This building effort (now called Basel Two) has been going on for many years and has also become, by all accounts, highly contentious. But no one doubts its importance. That is one reason why it is contentious.

Bilaterals

Not all the Bank's international work took place on the multilateral stage. For obvious reasons, our relationship with the US Federal Reserve was always close, although I continually had to disabuse Canadian contacts, official and otherwise, of the notion that we had any inside knowledge as to what the Fed was about to do in money markets. Still, our relationship with the Federal Reserve Bank of New York was in many ways more intensive than that with Washington, because the New York Fed undertook exchange market and money market operations for the system as a whole and also was heavily involved in the development and oversight of payments systems. Given the Bank's increasingly intensive work in improving the Canadian payments system—both to increase access and to enhance the timeliness of the final settlement of large transactions (a form of risk-proofing)—this led to regular exchanges conducted at the highest level to compare notes and to see where direct co-operation would be useful.

In 1992, with the North American Free Trade Agreement (NAFTA) becoming likely (it started officially in early 1994), we also stepped up our contacts with the Bank of Mexico, that country's central bank. It was not that NAFTA had, to my mind, any direct implications for monetary policy, any more than did the original Canada–US Free Trade Agreement. But it did seem appropriate to both of us to improve the links, if only to compare notes regarding experiences with our large partner in the middle, and especially as the Mexican economy opened up more generally. In fact, the co-operation became more intensive than this when, in a broad NAFTA kind of spirit, we entered into currency swap arrangements with the Bank of Mexico against which it had to draw on occasion in response to balance of payments pressures. I had a particular interest in this relationship. Having served on the desk for Mexico for a number of years when at the International Monetary Fund, I had always given a fair amount of attention to what was going on there. I also encouraged some of my colleagues to brush up their Spanish so that we could make the exchanges with our Mexican counterparts more dynamic.

Finally, yet another international flavour came from the particular role that the Bank played in regard to the development of the Czechoslovak (now Czech) National Bank after the Velvet Revolution.

One by-product of international meetings is that you sometimes get invited to places you would not normally think of visiting. In the dying months of Czechoslovakia's Communist regime, I was warmly invited to stop by Prague by the then governor of the central bank, having bumped into him at an IMF meeting in Washington in the late 1980s. I could not go then, but the invitation was renewed out of the blue by his post-revolution successor Josef Tosovsky (later one of the longest-serving European central bankers, and also briefly prime minister). So Bill White and I paid a three-day visit in 1990 right after a BIS meeting in Basel. We established a close professional relationship that enabled the Bank to provide hands-on help for a number of years, particularly in the development of the Czech money market. Some of the Bank's staff visited Prague, and some Czech central bankers spent extended time in Ottawa—learning how we did things and also improving their English, the undisputed language of world money markets.

This was a time of tremendous demand for technical assistance in all things central bankerly, especially of course throughout Eastern Europe. The challenges for the Bank were twofold. It was not our style to have people sitting around on the off chance that some emerging market economy would need our help, so what we could do was strictly limited, however worthy and interesting the cause. Also, we wanted to be sure that our help was targeted within a considered framework, because technical assistance of any kind is, on the evidence, so easily wasted. Both the BIS and the IMF were helpful in organizing useful support within a structure.

☙☟

The Canadian dollar has figured in this chapter quite a few times, but always in cameo form. In the chapter that follows I want to bring it into the spotlight. It should never be the star, since Canada's economic and monetary fortunes can hardly be expected to revolve around the currency. But it is all the same a key price in our economic and financial system. It is also one to which monetary policy must pay considerable and continual attention, to make sure that the signals the exchange rate is giving out are read correctly as our policy tries to do the right thing for the economy.

CHAPTER 6

ॐ

Exchange Rate Matters

Judging by the volume of media commentary, interest in what the Bank of Canada does or thinks about the exchange rate matches or even exceeds interest in inflation. Inflation is easily more important, but it is less dramatic in the short term, since spikes in domestic price levels turn up less frequently than jerkiness on the currency exchanges. But while movement is where the news is, currency issues involve far more than exchange rate management and events. They also relate to deeper questions regarding the kind of exchange rate system we can profit by, given the kind of economy we are and the reality of financial globalization. In recent years, these questions also attracted the media as our exchange rate fell to new lows against the US dollar.

So what kind of economy are we? By global standards, our economy is not small but not so very large either—let's say medium. In economic size, we rank about thirteenth in the world. Another pertinent way of looking at what we are is to recognize that we account for just 2 per cent of world capital markets. So understandably, the nation's publicity organs, both governmental and media, take pride in our ranking in such select groups as the G-7 and G-8 nations, with the political bragging rights that go along with membership. To that extent we are, as British politicians used to be fond of saying, "punching above our weight."

It is because we are not so very large that one can largely separate questions concerning our international financial relations (discussed in the preceeding chapter) from those connected to our exchange rate set-up and management. For a really large economy, this kind of separation would be more questionable. At the extreme, for the United States, the role of its currency and its relationship to other currencies is a fundamental and extremely complex issue in its international financial dealings because other countries worry so much about their own currency's relationship to the US dollar and often try to do something about it. It follows that the United States, because it is so very big, paradoxically has less say than many other countries over its own currency's external value. How much that kind of say is really worth is another question, and one that I will comment on later when discussing Canadian choices. It is sufficient to note here that the freedom to make exchange rate choices can even be a handicap if policymakers are in the habit of making economic choices that are poor, as quite a few countries have learned the hard way.

At the other extreme are the small countries. It is striking how many extremely small nations there are now. Close to 40 of the IMF's 183 member countries have populations of less than a million—my armchair definition of a small state. For those countries, the range of feasible exchange rate choices is also narrow. In a world of large financial capital flows, their Hobson's choice tends to boil down to one between, on the one hand, seeking to ensure financial stability by giving up their own currency, and on the other, fitfully trying to contribute to domestic economic stabilization through monetary policy actions—assuming of course that the country's government is not tempted to try to raise revenue through the inflation tax, for which it will definitely need its own, unstable, currency.

Canada, being medium-sized, has a fair range of options. We are minor enough that other countries don't bother too much about their currency's relationship to our dollar, but large enough to have an adequate domestic market for our money in a globalizing world in which financial flows loom large. What these facts boil down to is that we can, if we are sensible (not guaranteed, of course), have both good domestic inflation performance and some monetary room to manoeuvre in order to stabilize our domestic economy.

With all the chatter about globalization, it is also worth bearing in mind that the Canadian economy is, and has been for many years, about as global as any. Not only is external trade an exceptionally large share of our national income, but we have traditionally been extremely open to international capital, both in real investment and through financial assets. Sitting as we do on top of the New York markets, we began to experience large international flows before such global exchanges as those for Eurodollars were dreamt of. This means that the kinds of globalization events that have made headlines in recent years for so many countries, particularly in regard to money ebbs and flows, have been long-standing features of the Canadian scene. Our relatively lengthy experience also means that we have learned a thing or two about how to cope with some of the more challenging international market situations that are bound to arise from time to time—whether caused by events abroad or, as has been just as common, by disturbances at home. These are lessons that many other countries are just starting to apply.

We have profited greatly from this openness through the benefits of trade, advances in technology, and enhancement of our living standards. This openness also explains why over the years we have tended to let our dollar float in currency markets, even when the overwhelming practice for other countries was to keep their currencies fixed. Since many other industrialized countries were also inclined to hang on to exchange controls, their turn to try to find their way in a more financially open and more bracing market environment came later than here. Canada never went around trying to sell floating exchange rates to others, but it became apparent that we were preaching by example. Accordingly, the Bank of Canada was happy to provide help to the Scandinavian countries in the early 1990s, when they sought advice in dealing with their newly flexible currencies after their exchange rate pegs had been overwhelmed by capital market bets against them. Gordon Thiessen got a medal from Sweden for this.

Exchange Rate Management

Canada's long-standing policy since we abandoned the Bretton Woods pegged exchange rate formula in 1970 has been to let the exchange rate float. But what does it mean to float? This turns out to be a fairly complex question. One thing floating does not mean is forgetting about the exchange rate—not, at least, as regards how monetary policy is to be put to work. At the same time, neither does it mean that policy is at all likely to take a strong stand regarding any particular currency level. To do that would be tantamount to fixing the rate and would obviously be a contradiction of the basic policy of allowing adjustment to changing economic circumstances in part through the exchange rate. A more market-oriented reason for not taking a stand on the currency's level is that flexibility in the currency lessens the odds for speculators (no one-way bets). And in any case, a moving target is likely to deter them from the start.

But while the exchange rate is neither a target nor an instrument of monetary policy in Canada, it is undeniably an element in our economic system that monetary policy has to be very aware of and sometimes react to. In summary, monetary policy will in some way have to care about the exchange rate, and my discussion of exchange rate management that follows is about *how* it should care. Two basic kinds of situations present themselves—what, if anything, needs to be attended to when the situation is relatively calm; and what should be done when there is some kind of currency, or confidence, crisis.

The Currency in Calmer Waters

It took the Bank some time to take on board all the implications of a floating Canadian dollar. Senior management was not comfortable about Canada's exit from the global pegged exchange rate system in 1970, aside from any personal regrets that Louis Rasminsky might have had as a major contributor (chair of the drafting committee) to the post-war pegged (fixed but adjustable) exchange rate system established in 1944 at the Bretton Woods international conference. More broadly, when the Bank lost the fixed exchange rate policy anchor for its monetary actions, it then had to reconstruct a policy framework as it went along. And it had to do this in what had become a decidedly inflationary and economically ambiguous environment.

For a while, in the early 1980s, the Bank did focus policy informally on the Canadian dollar, trying not to let it go down too far too fast lest this re-ignite inflation. In a sense, policy was using the exchange rate as a target, at least of an intermediate nature if not as a more basic monetary goal. But this was hardly satisfactory. What this pointed to—something to be discussed fully in the next chapter—was the need to be as clear as we could as to what monetary policy was aiming for on a more lasting and more made-in-Canada basis. The only point to stress here is that aiming at domestic monetary stability was not just worthwhile in itself; it also provided a sound non-inflationary anchor for our floating currency. In this way, our basic approaches to the exchange rate and to domestic inflation would reinforce each other. They would also afford the Bank a proper sense of priorities in deciding how to act and react on a day-to-day basis in regard to developments in financial markets.

So much for the theory. How about practice? In particular, how could we best incorporate the exchange rate into our thinking about monetary policy actions? The broad idea that we worked with was to think of the transmission of Bank of Canada monetary policy to financial markets and then to the economy generally as a process that involved not just the domestic money market and short-term interest rates, but also the exchange market and the exchange rate. As I put it in a significant speech in Montreal in 1992:

> There is a useful sense in which we can look at developments in both short-term interest rates and the exchange rate to gauge the overall direction and intensity of changes in monetary conditions.

The basic notions were the following. First, an injection of liquidity from the central bank, other things being equal, ought to show up in a decline in both short-term interest rates and the exchange rate. Second, since both interest rate and exchange rate movements affect total spending in the economy, we could think of combining the effects according to their estimated impact on spending (e.g., the effect of a one percentage point change in interest rates compared with a 1 per cent change in the exchange rate) to derive a gauge for the change in monetary conditions. Third, this calculation, which came to be known as a "monetary conditions index," would help us to gauge the impact of monetary policy actions in a way that took intelligent account of the domestic effect of changes in the exchange rate and in interest rates.

This way of thinking was already very much in our minds in the late 1980s, when the exchange rate moved up strongly from about 72 US cents per Canadian dollar in 1986 to some 86 US cents by 1990. Our essential tack was to try, through our management of basic liquidity and consistent rhetoric, to hold short-term interest rates up at around 12 per cent. Whether these levels were really high enough to curb rising inflation, given the evident and very persistent strong expectations regarding costs and prices, was difficult to say. But we were also aware that additional downward pressure on spending and inflation was coming from a rising Canadian dollar. So monetary conditions overall were meaningfully tighter than might have been gathered through looking just at interest rates. The fact that, contrary to calls from some business and academia critics for action to curb the appreciation, we did not respond to the dollar's rise in this period as we had done in the 1970s, also helped to demonstrate that the Bank meant business.

One of the more persistently vociferous demands to bring down the dollar came from the head of Repap, a pulp and paper concern, who had gone so far as to set up a personal consulting forum that assembled from time to time in Montreal. This group consisted of a wide range of academic economists, and on one occasion I was invited to talk to the group. The meeting was chaired by Robert

Mundell—but not aggressively enough, it seemed, for our host's taste—and I must say that it was a tamer and odder affair than I had expected. While the hope evidently had been for a blunt confrontation over the iniquities of an appreciated dollar, what transpired was a much more diverse response—something like herding cats! Economists love to make contrary points and then debate them, so we soon were engaged more in an intriguing chat about currency issues and how to integrate a floating exchange rate into monetary policy through the use of a monetary conditions index than a debate about depreciating the currency.

A monetary conditions index is not too difficult to construct, and it has by now been used in many individual countries and widely by the International Monetary Fund as a way of sketching on a thumbnail basis the impact of monetary policy in an open economy with a flexible exchange rate. But interpreting the index turns out to be more complicated than originally thought. The product needs a clear warning label as "toxic if swallowed in the wrong circumstances." It works quite well as a guide when the purpose is to assess the impact of a monetary policy move or when the development is an independent, or autonomous, shift in capital flows. As I just indicated, the results of a policy move should pop out in both interest rate and exchange rate changes. As for capital movements, an outflow, for example, will push down the currency and should be counterbalanced by action to raise interest rates in order to sustain monetary policy on the same course as before.

The problem is that these two kinds of simple instances are far from exhausting the situations that might reasonably affect the exchange rate. For example, the shift in international economic conditions that occurred in 1997 and 1998, stemming from a series of economic and financial collapses in Asia and Russia and a downdraft in industrial materials prices, also had a major impact on expectations regarding the performance of major sectors of our economy. Naturally, this also affected the Canadian dollar, which fell from 73 US cents in the autumn of 1997 to 63 cents by August 1998. In those circumstances, the sensible thing was not to react to the gradual though sustained downward exchange rate pressure by trying to push up interest rates. Correspondingly, it was also appropriate that any Canadian monetary conditions index would also shift down.

But this downshift was disconcerting to anyone who had thought that the monetary conditions index was some kind of public indicator or even target for monetary policy. The incentive to think of monetary conditions in this way was compounded by the fact that beginning in 1995, the Bank had chosen to publish such an index regularly and, even worse, as a fairly lengthy historical series. However, it is far from clear what any historical series of this kind can convey that would be at all useful to an outside observer or, for that matter, to anyone inside the Bank. All in all, this was a case where commendable efforts at increasing transparency went too far. They led to confusion instead of clarity, and increasing clarity is, after all, what transparency has to be about.

One important moral of all this has been that in charting a course in monetary policy, the Bank should pay attention not just to movements of the exchange rate, but equally to differentiating the *sources* of any movements. For some movements, such as one caused by a large unexpected capital inflow, an offsetting interest rate reaction might well be called for. For others, for example where exchange rate strength mirrors economic strength, this is much less certain.

I have to allow that the cookbook on how to deal with the exchange rate does turn out to be a complex business, but the recipes are there and can be repeated if necessary. There is no real alternative to careful analysis of the circumstances and close attention to what financial markets are saying. My hope is that the kind of discussion here will help to inform, and at least mitigate, the sweeping statements about exchange rate movements that turn up so often in commentary and communication. The essential moral is that currency flexibility can be factored carefully into monetary policy in a perfectly sensible fashion, but that the circumstances need analyzing, and no doubt explaining, each time exchange rate movement becomes a significant issue.

Currency Crises

Capital flows are always with us, but when saver and investor confidence is at stake, they are front and centre. And with weakened confidence, the tendency is for funds to flow out, accompanied by a rise in market interest rates that also directly reflects the loss of confidence. In other words, exchange rate decline and the interest rate rise are two sides of the same coin. So it is not so much a question for monetary policy of raising interest rates in order to rebalance monetary conditions (market interest rates are already rising whether the authorities like it or not) as it is of trying to figure out how to help make the situation calmer.

Naturally, these events are very much connected to monetary policy actions and reactions, and some are discussed in fair detail in later chapters on monetary policy developments. One was the minor upset of early 1990, when the Bank tried to engineer an abrupt downshift in short-term interest rates before the next budget. Another was the far more dramatic setback of late 1994 to early 1995, sparked by Mexico's debt and exchange rate troubles and correspondingly intensified conjecture as to how much trouble Canada also would be in without stronger budgetary action. ("Hudson Bay peso" was one of the more scathing terms used for our currency on that occasion, although the shock to our modest Canadian psyche was no doubt tempered by the fact that we generally refer to our dollar somewhat dismissively as a "loonie.") Accordingly, here I can be relatively succinct, limiting myself to three related points.

My first point is that in such a crisis, the crucial thing for the Bank of Canada to do is to take back the initiative, to somehow get ahead of the market. One approach that does not work, tempting though it appears, is easing liquidity (injecting more money into the economy) to try to offset the market-induced rise in interest rates. This only nourishes further losses of confidence and finances more capital flight. The right thing to do—something at which the Bank became quite practised—is to *tighten* liquidity, thereby putting still more upward pressure on money market interest rates, especially overnight rates. Most dramatically, tightening can also involve selling treasury bills in the open market, thereby lowering their price and pushing up bill rates further still. Everyone would notice that. One effect of such measures is to put a financing squeeze on anyone speculating against the currency. More broadly, the actions would indicate that the Bank is going to be a force to be reckoned with and that there could still be two-way (i.e., riskier) bets in the exchange market. Once this becomes clearer, market uncertainties, at least as regards the approach the monetary authority would be taking, are lessened. And other things being equal, interest rates and currency values gradually return to a more acceptable state. Matters have turned out this way on quite a few occasions, not just the two cited earlier. It is not necessary to go over them all—post-Meech Lake, post-Charlottetown, and so on.

As my second point, I want to take a step or two back and recall the seminal lesson in what to do that occurred on account of a bout of exchange market and money market turbulence in late 1985 and early 1986. Earlier in 1985, the Bank had been attempting to ease Canadian interest rates relative to US ones. However, late in the year, a shift in market sentiment led to sharp downward pressure on the currency and the start of a market-led backup in Canadian money market rates. We had already learned that in those circumstances, it did not pay to inject further liquidity in order to try to bring interest rates back down. The interesting question, however, was whether such a "watching brief" kind of approach would restore confidence with enough dispatch.

A significant feature of the 1985–86 episode was the particular attention displayed by Michael Wilson, who was keen for the Bank to be more aggressive in countering these adverse market developments, and keener than the Bank initially cared to be.[1] I think that his interest reflected two factors: his earlier investment banking background and consequent close appreciation of market dynamics and interactions—in particular, what the market would pay attention to; and the fact that we were, as with the later episode in

---

[1] For Michael Wilson's perspective on this episode, see the *Globe and Mail*, January 25, 2002.

1990, getting awfully close to a budget. This always makes a minister of finance edgy. In early February 1986, with the dollar down to 69 US cents from over 73 cents the previous October, more drastic action was finally taken. The government intervened aggressively in the exchange market (also announcing a foreign borrowing for this purpose), while the Bank sold treasury bills and tightened overnight liquidity. As the exchange rate strengthened, short-term interest rates came down, and by May 1986 they were back to where they had been the previous autumn. The Canadian dollar stabilized at around 72 US cents.

My third point, and now more broadly again, is that it may be objected that I have painted too rosy a view concerning what can be done. The objection would note that pushing up interest rates further in this kind of situation can bring its own set of problems—for example, worsening a governmental fiscal position through increasing debt service, pushing up borrowing costs for businesses, and even causing bankruptcies. Besides being problems themselves, they could also erode confidence. However, those objections do not persuade. In the first place, in our floating exchange rate situation the currency will already have moved down by a notable amount, since this is not a case of defending a fixed currency peg, as in the notorious Swedish case of 1992 when even short-term interest rates at triple-digit (and therefore patently unsustainable) levels did not prove adequate. So in contrast to the kinds of defences that have to be mounted for a fixed exchange rate, with a floating rate we do not have to do so much on the interest rate side to establish our point. In the second place, the proof of the pudding is in the eating, and the approach has worked well for Canada on too many occasions to be a fluke.

Whose Dollar?

From time to time over the years, I have run into Domingo Cavallo, architect and once designated resuscitator of the currency board system that tied the Argentine peso into a one-for-one relationship with the US dollar. On the latest occasion, in the fall of 2000, he was once again arguing that if Argentina were to quit its currency board (that is, go onto a float as had its trading partners, Brazil and Chile), then it would choose to do so in circumstances where it would see its peso float *upwards*. This, as far as currency market sentiment is concerned, would be equivalent to a corporation achieving a successful initial public offering when it enters the stock market.

I told him that based on Canada's experience, there was good news and bad news. The good news was that while it was certainly unusual for a country's currency to appreciate in its initiation as a floater (indeed, currencies almost always take a dive, though not necessarily as much as Argentina's when it went off its currency board arrangement at the end of 2001), Canada provided an appropriate precedent. In both 1950 and 1970, our newly floating dollar went up against its US counterpart. On both occasions, we had floated on the back of a strengthening current account and large capital inflows. The bad news was that the first float ended in disarray in 1962, after our government tried to manipulate the currency down on the grounds that it was too strong. The second float has, in the end, been more successful. But it took us well over a decade (and perhaps as much as two decades) after the decision to resume floating in 1970 before we became fully comfortable with what we were doing and why we were doing it.

Even though a body of Canadians has been arguing strenuously to the contrary, Canada is now viewed by the rest of the world as a country that knows how to run its flexible exchange rate regime successfully—at least the Bank of Canada knows, and no doubt the Department of Finance does as well. Admittedly, we will give a better impression still as to what we know if Prime Minister Chrétien continues to refrain from congratulating the country on having a depreciating dollar, since such comments leave the erroneous (I hope) and potentially damaging impression that our policy is one of promoting currency decline. Still, this has been a minor issue to date, even though it makes for easy and unfortunate headlines.

But that is not the end of the affair. Even if we are a competent floater by global standards, it is still reasonable to ask, as critics also do, whether a flexible exchange rate regime is, all things considered, the best one for Canada to use. Not so long ago, the market for such a question would have been extremely small. But the march of events in the past few years, above all the lengthy decline of our dollar against the US currency, makes the whole issue rather more real from a Canadian angle. However, as I will also show, the issue is now not real enough or well-defined enough for us to change what we do.

How to decide what exchange rate set-up works best for a country is truly a question in the realm of the broadest political economy. To bring some order to what I have to say, I will break it down three ways: economic considerations, financial ones, and those that are of a more political cast—though the political factor seems to enter everywhere, however much one tries to keep it in its own box.

Economic Considerations for the Currency

Probably the single most important economic event shaping Canadian views about desirable exchange rate regimes has been one of precedent—namely, the inauguration of the Eurozone, with a common currency, the euro, to replace the deutschmark, French franc, etc. Simply put, the question is: If the Europeans (or more precisely many Europeans) think it is such a good idea to give up their national currency, why shouldn't we?

To go over all the ways the European choice differs from the realistic decisions facing Canada would be tedious. But the essential point is that we do not, in fact, have the option of setting up some kind of multi-country condominium arrangement, with the range of common institutions and common, unweighted decision making that Europe has developed. Rather, our decision would be whether we are prepared to tag along behind US institutions, US national choices, and the US national currency. And this is true even if Mexico were to join in as well, although some Canadians fantasize that Mexico would make a difference to the power equation. Furthermore, any decision to tag along has economic costs. One important consideration is that unlike the situation for Europe, Canadians cannot freely cross the border to take jobs, although this would help to offset the rigidity entailed by a shared currency.

A deeper and more contentious issue is the extent to which we are falling behind the United States in our productivity and living standards, and whether this is at all due to the fact that we have not fixed somehow to the US dollar. Professional debates rage over where, why, and how much our productivity levels differ from those in the United States. The statistics are difficult to interpret. Some prominent voices argue not only that the difference is very large, but also (crucially, for what we are discussing here) that it exists precisely because our currency has tended to depreciate. Key figures pushing the argument that a flexible, and above all depreciated, Canadian dollar has been at the root of a major relative drop in our living standards are economics professors Thomas Courchene and Richard Harris. However, they have been more successful in getting the ears of provincial politicians and journalists than in convincing other economists that their reasoning is more than merely imaginative.

The story they construct—that a chronic tendency to let the currency depreciate has lowered living standards by allowing Canadians to avoid the tough decisions needed to raise our productive efficiency—is internally consistent. But it is hard to fit that tale to the actual Canadian facts. In the first place, it is easier and more plausible to tell any productivity story the other way round, *starting* from weakness in improving productivity and *finishing* with weakness in our currency. Second, there are solid explanations for the Canadian dollar's performance over the years (principally through a trend decline in the prices of our major commodity exports) that do not require any link to productivity performance. It is also worth pointing out that our dollar has depreciated only against the US dollar, which has been strong against all currencies. Canada's currency has held up quite well elsewhere—notably against the euro and the yen. And in 2002, as the US dollar began to weaken in currency markets, Canada's currency, logically, started to improve again.

I am not suggesting that we do not have a productivity challenge, although it is probably less than the critics suggest and exists for reasons different from the behaviour of the exchange rate. Neither am I saying that Canada's economic future may not be better if it relies less on our being "hewers of wood and drawers of water." That depends on the future prices of commodities such as wood, water, copper, oil, etc. But I am arguing that we are better off tackling such issues directly, to the extent that we can agree that they are real, rather than using an exchange rate fix as some kind of cure, especially, of course, when the exchange rate is not the cause. In short, we should be comfortable with the economic consequences of a floating Canadian dollar. My sole qualification is that this assumes that Canadian domestic financial policies are run well.

Financial Considerations

I confess to feeling strongly about the financial, or monetary, aspects of the matter. If there is one force that has proved powerful in pushing countries to fix their exchange rates in a way that seems irrevocable—that is, through a currency board or, more thoroughly, through dollarization—it is their demonstrated incapacity to run a sound financial policy. But that seems, to me at least, to be a counsel of despair about what monetary authorities should be able to do. It also puts the cart before the horse.

Latin America is in the unfortunate position of providing some excellent examples of monetary mismanagement. The consequences, whether for Argentina or for Ecuador (another cautionary example that has been in the dollarizing news), have been financial disarray, soaring inflation, spiralling interest rates, and a diving currency. Hence the recipe—fix your currency and thereby turn monetary management over lock, stock, and barrel to someone (i.e., the United States) who can do it better than you can. This Latin American tendency has been cited as a reason why we should move in the same direction, and why we are somehow missing the continental boat if we don't.

But as far as Canada is concerned, that boat looks like the Good Ship Lollipop. We deserve better. Exchange rate fixing in Latin America comes down to a call for a quick, definitive solution for more domestic monetary confidence, the prize being much lower— i.e., US-made—interest rates. But in Canada, given our better recent inflation record, moving to the US dollar could well mean higher interest rates. That at least should make people think twice.

The South American currency debate is far from settled. Some countries are showing promising progress and capability under a floating exchange rate. Chile and Mexico come readily to mind. Argentina, in contrast, found matters impossible with its currency board, being chained to a high US dollar in spite of its large export markets in Europe and Brazil. It had to go to the International Monetary Fund for support. Its difficulties also showed in the astonishingly adverse risk premium in its local interest rates that emerged in 2001 notwithstanding low inflation and its US dollar link. More profoundly, over the years immediately preceding 2001, it could not generate the domestic economic flexibility and disci- pline in its public sector finances that it needed to live within its currency straitjacket. In fact, if it could not raise its productivity performance substantially and the United States continued to turn in decent inflation, it would have been required to *deflate* its price level continually to stay competitive—and that would have taken some doing. Clearly, Argentina has had economic policy and per- formance problems above and beyond its (almost) unyielding fix to the US dollar. But the collapse at the end of 2001 of its currency board arrangement should make those advocating a fixed currency in Canada much more careful about what they wish for, especially when they want the experiment to solve perceived internal prob- lems. They may get what they wish, in spades.

One currency step that Argentina did not take, at least not wholeheartedly, was actually to dollarize—that is, to abandon entirely its homegrown peso unit as legal tender in favour of the US dollar. The immediate advantage of such a step is that it becomes more difficult to devalue, simply because there is then no domestic currency unit to be devalued. The country would have to create one from scratch, and that is difficult. The deeper advantage is enhanced currency credibility, and therefore less of a risk premium in domestic interest rates because of the greater difficulty of then going back to a local currency unit. But two things that Argentina has taught us are first, that no one should underestimate the political determination to invent, or reinvent, a currency when it seems the immediately right thing to do, and second, that setting the currency in what you think is concrete by no means guarantees an end to domestic policy problems.

Weighing the Politics

Rare is the national politician who feels that significant advantage will come from giving up a nation's currency in favour of dollarization. Matters have to come to a terrible domestic pass before a body of political weight would shift in that direction. Conversely, it would no doubt be a pleasant political thought in the United States (manifest destiny and all that) to see its dollar used officially not only from sea to shining sea but also south of the Rio Grande, and perhaps north of the forty-ninth parallel as well. A few years ago, a bill was introduced in the US Senate to make this easier to happen by granting a country some part of the homegrown seigniorage profit it must give up when it officially adopts the US dollar. The bill lapsed, but it may get reintroduced.

The position of the US administration on dollarization has been cautious to date. There is no objection in Washington to other countries using its dollar, officially or unofficially. After all, the seigniorage then accrues fully to the US Treasury. But so far, the welcome does not go beyond this. In particular, it has been made clear that no liquidity support to other banking systems would be automatically forthcoming from the Federal Reserve, even though in surrendering its currency a country would also be giving up any homegrown monetary support for its financial system. More generally, the Federal Reserve is clearly not enamoured of the prospect of being pressured to decide how to run monetary policy for other countries in addition to the United States.

But the demands and opportunities of geopolitics may eventually change this. Many will no doubt recall the shift in US attitudes over Canada–US free trade, from one of relative indifference when Canada first came calling to positive engagement after further US reflection on what might be happening in Europe and Asia. I vividly recall James Baker, who as US Treasury Secretary engineered this shift in 1987, stating in a speech in Ottawa, "If we can't have multilaterals [on free trade] we can have minilaterals." A similar shift might be forthcoming one day regarding currency blocs. "If they can have *their* currency blocs, then we..." At that point, the choices for Canada could become more politically interesting, although they would always, ultimately, remain in the gift of the United States.

In Canada, national politicians are not biting at the lure of a strongly fixed currency (or, alternatively, at no national currency at all), but provincial political interests do not necessarily line up with national ones. So no one should have been surprised to see the quick concern shown in 1999 by Quebec's then minister of finance, Bernard Landry, over Canada's apparent lagging productivity and the conviction he displayed that fixing to the US dollar would cure it. Not to suggest that there is a hidden agenda here—in fact, the agenda is very obvious.

Quebec's possible separation from the rest of Canada would not only have political repercussions but would generate major economic and financial dislocation as well. Concerns about the rocky road ahead, together with inevitable firebrand rhetoric, would cause a run on the Canadian dollar, hurting not only those in the rest of Canada, but also Quebeckers. This is not a good stage on which to play out separation. But the exchange rate factor, at least, could be alleviated by dispensing with a national currency in favour of the US dollar. Of course, to be effective, such a manoeuvre would need to be undertaken before the breakup happened. This separatist political incentive to promote Canada's dollarization right now, however flimsy the general arguments, could not be plainer. Bernard Landry, now (in the fall of 2002) Quebec's premier, would certainly be sensitive to it.

Including Gold?

The mighty foundation of the international financial system for decades, starting in the nineteenth century, was gold, and central banks were its guardians. No longer. Central banks are still the repositories of a very significant portion of the world's stock (made up of virtually all the gold mined since the beginning of time), but gold's monetary function has largely evaporated. In effect, this is because its supply was not elastic enough to meet governments' expanding, and increasingly expansive, demands on the financial system, both domestically and internationally. Furthermore, those central banks have developed a disconcerting instinct to sell the metal off and depress its price. That is not good news for the people or territories that produce it, and it also puts central banks in their bad books. There are other complications as well.

A small one is that here the term "central banks," despite the common usage, is something of a misnomer. In the context of gold operations, the expression is more accurately seen as a euphemism for national governments. A central bank may well house a nation's gold in its vaults, but no matter what the newspapers say, that does not necessarily mean that the bank owns the gold or will decide when to sell it. In Canada, the government has title to the country's gold reserves, wherever they are held. So when it was resolved to start unloading official gold back in 1979, it was then minister of finance John Crosbie who pulled the trigger.

The Bank of Canada was consulted and did not raise any particular objection. Its role since then has been to arrange the selling of gold on Department of Finance general instructions. The same would also be true, to cite a more news-catching and more recent example, for Britain. The Bank of England may well have conducted regular gold auctions, but anyone who wanted to complain about the policy or direct compliments should have addressed the Chancellor of the Exchequer. Even in countries such as Germany, where the central bank has greater say over such matters (gold is held on the books of the Bundesbank), it is hardly likely that a program of gold sales would get under way without a nod of approval from the government in question. The Swiss National Bank, one of the more independent central banking institutions by any score, went one better and got a constitutional amendment.

The disquiet of gold producers is easy to understand. Their production is squeezed and commercial prospects are put into question. What is more complex, and in some aspects debatable, is the reasoning that goes on behind official gold disposal—in particular, how central banks judge that it works to their financial advantage.

One motive for selling comes from the realities of currency management. If a government is inclined to undertake market interventions to support its currency, what it needs is foreign exchange, not gold. From that reality, it can be a short step (if the central bank does not want to get into such operations as short-term swaps of gold for US dollars) to disposing of gold for foreign exchange, which can be mobilized almost instantaneously for exchange rate support.

Another argument that can persuade a vacillating central bank is the fact that gold bars do not pay interest. Foreign currency reserves, on the other hand, are invariably held in revenue-bearing instruments—US Treasury bills are a prime example. So apart from any merit that gold has as an alternative asset for portfolio diversification, the only financial value from holding it would be the expectation that it will appreciate over time at a pace faster than the rate of interest. But the currency price of gold fluctuates quite a lot, so good timing when selling gold is important. Compared to other central banks, the Bank of Canada sold virtually all its holdings (some 21 million ounces or over 600 tonnes) into the market at relatively good prices, averaging over US $350 per ounce.

This highlights a third approach, focusing on "extraordinary income"—the apparent profit that can be made when gold is sold at a price above the value at which it is carried on the books. Such considerations seem to have been a particular spur in Canada, where officials were much taken with the large spread between the gold price to be realized in the market and the arbitrarily modest carrying value per ounce in our public accounts. Opportunity knocked particularly in the latter part of the 1980s, at a time when our deficit-challenged colleagues at the Department of Finance were searching for every revenue cent they could find, whether through limiting tax bracket indexing, imposing income tax surcharges, or as in the case of gold, selling assets.

More than one European government hit on the same idea in the mid-1990s, when national debts had to be cut significantly (except for happy Luxembourg) if the fiscal performance tests decreed under the Maastricht Treaty for entry into the European Monetary Union were to be met. One of the issues was whether the sale of an asset to reduce public debt was a bona fide reduction in debt. Since you would not have to be much of a purist to say that an asset sale was not Maastricht eligible (i.e., not an ongoing budgetary improvement and not an improvement in debt on a net basis), it is curious that the really egregious example came from Germany, normally a preacher of financial rectitude. There, the government aimed in 1997 to get the Bundesbank's gold reserves revalued to market prices and have the accounting profit applied to reducing public debt. The manoeuvre failed on account of the Bundesbank's strenuous and very open objections. But it's an ill wind. Market expectations that Italy would qualify for Eurozone membership strengthened on the news that the German government had tried a creative interpretation of the Maastricht rules. With this precedent, bending the rules on Italy's behalf might become more acceptable.

Since Canada started selling gold early, we enjoyed a first mover advantage. For this reason, and because we are a country that is not in the sights of most other gold holders, we were able to go about our affairs in relative tranquillity. In the 1990s, after Canada's holdings were already considerably reduced, gold selling generally became more complicated as more and more central banks got into the act.

A particular stir was created early in 1993 among European central banks when it was learned that the Dutch had very quietly sold off 400 tonnes, about a quarter of their stock. Some felt that European solidarity had been breached and that this could pressure others to sell. What would happen to the gold market then? When G-10 governors next met at the Bank for International Settlements,

I suggested that Canada was a special case, and not just for having started selling much earlier, being open about it, and not being in Europe. I pointed out that decades before, when the official world price of gold had been held low, at US$35 an ounce, Canada had bought gold at a higher price (under special legislation—the 1948 *Emergency Gold Mining Assistance Act*) to support small mining communities in our hinterland. Otherwise, the jobs and communities would have disappeared. (To do this, we needed special dispensation from the International Monetary Fund.) So, I contended, it was only fair that we should eventually sell high the gold that had been bought high more than 20 years earlier. I chose not to rub in that the whole operation had been an excellent deal because the premiums per ounce paid by the federal government in that earlier period had averaged only some $5 more than the low official price.

The problem central banks pose for themselves when interest in selling gold catches on in their ranks is the ages-old cartel difficulty—how to sell without pushing the price against themselves and each other. Clearly, pressure builds up to steal a march and get a better price before your neighbour goes ahead and before the bottom falls out of the market. A rush toward a selling window can easily ensue, itself causing the price to fall. Then, so much for vaunted central bank cooperation—more likely instead recrimination.

Matters have been complicated further by the fact that quite a few central banks have aimed to have it both ways. They have retained title to their gold but also, particularly in more recent years, have lent it out to earn some interest. The return is not large, generally no more than about 2 per cent annually. Still, they have probably thought that such a return is better than nothing. In fact, taking into account the effect on the value of their gold holdings, it may be worse than nothing because lending gold adds to market supply and therefore depresses the price. It is doubtful that central bank lenders realized fully what they could be doing to themselves—not because they could not understand the ramifications of their actions if they put their minds to it, but rather because they were not paying much attention to the financial dynamics of the gold market. This was itself eloquent if mute witness to the vastly reduced place of gold in monetary thinking.

Later in the 1990s, the role of central bankers in creating gold market uncertainty and downward price pressure—a role that was out of all proportion to the amounts they were actually selling at that time, but did reflect the vast overhang of central bank gold stocks—did get their attention. The result was the Washington Agreement, an accord among quite a few major gold holders, announced in September 1999, to limit their collective annual sales over the next five years to not more than 400 tonnes, or about a sixth of new yearly production. Just as significantly, they also agreed to cap their lending. These moves had the effect of mitigating, though not eliminating, downward price pressure. Conversely, they also helped to maintain the value of the stocks that these institutions still held. Canada was not a party to the agreement, but with the federal government's inventory down to the bare bones, this was academic. By 2002, the market value of our gold holdings was under US$300 million (less than a million ounces or 30 tonnes), compared with total international reserves of some US$28 billion. In the rankings, Canada held more gold than Ecuador but less than Bolivia.

Less academic, given the enormous size of its Fort Knox reserves (over 8,000 tonnes), is the fact that the United States did not sign the Washington Agreement either. One can only guess why not, but even if the United States had been, improbably, of a mind to sell, there would have been concerns over joining what could perhaps have been considered a commercial cartel rather than an example of international financial cooperation. The US government did sell gold for a while in the late 1970s, in part at least because its dollar was under pressure, but this will not be a motive in the future as long as the US dollar is highly regarded. For a brief while though, in 1987–88, the United States did seem to flirt with finding a stronger place for gold in the international economic system. Treasury Secretary James Baker created quite a stir by pushing in G-7 circles the notion that the group should incorporate into its analytics a commodity price indicator for global inflation that would, above all, "include gold." But quite what was going to be done on the basis of this special indicator was never made clear, even for other G-7 participants. Perhaps the US Treasury did not know itself. In any event, the idea soon faded away, and with it any notion that gold would be playing a special role internationally through the G-7.

If gold is no longer the foundation of the international financial system, what is? Many would answer that it is de facto the US dollar, at least while it remains strong. And when it is not, the euro will vie for attention, perhaps eventually also with some currency out of Asia. What this really means is that in the end the foundation is built on trust in paper—that is, on central bank balance sheets, augmented by a dose of competition among major currencies. In such an environment, admittedly not without its ambiguities, gold may not have a well-defined public place. But given those ambiguities, there will be persisting private demand, in inverse proportion to the amount of trust that a foundation based on paper can provide.

In such an environment, the best Canada can do is aim to cultivate its garden by clearing away its own ambiguities—to sustain its currency's domestic purchasing power and thereby build homegrown confidence. This is an issue that I return to in my final chapter. Here, I will limit myself to noting that a more solidly based Canadian approach—generating more trust in the Bank of Canada's balance sheet—would also set a good international example, even if, of necessity, one that is only medium-sized.

PART III

How Monetary Policy Has Evolved

CHAPTER 7

ଚଡ଼

Monetary Policy in the 1970s and 1980s

Nowadays we seem to have a fair consensus on what Canadian monetary policy should be doing. "Low inflation" (as opposed to "high inflation"?) is seen as desirable. It also seems to be widely accepted that the Bank of Canada had better focus on sustaining this relatively happy state. And perhaps now the consensus extends further, not just to seeing this as the best way to sustain low interest rates through monetary policy, but also to the broader consideration that it is the surest way for monetary policy to contribute to a good economy. Of course, nothing helps like seeing the economy do well when inflation is low—low at least by the relatively elastic standards of the past 30 years—and having seen the economy do poorly under higher inflation.

If it seems so agreeable to be where we are, why did it take us so long to get there? A broad but incomplete answer is because inflation expectations were persistently pessimistic over a long period. A more complete response recognizes that while the Bank was committed to restoring monetary confidence in Canada after the massive inflationary setback of the 1970s, there was no wider policy consensus that the effort was important or even worthwhile. Quite what else monetary policy was expected to do was not clear either, so the Bank was pretty much on its own. Even though there was a genuine underlying concern that government spending and deficit policies were no help, a swath of commentators thought that such policies were about right, that monetary policy was too tight, that inflation and inflationary expectations did not matter too much, but that if they did, substantial mileage could be gotten from a regime of price and wage controls. And they were keen to let everyone know these things. They also thought that the Bank controlled interest rates and could, and should, keep them down whatever the state of financial confidence. No wonder inflation expectations remained strong.

The difficulties I have just referred to were, of course, not just Canada's. In 1979, Arthur Burns, notable economist and chairman of the US Federal Reserve from 1970 to 1978, delivered his contribution to the Per Jacobsson Lecture series. The poignant title he chose, "The Anguish of Central Banking," was both very appropriate to the times and no doubt heartfelt. His anguish lay in the paradox represented by the fact that "central bankers, whose main business one might suppose is to fight inflation," had "been so ineffective in dealing with this worldwide problem." His search for an explanation led him well beyond central banking activities, but he did not excuse central bankers either. As he put it:

> Every central bank has some room for discretion, and the range is considerable in the more independent central banks. As the Federal Reserve, for example, kept testing and probing the limits of its freedom to undernourish the inflation, it repeatedly evoked violent criticism from both the Executive establishment and the Congress and therefore had to devote much of its energy to warding off legislation that could destroy any hope of ending inflation. This testing process necessarily involved political judgments, and the Federal Reserve may at times have overestimated the risks attaching to additional monetary restraint.

But that, fortunately, was not the end of the story—in the United States or elsewhere. In fact, at about the time that Dr. Burns was giving his lecture, things were beginning to change for the better. Ironically, they were improving because inflation and its consequences had by then gotten so very bad. The obvious question that I asked myself at the time was whether there was a better way— whether a strategy of prevention would have been better than coming to confront the issue only after the damage from inflation, and the expectations about inflation that came to be embedded in economic and financial behaviour, had become so severe. In other words, I did not see why central bankers really needed to become so anguished.

Turning back to Canada, what fortified the Bank and helped it plug away over the more barren years were two crucial considerations. It could not pass its buck. Besides being the ultimate supplier of the nation's money, it was also the institution most directly responsible for confidence in its product. The other consideration was a practical one. What, realistically, were the Bank's policy alternatives to applying the instruments it had to the task of improving monetary confidence? None made sense over any horizon longer than a few months. So while the Bank's doggedness won it many critics (and some supporters), in the end its general sense of direction was unassailable.

Inflation Worsens

In 1970, when Canada kicked off the current era of exchange rate floating, it already had an inflation problem coming from the wage and price pressures that had built up during the North American spending boom of the 1960s. Toward the end of that decade, the government had tried its hand at a program of voluntary restraint overseen through the Prices and Incomes Commission, but to little avail. Canadians, and particularly the Bank of Canada, might worry about where this inflation might go, but not much could be done, given our fixed exchange rate and the escalation of inflation in the United States under the twin pressures of the Vietnam War and the spending required by President Johnson's "Great Society" agenda— guns, butter, and a few other things as well.

Despite professions regarding the importance of monetary control that were made (at least to the IMF) when Canada floated its dollar in 1970, that did not prove to be an inflation turning point—at least, not in a direction that could be considered good. The temper of the times meant that the Bank's concerns got little audience, and worry over the Canadian dollar being "too high" soon became the norm in Ottawa. The then popular view, and one that still has many adherents outside the economics profession, was that the authorities could pick the low unemployment rate they naturally wanted, get there through combined doses of fiscal and monetary policies, and at worst see a somewhat higher but stable level of inflation. It took some years for that view to get dug up and exploded, at least professionally. Also, it might well be that the Bank's own willingness to take more of a stand over what was happening had been affected by the institutional trauma it had suffered from the events surrounding James Coyne's forced departure a decade earlier.

The official government body set up in the early 1960s to pronounce expertly on these matters, Ottawa's Economic Council (discussed in more detail in the next chapter), tried to be guarded in its analysis. While it did set specific national unemployment goals (coyly called "employment goals"), it also talked about the need for improvements in the economy's structure (more flexible labour markets, for example) to make those goals possible. It nonetheless handed down medium-term inflation/unemployment scenarios that went beyond being merely rosy and impinged on fantasy. Its report for 1969 was a classic, setting down targets for the mid-1970s of a combination of 3 per cent unemployment (a figure not seen annually since 1956) and 2 per cent inflation. This rate of inflation had been about the average for a stretch of previous years, but only if one excluded the inconveniently worsened experience from 1966 on, when inflation had been running at 4 per cent.

Little wonder, then, that Governor Louis Rasminsky bowed out in early 1973 on a pessimistic note, writing that:

In a certain sense, I think it is really impossible to succeed at the job of being a central banker under today's conditions when economic arithmetic counts for so little and all the social and economic pressures favour inflation.[1]

At that time, Canada's dollar had been floating for almost three years. So technically, at least, monetary policy had the wherewithal, not being hemmed in by an exchange rate that was fixed, to combat cost and price pressures.

If the challenges for monetary policy in confronting inflation seemed tough then, they soon became worse. In 1972, oil prices started to move up because of worldwide shortages, in part induced by OPEC muscle flexing. Grain scarcities were another source of inflation pressure worldwide. But Canadian policy added its share—all hands to the inflationary pump in the interests of lowering unemployment. The February 1973 budget introduced by Finance Minister John Turner (which confronted Gerald Bouey in the same month that he entered office) was firmly stimulative at a time of soaring aggregate demand. His budget speech did not argue that inflation was not a problem, but rather that unemployment was the greater one. Government policy was, in effect, saying that one problem could be traded off, if not solved, against the other. The speech concluded by stating as much:

> We shall be attacked in some quarters for still not doing enough to stimulate the economy. Others will say that we are doing too much and that by over-shooting the target, we will aggravate inflation. We recognize that we are running a risk, and that the risk is on the side of over-shooting. That is a risk worth taking at this time in the interests of dealing more effectively with unemployment.

Monetary policy was also touched upon when the minister noted that "a generally expansionary monetary policy fostered economic

---

[1] Quoted in Muirhead, 1999.

expansion and encouraged Canadians to borrow in domestic rather than in foreign markets." The latter part of this phrase is code language for the help an expansionary monetary policy had been giving in holding the exchange value of the Canadian dollar back from further appreciation.

By 1974 the overall rate of consumer inflation was up to double digits, from under 5 per cent two years earlier, and in the same period short-term market interest rates went from 5 to over 10 per cent. Measured unemployment declined slightly, from more than 6 per cent to just over 5 per cent. But it should be noted that this slight improvement occurred at a time when policy changes were pushing unemployment up. The drastic easing in eligibility rules for unemployment insurance introduced in 1971 had begun to change the way people behaved in relation to the job market. With the reduced cost of being out of a job for a while (thanks to larger, longer, and easier-to-obtain unemployment benefits), people naturally left jobs more readily and were less keen to get a new one than before. The upshot was that they were more likely to be recorded as unemployed. In this way, unemployment insurance changes had also changed the economic meaning of the unemployment statistics.

By the fall of 1973, the Bank at least, if few others, could see this. As Gerald Bouey pointed out then, in classic Bank understatement on an admittedly politically white-hot question:

> It is far from easy to reconcile virtually all the other evidence bearing on the state of the Canadian economy with the report from the Labour Force Survey that as recently as August of this year, the number of Canadians unemployed was still a full 5½ per cent of the labour force....

The eventual professional consensus, when sufficient time had elapsed to allow a fuller statistical analysis, was that insurance changes had by themselves increased unemployment (as statistically recorded if not as a measure of hardship or the number of people actively looking for work) by at least a percentage point.

The Canadian authorities had, like other governments, been dealt some bad economic cards through the grain and oil scarcities (a type of problem that later became known under the general heading of "supply shocks"). But they also played the ones they already held in a way that would compound their problems. For the rest of the decade and well into the next one, both unemployment and inflation would go much higher. Furthermore, the Canadian dollar fell sharply in the latter part of the 1970s. While the drop was initially triggered by uncertainties caused by the debut of the separatist Parti Québécois government, the fact that our inflation had for some time been running persistently ahead of that in the United States (in the six years through 1976, consumer prices in Canada increased by 49 per cent overall, compared with 40 per cent in the United States) finally caught up with us. This delayed reaction, resulting in a sharp plunge in our dollar, added further to the homegrown inflation pressures that had already started to erupt in the first half of the 1970s, notwithstanding the stronger Canadian dollar in those earlier years. All in all, this was not a great way to benefit from the policy flexibility afforded by a floating currency regime.

Wage and Price Controls

In 1975, with standard economic policies clearly not coping, the federal government introduced a policy of general wage and price controls: the Anti-Inflation Program. Senior staff at the Bank were significantly involved in the prior analytical work—particularly George Freeman, one of the Bank's deputy governors and a veteran of the voluntary wage–price guideposts of the late 1960s, supported by myself as head of the Research Department. Staff were also seconded to the Anti-Inflation Board to help in its operations, as they had been to the Prices and Incomes Commission a decade earlier. Robert Johnstone went in from his senior position at the Bank to become the board's executive director, and I also was over there for a while. Other younger folk from elsewhere in Ottawa who put in time there included Edmund Clark, now number two at the

Toronto-Dominion Bank, and David Dodge, now in charge of the Bank of Canada.

While the Bank supported this controls policy initiative in word and deed—after all, if it worked even halfway decently it would take a load off monetary policy—it also had reservations. Earlier experiences, especially in the United States from 1971, had shown that widespread controls on prices and wages were very difficult to operate in a sophisticated market economy for any extended period in the face of accumulating market distortions (in particular, any shortages of supply were compounded because prices could not adjust upward at all readily) and a spreading sense of unfairness. My sense was that such controls reached the height of their popularity on the day they were introduced. And any initial reservations were soon compounded by the hard reality, learned fast by those of us who spent time at the board, that wages were far easier to constrain by administrative means than prices, or even than profit margins. In fact, this did not matter much for the success of the program except in terms of the perceptions of fairness in the way the scheme was implemented, because if increases in money wages were curbed, prices, which were a good deal more responsive to market conditions, would quickly fall into line. That is, prices would respond provided fiscal and monetary policies were tight enough to ensure that total dollar spending in the economy also rose more slowly than before.

Naturally, such concerns were not limited to Bank of Canada officials. No one with whom the Bank dealt, certainly not officials in the Department of Finance, thought that controls could play more than a supporting role to other broader and more long-term economic policies. The hope was rather that the controls could help to slow the sheer momentum of inflation brought about by exaggerated changes in some prices and wages, which caused attempts to catch up and leap ahead in others. The homely analogy often used at the time was that of getting everyone at a football game to sit so that all could view the match from a position of comfort.

Targeting Money

It was comforting that the government was addressing the inflation problem. However, the deeper question facing the Bank at that point was the future trend of inflation, and monetary policy's role in this. To put the point in business jargon: what was the macro-economic exit strategy? Here the Bank parted company with many commentators, since it saw controls as more a support to an anti-inflationary monetary stance than a replacement. In other words, the Bank was skeptical of the notion that controls would allow monetary policy to be particularly expansive. More likely, controls could at best smooth the overall path to a sustained better price performance. But that better performance needed to be validated, or even ensured, by monetary policy. It was this kind of thinking that brought Gerald Bouey finally, in 1975, to adopt explicit public targets for monetary expansion.

The notion of using some kind of publicly announced money supply target had been examined and vigorously debated around the institution for quite a while, and considerable research had been done over a number of years. One important advantage would be that a well-designed target would surely provide a better sense of the stance of monetary policy than would the level of short-term interest rates. The reason is that in a climate of high inflation and correspondingly volatile expectations about infla-tion, it is almost impossible to assess confidently how high interest rates really are. Credit could seem expensive or cheap depending on one's outlook for inflation, and at that time, on the track record, anyone would find it difficult to gauge where inflation might go.

But there was also much skepticism at the Bank as to how well a target on the drawing board would actually perform in the field. Here, the doubters might have been anticipating "Goodhart's Law"—the point made about that time by Charles Goodhart, then a senior officer of the Bank of England, to the effect that when a monetary aggregate changes from being merely observed to being a target that has to be in some way managed, its actual behaviour, unfortunately, changes as well.

In any event, the target needed to be a good one, not only because the Bank would be hanging its hat on it, but also because the institution would be attracting some nasty reactions. The epithet "monetarist," not used in a kindly way and not seen popularly to be as kind as "Keynesian," would regularly be thrown at it. The Bank, because of its increased focus on the pace of some measure of monetary expansion, would inevitably be portrayed in some vociferous quarters as having no concern over the real economy, living on another planet, occupying an ivory tower, and so on. The staff got to know the stock phrases very well. On the other side, a catch phrase that some of us thought might be usefully turned into an illustration for our annual report was "carrying the burden."

What particularly seemed to infuriate the critics was the notion that this change in monetary policy technique—adopting a target for monetary expansion rather than trying to gauge directly whether interest rates were appropriate to the circumstances and, presumably, to the policy objective—might conceivably represent also a change in underlying monetary policy objectives themselves. For example, in 1979 Dr. Arthur Donner (then an academic) and Dr. Douglas Peters published a sharp critique, entitled *The Monetarist Counter-Revolution,* which set forth a solemn and lengthy characterization of what the Bank was supposed to be thinking—its "monetarist doctrines"—that left Bank staff shaking their heads in puzzlement. We were mystified at their interpretation of what we were aiming to do and also by their views as to how monetary policy worked. The way we saw it was that the Bank was merely getting more organized in managing demand in a less inflationary way. Was that the problem?

One notable irony in their hostility toward using information from the growth of monetary aggregates in setting the course of monetary policy seemed to have eluded Donner and Peters. There is compelling evidence that the US Federal Reserve could have done more to relieve conditions during the Great Depression if it had paid more attention to the path of money instead of looking at interest rates. Interest rates during the Depression were historically low, and this misled the Fed into believing that monetary conditions were easy. But given the declines in prices generally, they were not. All this is documented in the monumental study, *A Monetary History of the United States*, authored by Milton Friedman and Anna Schwartz—especially the chapter titled "The Great Contraction."

The situation in Canada at that time cannot be compared because the Bank of Canada did not come into being until the mid-1930s. But Canadians may be interested to note that in their study, Friedman and Schwartz make a point of citing the sensible (if unusual for the time) thinking of the Royal Bank of Canada on the causes of and remedies for the US distress. In its July 1930 monthly letter, the Royal Bank observed that "the present low [interest] rates do not indicate as easy money conditions as surface appearance seems to imply." Later in the same piece, it pointed out that "the decline in circulation [i.e., money supply as the Royal Bank measured it] has corresponded closely to the percentage decline in prices." What to do then? The Royal Bank's answer was that "immediate and decisive action on the part of the US Federal Reserve Bank in putting new funds into the market in large volume is what is necessary," meaning, in more modern terminology, aiming specifically for a more rapid expansion of the money supply by injecting central bank liquidity into bank reserves.[2]

The Bank took the plunge into announced money targets because it was convinced that with the path of declining inflation to be spelled out in the Anti-Inflation Program, there had to be a matching response from monetary policy. The announcement of such targets, defined in terms of M1 (currency and demand deposits), was foreshadowed in a notable speech by Governor Bouey delivered in Saskatoon in September 1975, one that became widely known as the "Saskatoon Manifesto." The essence of the Bank's position (or is it "monetarist doctrine"?) is clearly seen in the following brief passage:

---

[2] I have conjured enthusiastically with the possibility that one of the forces behind the Royal Bank's views was Graham Towers, who had shone in economics at McGill (where he had been an esteemed pupil of Stephen Leacock). However, while my correspondence with John McCallum, then chief economist at the Royal Bank, has made it clear that Towers did occasionally contribute to the monthly letter, it was not possible to establish any direct link to these particular views.

Whatever else may need to be done to bring inflation
under control, it is absolutely essential to keep the rate of
monetary expansion within reasonable limits.

You really cannot argue with that at the level of principle, however much critics might have railed. But first catch your target.
Despite much Bank effort and worry, the results of the monetary
targeting episode were mixed at best. It was one thing to envisage
monetary targets as showing a clearer path for interest rates that
would be high enough to lead to a less rapid escalation of total dollar spending in the economy and, over time, to lower inflation. It
proved quite another to assess what was happening to money quarter by quarter and explain why the particular money numbers were
where they were and what they meant in terms of broader economic objectives—or increasingly, as time passed, what they did,
not mean.

The basic problem, and one that seemed to get worse over time,
was that the relationship between the money numbers and what
was happening to overall spending in the economy changed a great
deal. These changes proved difficult to gauge and predict, as had
the changes in unemployment statistics caused by changes in
unemployment insurance legislation a decade earlier. The underlying reason, which probably stemmed more from Murphy's Law
than from Charles Goodhart's, was the unhappy reality that rapid
inflation brings high interest rates. (After all, why would anyone
lend or even save money at low interest rates in such a climate?)
Higher interest payments on deposits, together with the increasing
application of computer technology that allowed the introduction
of daily rates of interest on deposits, was provoking a sea change in
the kinds of money balances used to finance transactions. In these
circumstances people had less incentive to hold non-interest-bearing demand deposits—the main component of M1.

But the point of focusing on M1 as the target had been precisely to capture the link between money balances and purchases of
goods and services. By targeting the pace of expansion of M1, it was
hoped to exploit the apparent historically stable relationship

between such transactions balances, short-term interest rates, and total spending in the economy. The hoped-for policy sequence was from central bank actions to the effect on short-term interest rates, to the effect on demand for M1 and on total spending in the economy, and finally to the effect on inflation—plus whatever help controls taken by themselves might give. The most glaringly weak link in this chain of effects turned out to be the vanishing demand for M1-type balances. The presumed stable relationship of money to interest rates and to spending turned out not to be there.

By the early 1980s, the casting of monetary policy's direction in terms of the M1 target had become untenable. With deposit holders flocking out of conventional demand deposits, M1 was growing extremely slowly, and occasionally not at all, even as inflation was accelerating. At the same time, we were being called upon to try to slash interest rates so as to offset the apparent slow growth in our announced target numbers. Rather than do this, in late 1982 the Bank abandoned the M1 targets—or more accurately, as Gerald Bouey pointed out shortly after, it was M1, through its bad behaviour, that abandoned the Bank.

What about other money aggregates using broader definitions of "money," such as M1+, M2, M2+, and so on? Could we not have found a better target? We certainly got advice to this effect, but our work did not reveal any series purporting to be money that looked sufficiently reliable to use as a plausible successor to M1. We were still putting a lot of effort into the search when I became governor, and the pros and cons of monetary targeting took up a lot of space in my 1988 Hanson lecture.

Monetary aggregate targets do express rather cogently, if in proxy form, the fundamental fact that the central bank's leverage comes through its unique ability to supply a special form of money that is the ultimate legal means of payment for the Canadian economy. They also put clearly in the shop window for all to see the fact that a central bank is above all an institution that works in a monetary dimension. However, the practical problems in targeting money have been enormous, as most countries have discovered by now. To paraphrase the late Herbert Stein, a wise American economist, there may well be a stable relationship between some measure of money and total spending in the economy, but it seems to exist only if the *definition* of money is allowed to swing around in a wide and unpredictable way. So why not move on? That is to say, instead of focusing on an intermediate target such as an M, why not go further down the transmission belt to the long-term consequences of M, and other monetary elements as well? Why not target inflation itself?

This line of thinking is very persuasive from a technical point of view, but there are also, as was noted earlier in Chapter 2, some issues concerning the increased direct involvement of government in monetary policy decisions that will need further discussion. It is sufficient to note here that while, like Canada, quite a few countries (including the United Kingdom, Mexico, Australia) do have official, explicit inflation targets, some extremely important ones (the United States and Japan) do not. The newly formed European Central Bank has, for now, a combination of monetary aggregate *and* inflation targets. However, the European monetary numbers do not seem to work any better for it than similar German aggregates did earlier for its philosophical parent, the Bundesbank.

Back to Eclectics

At the start of the 1980s, the Bank's monetary policy hand was to all intents forced by events outside our borders—namely, the great American disinflation led by the Federal Reserve's Paul Volcker. Mr. Volcker was invited in as chairman in 1979, when US monetary policy was in disarray. It had become increasingly difficult to understand what the Fed was trying to achieve, and there was a plunge in confidence, both domestic and international, in American financial policies in general. He was in effect given the political mandate to deal with inflation, and this he proceeded to do vigorously, in the process pushing US short-term interest rates up to about 20 per cent and thereby giving the world a whole new set of criteria for the stock term "monetary tightening."

Confronted itself with the fallout from the US decision to confront inflation, the Bank of Canada decided to try to hang on to the

US dollar exchange value for our currency. This meant, in practice, at least matching US rate increases. And given the frequency with which US rates were changing, the Bank also decided, in March 1980, to move from a fixed to a floating bank rate. That is to say, the minimum rate at which it could legally lend to client institutions was then set to be a quarter of a percentage point above whatever proved to be the average rate for the weekly tender of three-month Government of Canada treasury bills. In that way, the bank rate came to reflect rising money market pressures in a pretty automatic fashion. And in that sense it floated week by week, but in strict relationship to the yield on the instrument most widely held and most frequently traded in the Canadian money market, and therefore the one most likely to reflect broad market conditions.

The year 1981 was one to remember but not to enjoy, as Canadian interest rates climbed alongside US ones. The chartered banks' prime rate reached a peak of 22.75 per cent in August 1981, and Canada Savings Bonds that year had to be offered for sale at the unheard-of one-year rate of 19.5 per cent. Calls for a halt to the process became louder and more widespread. A popular accompanying slogan was for Canada to have a "made-in-Canada" monetary policy, and in effect, try to take whatever monetary medicine the United States would dish out by allowing our dollar to depreciate further. Thereby, it was hoped, we would avoid the pain of such high Canadian interest rates.

In the previous chapter, I explored at some length how in difficult economic circumstances interest rates and the exchange rate interact in volatile ways, with one market aggravating the other. So let me just note here that a policy of, in effect, trying to peg Canadian money market interest rates at a relatively low level by pumping out liquidity while letting the Canadian dollar "go" (or as it was also often and more gently put at the time, "find its own level") depends tremendously on the extent of underlying confidence. But one confidence deficiency from which Canada then suffered was that it too had a bad inflation problem. Here also, the rise in living costs was already into double digits (almost 13 per cent in 1981) and would have gone higher still if such a naive course had been attempted. So whether one checked it out against the interest/exchange rate market dynamics provoked by a falling currency in highly uncertain circumstances, or against the likely inflation fundamentals, the belief that domestic interest rates would stay down looked like a proposition that was highly wishful at best. A more convincing proposition was that we should have tried harder to keep inflation down in the first place, that the need now was to instill more confidence in domestic financial management, and that we had better buckle down to the task.

All this leads to a deeper and more purposeful interpretation of what the Bank was up to. Hanging on to the exchange rate as best we could was not the real objective but rather, with the crumbling of M1 targets, another way of guiding monetary policy in an anti-inflationary direction. In other words, shadowing the US dollar was a means to an end. That end was a better inflation performance, using the instrument and the rationale that was immediately available—the exchange rate—as a means for nudging Canada along that path.

A more thoroughgoing approach to a made-in-Canada monetary policy did come later in the decade. But this again was evidently not to everyone's taste, even for some who were otherwise rather nationalistically minded. The reason seemed to be that the policy was more directly, and more avowedly, anti-inflationary. Presumably a thoroughly made-in-Canada, thoroughly inflationary, policy was one preferred nationalist outcome. This is not difficult to arrange if you have a pliable central bank, and it is something many nations have tried. But where would that lead?

Nineteen eighty-two was another exceptionally hard year for the economy. It was also an exceptionally difficult time for figuring out what should be done with monetary policy, and not just because the M1 target was not working. The economy shrank, inflation was still around double digits, and so were interest rates. After a few years of relative stability, the Canadian dollar came under more downward pressure against its US counterpart, moving from 84 US cents to close to 80 US cents. Unemployment rose to over 12 per cent.

It was also a year of protests, bracketed by a mass rally over high interest rates organized in late 1981 by the Canadian Labour Congress, and the publication in early 1983 by the Canadian Conference of Catholic Bishops of *Ethical Reflections on the Economic Crisis*. In phrasing reminiscent of the unfortunate February 1973 budget, those musings called, among other things, for "unemployment rather than inflation" to be recognized as the number one problem to be tackled.

The bishops clearly favoured a highly interventionist, almost syndicalist, approach to national economic management. They sought, among other things, "assurances that labour unions will have an effective role in developing economic policies..." including no doubt a role in developing monetary policy as well. One can perhaps wonder what the bishops thought about representative democracy, better expressed in this instance through the endeavours of the New Democratic Party rather than through trade union actions. But then, their own governance set-up was itself hardly a representative democracy. In any case, when it came to intervention, both the bishops and the unions were hostile to the 6 and 5 wage control initiative that the federal government had introduced in June 1982 for its own employees, limiting wage increases to 6 per cent in the first year and 5 per cent in the second. Their fundamental objection was its focus on wages "rather than controls on profits and prices," as the bishops put it. Public sector unions of course felt doubly sinned against by the perceived unfairness of controls on their wages but not on those of others.

Since this 6 and 5 program was so contentious, it is worth spending a moment considering why general controls were not held to be a serious option. To introduce widespread controls was, as the Anti-Inflation Program's experience had demonstrated, not only an extremely complex and ultimately unworkable task from a technical viewpoint, but also something that was very likely to be seriously challenged on constitutional grounds. By focusing on controlling wage movements in its own sector, and cultivating also the clear willingness of other levels of government to go the same route, the federal government could avoid the constitutional issues but still cover a large slice of the wage determination process.

The willingness of other levels of government to join is easy to explain. For years, there had been an evident problem in figuring out what the economic basis of public sector wage bargaining should be, even at the best of times. Many dated the problem back to the precedent of a dramatically inflationary settlement with the St. Lawrence Seaway workers in 1966. Both sides to the bargains were virtual monopolies, but the unions were clearly much more adept at the game than their public sector employers. The champions were the inside postal workers under some flamboyant leaders. They could quite easily lever the hardship caused at that time, when regular mail was a much more critical element of communication than it is now, by shutting the postal system down, which they did or threatened to do on several occasions in the 1960s and 1970s.

Several more years had to pass before governments would be pressed into more discipline in their bargaining by unsustainable levels of indebtedness, the unwillingness of the general public to accept still higher taxes, and/or a more determined monetary stand that made it clearer that inflationary wage settlements would be expensive settlements. In the limbo of that earlier time, blunt controls on public sector wage outcomes looked like an attractive way of setting limits. And from a social equity angle, the poor economic conditions meant that profits were bound to shrink anyway. This squeeze would not only demonstrate that, contrary to the bishops' assertions, capital was not taking "priority over labour in present strategies for economic recovery," but would also act as a force constraining wage settlements in the private sector. Indeed, all things considered, the 6 and 5 program worked rather well, especially considering the miserable economic circumstances overall.

In addition to union and episcopal protests, a broadside was issued in October 1982 on behalf of some 50 Canadian economists. This "Statement by Canadian Economists" evidently was designed to follow the famous example set in 1960 by the "Economists' Letter" (more widely known as "The Economists Versus the Bank of Canada"), which was issued at the height of the Coyne Affair. The 1982 communication was similarly scathing regarding the Bank, this time over what it termed the Bank's "high interest rate or mon-etarist policies." These economists considered that the thing to do was to lower interest rates "by 2 to 3 percentage points" and not worry overmuch about where the Canadian dollar went. They also were keen on a broader incomes and prices policy—"preferably through negotiations with business and labour," another triumph of hope over experience that could only occur in the cloisters of academia. Above all, they said, "we wish to express unambiguous-ly our condemnation of present government monetary policy."

Quite how the signatures were collected is not clear. Some uni-versities figured in substantial numbers and some not at all. But the church of protest was not, it would seem in retrospect, that narrow. Among the signers were a future Liberal Cabinet minister (but not then in Parliament), a future pillar of the C.D. Howe Insti-tute (a place not known for attacks on sound money), and a future deputy governor of the Bank of Canada (but not in its employ at the time).

Still, the Bank continued to see matters differently. As before, it had no philosophical objection to the government trying controls to improve matters. But for the kinds of reasons set out earlier, it was far from convinced that more comprehensive price and wage controls of the kind these economists were advocating were actual-ly workable. As noted earlier in this section, it also saw problems in the notion that monetary policy could manoeuvre short-term interest rates to the degree advocated without risking a confidence crisis on the exchanges, further inflation, and, therefore, upward market pressure on interest rates—the reverse of what these econo-mists, or anyone else, wanted.

But broader still, the issue was again being posed, as in the mid-1970s, as to the extent that controls could be used to validate a drastic loosening of monetary policy. In the Bank's view, it was wiser, as it had been a few years earlier, to see controls as a com-plement to a counter-inflationary monetary policy rather than as a licence for monetary policy reversal. In this way, the policy contri-bution of the controls would be the auxiliary, but still helpful, one of speeding a return to less inflationary expectations, lower interest rates, and other good things. The Bank's skepticism here was reinforced by the fact that these economists were insisting on a drastic loosening of monetary policy even if controls were not tried.

In fact, the emergence of somewhat better economic conditions happened quite quickly. Output rebounded sharply in 1983; unemployment stopped going up; money wages rose much less rapidly, in the private as well as the public sector; price inflation slowed a lot; and interest rates came down more sharply than the cuts that had been called for in the letter. The Canadian dollar also became less volatile, although it continued to move down on balance (from around 80 cents to some 73 cents by 1985) as the Bank, in these more promising circumstances, increasingly tested the scope for encouraging a decline in Canadian short-term interest rates relative to those in the United States. However, this period was also marked by an accelerated buildup of fiscal deficit and debt problems—problems that would become enormously challenging by the end of the decade.

Recognizing the time bomb nature of this deficit/debt problem was delayed by changes in the way the short-term impact of fiscal policy came to be assessed. It had by then become customary in academic and policy circles to analyze fiscal policy and fiscal developments not so much in actual numbers as in numbers that were adjusted in various ways to offset what were seen as transitory and distorting factors. One adjustment was to eliminate any impact on fiscal magnitudes of where the economy was judged to be in the economic cycle. For example, if the view was that the economy was operating with too much slack, it then followed that the tax base was also running below par, that revenues would be higher on a cyclically adjusted basis, and that the deficit would be lower. Another adjustment was to recalculate government interest payments down so as to reflect the fact that in times of high inflation, an important component of the resulting higher interest rates represented the repayment of capital. This is because those higher interest rates paid also reflected the fact that the purchasing, or "real," value of dollar debt was declining at the rate of inflation. The result of such calculations was, again, a lower deficit than from conventional financial accounting.

On this basis, critics of monetary policy were also prone to argue—as, for example, had Drs. Donner and Peters and also economics professors Clarence Barber and John McCallum at greater length in their 1980 book-length critique of policy, *Unemployment and Inflation: The Canadian Experience*—that there was ample scope, among other things, for a more expansionary fiscal policy. But this approach was more limited than the authors seemed to realize. A crucial problem, and one that showed its full dimensions later in the 1980s, was that it was the *actual* deficits and debts that had to be financed, not the theoretical ones. The Bank knew this very well because it was by statute the government's fiscal agent and therefore had to arrange the successive debt issues. Hopefully, it would not have to print a lot of money to make those issues succeed, though probably the critics conjured with the possibility that this was precisely what the Bank would be forced into doing.

Compared to the furor of 1982, the next several years were relatively quiet for Canadian monetary policy. The overall economic and financial situation stayed relatively benign. This was doubly welcome at the Bank because it was heavily preoccupied by the dramatic failures in 1985 of the two Western Canadian banks and its response to the subsequent commission of inquiry.

The main crises that monetary policy had to cope with in the period through to the end of 1987 were more one-shot asset market disturbances than drawn-out affairs. The first was the plunge in the Canadian dollar in late 1985 and early 1986, and the second was the US stock market mini-crash that spilled over into Canada in the fall of 1987. While both these disturbances had potential implications for the economy in general, their actual effects were short-lived. A more basic issue to address is how thinking developed on the direction to be taken by monetary policy in the years ahead.

Where Next?

By the mid-1980s, inflation in Canada had been hauled back from double digits to what seemed a floor of 4 per cent or so. At the same time, output was expanding rapidly, and unemployment had fallen to around 9 per cent by the end of 1986. So far, so good. Where next? What could monetary policy do now to contribute to ensuring further improvement in Canadian economic performance?

Soon after my appointment as governor in early 1987, I felt that it was an appropriate time to start using my public addresses to make the case for a monetary policy framework that would provide a consistent long-term basis for such improvement. Certainly, embarking on a program for long-term monetary stability at a time when circumstances were reasonably calm should be a better way of going about matters than the more common approach—raising the rhetorical tone in response to adverse developments.

This thinking did not, of course, come out of thin air. For one thing, the experience of the previous 20 years had disabused many people (but certainly not all) of the notion that ever more output and employment could be squeezed out of the economy by allowing a bit more inflation. And while people might debate how much inflation, if any, was really necessary, surely the problem was not that there had been *insufficient* inflation, although some persisting commentary in Canada seemed to suggest so. The thinking in most of the economics profession had also come a long way in its understanding as to how expectations were formed and how, in particular, short-term trade-offs and policies aimed at the short term were likely to disappoint beyond that horizon. It was increasingly accepted that policies that were consistent over time were indeed better policies. In particular, you could not expect to get a real economic advantage by surprising all the people with inflation all the time. More than a few would catch on and take protective action according to the way they saw the policy wind blowing. And as they caught on, even the short-term trade-off between inflation and unemployment would get worse.

So what I was putting forward in 1987 and early 1988 in a series of speeches and lectures was both the outline of a program for monetary policy and a subject for general and professional debate. My first formal public speech, in Toronto in April 1987, made reference to the primary goals for monetary policy, observing that "the objective to which monetary policy should give central attention is maintaining confidence in the value of the money we use in Canada—in other words, the goal of price stability." Succeeding speeches that year, in Calgary and Halifax, expressed the same thought, and the Hanson lecture in January 1988 dealt with the matter at some length. This was noticed. I was invited to give an address at the Canadian Economics Association annual meetings in June 1988, where I again visited the topic, and the reaction to date.

In highlighting earlier in this chapter the 1982 economists' statement, I emphasized the persistence and vehemence of the inflation-support school within the Canadian economics profession. Did I overdo it? While some critics still apparently want more inflation rather than less and will, unfortunately, always consider me to have been a great disappointment, today most seem much more quiet on this issue, including those who signed the 1982 statement.

More positively, the global shift in the intellectual climate regarding inflation and the need to confront it through an independent central bank did make its mark in Canada as well. The noted Canadian economist Richard Lipsey was quick to recognize the importance of the issues that the Bank was beginning to address and the leadership it was giving. Economists—notably Peter Howitt, David Laidler, and Michael Parkin at the University of Western Ontario, as well as Douglas Purvis at Queen's until his untimely death in 1993—were thoughtful and timely participants in the policy debate that ensued and went on for some years. David Laidler in particular provided a stream of lively and constructive analyses of the issues through his association with Canada's major private economic and social policy think-tank, the C.D. Howe Institute.

The Bank of Canada has always kept in close touch with the Canadian economics profession. It has also had a relatively strong research function compared to other governmental bodies, which is one way of attracting good minds into the institution. Since the Bank, unlike a government department or a minister, can hardly claim political necessity as the basis for its actions, it always stands in need of support from serious economic thinking. So a strong interest in economic research is also a way of ensuring that the central bank can harness economic science to improve its policies, to

promote good policies, and to defend them against bad ideas—
some of which might conceivably be put forward by groups of
economists themselves.

Returning to my narrative of unfolding monetary events, Professor Laidler and William Robson of the C.D. Howe Institute, in
their valuable study of monetary policy over the period 1988–93,
The Great Canadian Disinflation, give a fair amount of attention to
what they see as "the uncertainty in [the Bank's] public pronouncements" and the "tentativeness with which the Bank set
about resetting monetary policy during the balance of 1988."

Admittedly, the monetary program put forward in 1987 and
early 1988 was not as concrete as one might ideally have liked to
see. As already noted, at no time did I spell out what price stability
meant in terms of actual price behaviour, although the clear impression was left, intentionally, that if it meant any inflation at all, this
was distinctly less than 4 per cent. Contrary to many assertions,
"zero inflation" was never put forward as the policy target, although
I also saw to it that it was not excluded out of hand from the menu.
Furthermore, distinctions that might have been made between stability in the price level and zero inflation were not addressed at all.
In general, what the Bank was doing was underlining two things.
First, those who favoured inflation as a systematic policy needed to
demonstrate why it would be good for monetary policy to provide
it, and by how much. Second, the Bank was not thinking of going
in the direction of inflation as a systematic policy.

Why did the Bank not spell out further the arithmetic of price
stability? In part, it was merely exercising caution—don't cross
bridges before you have to. Beyond the whole range of technical
questions—for example, which price index to use in measuring
inflation, or over which time period to specify the path and the
goal—it seemed sufficient at the time to make clear that we really
did give price stability, or, more broadly, confidence in the future
value of Canadian money, abundant priority. That itself, as the vigorous and often vituperative reaction demonstrated, would likely
be plenty for commentators to chew on, even if it was not so very
different from what had been said before. Perhaps the difference
was that I said it more often or more systematically.

Beyond this, what I had said in the Hanson lecture might be just about as far as the Bank could expect to go without engaging government in major discussions—discussions that it was not at all clear the government in general would be keen to conduct in the long-term spirit that the Bank needed to if it was to spell out monetary policy properly. Even at this broad level of exposition, we understood that alarm bells had been ringing in the Department of Finance. Michael Wilson was fundamentally supportive, but some of his top staff appeared to see matters differently. What policy strategy they might have preferred was never made clear—possibly no strategy at all except, perhaps, to grease the wheels of the fiscal deficit and adjustment to the Free Trade Agreement. All things considered, better to let our views percolate through repetition and generate considered reaction and, hopefully, support that way.

It was never very clear to me where the government in general stood in regard to Canadian monetary policy. My impression (bearing in mind that I was never present at Cabinet discussions) was that Michael Wilson's views were pretty authoritative, given the lack of background of other ministers in these matters. Still, while one is generally entitled to presume in the central banking business that government silence is indeed support, there must have been rumblings.

In 1993, toward the end of my term, I learned from Raymond Chrétien, Canadian diplomat and by then himself exiled temporarily to Brussels, that there had been discussion earlier within government circles of inviting me (if "inviting" is the right word) to become Canada's ambassador to Moscow. While the fact that I speak Russian may have provided some cover, I have to believe that the thinking was more to engineer an exile in the style of Raymond's—but in my case, even further away from Ottawa. In any event, the idea was never broached with me. This was just as well because I would have turned it down flat.

But to return to the question of the Bank's tentativeness in resetting monetary policy, it should be borne in mind that October 1987 had brought a stock market correction of initially violent proportions, both in the United States and consequently in Canada. The economic after-effects were initially uncertain. The Bank's view was that these would turn out to be less than many anticipated, and before the end of the year it was again tightening liquidity in the face of robust aggregate demand. The standard Ottawa outlook outside the Bank was not for strong economic demand, either then or through 1988. But strong demand there was, and the Bank persisted in tightening. By the end of 1988, the yield curve was, unusually, inverted. That is, short-term interest rates, at close to 11 per cent, were then higher than long-term rates, suggesting that money was getting very tight. The Canadian dollar had also moved up, to 83 US cents. However, inflation was still showing unmistakable signs of accelerating, not slowing. It was also clear that the move up in inflation had been totally the result of plain and simple spending pressures on the economy's productive capacity, even if unemployment, at above 7 per cent, looked high. Unlike the experience of the 1970s, there was now no adverse shock to prices from supply shortages to complicate matters.

The following year was a repeat of 1988, only more so. In the face of a further strong surge in demand in Canada and a climb in inflation to over 5 per cent, the Bank kept a tight rein on liquidity, in effect holding short-term interest rates up at around the 12 per cent level that they had reached early in the year. It hoped to make it progressively clear, for the present and the future, that inflation was to go down, not up. The price stability framework that had been publicized, even though it was couched in general terms, appeared to be helpful in that regard.

Fiscal Complications

Canada's demand pressures in this period, with total dollar spending in the economy rising by about 8 per cent annually, did not originate solely in the private sector of the economy or from abroad. Notwithstanding concerns about deficits and debt, federal government fiscal policy underwent some easing in 1988, apparently in response to a forthcoming election. (Admittedly though, opposition parties were competing through promises to spend much more in the way of government funds if they got into power.) Into the bargain, the policy of Ontario—a province that accounts for some 40 per cent of total GDP—was one of strongly sustained budgetary expansion.

The lively issue of the relationship between monetary and budgetary policies in Canada is discussed further in Chapter 9. But what I can emphasize here is the situation of Ontario and the curious response that it generated. An astonishingly expansionary spending policy under its then Liberal government, piling on top of already surging private demand and a provincial economy that was popping its rivets, provoked not so much criticism of Ontario by other provinces as intensified interest in exploring whether there was any scope for a monetary policy that was regionally differentiated. Could there not be a monetary policy that was tight for Ontario but easier elsewhere? It seemed to me at the time that this was an instance of peer protection rather than peer pressure. In any case, and as already pointed out, the reality of a common currency and well-developed credit markets meant that any such interest rate differentiation was a non-starter. Another reality, irksome both in the West and in Quebec, was that the "weight" of each province in the overall stance of monetary policy had to be in direct proportion to its share of the total economy. Even if this meant a 40 per cent charge for Ontario alone, no other basis made national economic sense.

Could the Bank have remonstrated more with various fiscal authorities against adding demand to an already inflationary situation? Perhaps, but it was doubtful that they would have taken much notice, given the way these things were decided. What I did try to make clear were the overall implications for inflation and interest rates, and in particular that monetary policy would not budge for purely fiscal developments. That is to say, if demand was strong overall, a given monetary policy would appear tighter than otherwise, whatever the sources of that demand. The converse also applied if overall demand was weak. In this analysis of monetary policy's broad responsibilities, I was trying to emphasize that fiscal demands had no special or privileged place. They were just a source of spending like any other.

In part, this was done through parable, using in particular the unfortunate British example of the mid-to-late 1980s. The Chancellor of the Exchequer, Nigel Lawson, who in the British set-up of the time controlled the Bank of England's policy actions as well as the budget, had commanded an easing of monetary policy specifically to offset fiscal tightening. His terrible problem was that other forms of demand, especially consumer spending, happened to go through the roof as a result of financial sector liberalization. The result was another British monetary misfortune. So the moral is that you should keep your monetary eye on demand in total, not on particular components, even if they are officially sponsored.

Staying on Message

In 1989 and 1990 the truly challenging issues for monetary policy began to be joined. Inflation, and inflation expectations, remained stubborn, but it also became increasingly clear that the Bank meant business. It stayed on message, and for 1989 kept liquidity tight enough so that short-term interest rates remained at about 12 per cent even as US rates began to ease back. The economy expanded during that year, but unemployment stopped declining.

By early 1990, it had become apparent that the economy really was slowing, and in January we tried to embark on a process of easing bank liquidity and encouraging some decline in short-term interest rates. The timing was tricky because it was just before the federal budget and we needed to be out of the market's way as the budget was being presented and digested. Unfortunately, this initial easing manoeuvre was not successful.

The Bank's moves were seen by financial markets as very abrupt, generating much uncertainty as to where it was going. The result was a sharp plunge in the currency—a drop of about three cents to 83 US cents between mid-January and mid-February. We wanted monetary conditions overall to ease, but not that fast, and we certainly did not wish to give the impression that our strategy had been abandoned. Domestic inflation was still in the 5 per cent range notwithstanding the stronger dollar, and wage increases were still accelerating. The currency's plunge therefore provoked a vigorous reaction as the Bank again tightened liquidity, pushing up interest rates to stem the dive. In the annual report for 1989, completed at the end of February 1990, I noted that "taking into account the offsetting effects of the higher interest rates and lower Canadian dollar, there appears on balance to have been some easing in overall monetary conditions in Canada."

But while monetary conditions overall may have undergone some easing, the total experience was decidedly unsatisfactory. From then on the Bank would proceed less abruptly, letting air out of the currency more gradually and being less prone to upsetting expectations in the Canadian money and bond markets and thereby pushing up interest rates.

However, for the next few months matters were largely taken out of the Bank's hands by political events—a premonition that the Meech Lake deal that had to be ratified provincially by the summer of 1990 would fail to settle the place of Quebec in Canada, and notably the dramatic departure of Environment Minister Lucien Bouchard from the federal government in May in order to lead the separatist movement in Quebec. Financial markets did not take kindly to these developments, and interest rates, both long and short term, pushed up to a peak in that month, while the dollar tended to weaken. But for the balance of the year, the Bank was able to help interest rates move gradually down. The interest differential against the United States also began to narrow. But notwithstanding, the currency moved up to a high point of some 89 US cents in the fall, in response to the Gulf crisis and the spurt in energy prices.

As the year 1990 drew to a close, it seemed to me that the Bank was beginning to get across the important basic messages about monetary policy and monetary confidence, and that we would be staying the course, even as monetary conditions had begun to ease in the face of a distinctly slowing economy. Those messages had been repeated many times and in many ways over the past four years, but repetition is, after all, also reinforcement.

This is not to say that everything was staying the same. It was just about that time that intensive work was going on in Ottawa on a new monetary initiative: inflation targets. Introducing inflation targets did not change the Bank's message, but it meant a big alteration in how the message was packaged. As such, that process and its immediate sequel deserve a chapter to themselves.

Creating
Inflation Targets

The introduction of inflation targets—in then Bank of Canada terminology, "Targets for Reducing Inflation and Establishing Price
Stability in Canada"—was a far-reaching innovation. Besides continuing to play an important role here, targets have caught on in
many other countries since.

Process

Inflation targets were announced by Michael Wilson in his February 1991 budget, but in effect the announcement was a joint one.
The minister made the necessary initial statement in his budget
speech, and the Bank simultaneously issued a press release, together with background notes covering a range of more specific issues.
The day after the budget was tabled, I held a media conference on
the targets.

   The media were in a challenging mood. Perhaps this was due to
the awkward venue. Since we could schedule the conference only
after the budget speech, we found that we had to hold it at the
Bank instead of the usual place, the National Press Centre down the
street. Unfortunately, our classy (but ancient) main elevator chose
that day to break down, obliging our puffing visitors to walk up to
the fourth floor, some with equipment.

   More likely though, the charged atmosphere reflected the fact
that the media thought that there might be a real story—not so

much in what had been decided as in *how* it had been decided. There were all kinds of questions, but one line of enquiry stood out: what did "joint announcement" mean with regard to this particular initiative and, more broadly, with regard to the relationship between an "independent" Bank of Canada and the government? As one scribe phrased the point: "Who has the last word?" Or as journalist Michel Vastel more bluntly put it: "Who twisted whose arm?" Good questions.

I limited myself to noting, accurately, that the targets had been arrived at after discussions between Finance and the Bank and that they were, as a result, targets that had been agreed to by both parties. I also argued that the statutory relationship between the Bank and the government spelled out in the *Bank of Canada Act* (discussed in Chapter 2) had not been upset by the agreement on targets. While this was correct, it no doubt did not respond at all wholeheartedly to what these astute journalists were zeroing in on—nor was it intended to.

What I could have added but did not was that as indeed the act contemplates, there had been genuine and quite strenuous consultations—give and take—between the minister and myself, followed up by discussions between Bank and Finance staff. I was acutely conscious that the Bank was not obliged to agree to whatever Finance proposed, including whether to have and how to set inflation targets, simply because it was put on the table. At the same time, we did want to arrive at a constructive outcome for reasons of substance as well as process, as I am sure Michael Wilson did as well. While some of the Bank's priorities in the negotiation were evidently different from those of Finance, a constructive outcome is what I think we both achieved. I could also have speculated at the time, for example in response to Mr. Vastel's question, as to whether the very existence of these targets was likely to change in some way the dynamic of the Bank's relationship with the government. Of course, I chose not to opine then, but that interesting and in fact very pertinent question can be tackled now—at least, it will be three chapters on. Let me just note here that as things have developed, the journalists were on to something.

Substance

Precedents were scarce. By now there is considerable literature on inflation targets, but it only emerged after central banks started using them. (Some 30 countries now sport explicit inflation targets.) So we had some memorable discussions at the Bank, and did some path-breaking work on how exactly to go about framing them. In this area as in so many others, much of the basic work was undertaken by Deputy Governor Charles Freedman, in this instance (as often before and since) ably backstopped by David Longworth, then a departmental advisor. In 1990, when Canada started thinking about targets seriously, the only example available was New Zealand, where they had been introduced earlier that same year. The Bank did not send anyone to New Zealand to check matters out, but at one point in our process Gordon Thiessen did go over some key points by telephone with the New Zealand Reserve Bank's senior deputy governor—taking care, as central bankers must, to be as vague as possible about why we wanted to know what we wanted to know.

I had made what might have been seen as a slighting reference to inflation targets in a speech that I gave in December 1989 at a meeting of the British–North American Committee:

> But what does "living with inflation" mean? Does it mean a chosen target for inflation? In my experience, if a target is suggested it is almost invariably whatever the rate of inflation happens to be at the time. Some target!

However, there I was not so much casting doubt on the general case for inflation targeting as cautioning against using a target to prop inflation up rather than to trace a path for bringing it down. I do not recall whether I had the views of the Economic Council of Canada in mind at that point, but I might have—as I now want to illustrate.

In Canada, the only extended public reference to inflation targeting before the official announcement had been made by the Economic Council in its *1990 Annual Review*, published in early

October. There, the council reviewed Canada's overall inflation reduction experience and, as was typical of the council's consensual approach to economic policy matters, came down from the mountain with a recommended mixture of approaches, starting off with a discussion of the possibilities for a "social partnership." This phrase means some type of general agreement—in particular between labour and business—as to how the national economic pie will be divided. It was thought to be working well in some countries in Europe—particularly in Sweden. But having delicately concluded that social partnership methods were unlikely to be fruitful here because "Canadian institutions, both economic and political, are characterized by fragmentation rather than centralization of power," it then moved on to "coordinated and credible inflation targets." The following excerpt provides the essence of the council's view:

These observations lead to two main conclusions with respect to anti-inflation policies:

1. The Bank of Canada's objectives must be both clearly defined and perceived as feasible in the medium term, if there is to be an adjustment in inflation expectations; and
2. To fight inflation more effectively, all levels of government and all public authorities must assume greater responsibility for controlling inflation.

The Council believes that monetary policy would be more effective if the bank's objectives were stated in terms that are easier to understand and to relate to. Currently, the bank's objective is defined as "achieving and maintaining stable prices." No time frame is given for the accomplishment of that goal. Furthermore, the term "stable prices" suggests a zero-inflation target—an objective whose feasibility is questionable in view of the fact that Canada has not achieved zero inflation for any significant length of time during the postwar era.

The council, as it almost always did, also called for more coordinated fiscal policies and more coordination between "federal fiscal and monetary policies." Fiscal–monetary coordination issues deserve extended critical examination, something I will undertake in the next chapter. Let me simply note here that it seemed ironic at the time that the council would once again call for more coordinated fiscal policies between the federal government and the provinces when no such thing had ever been seriously achieved in Canada (before or since), but at the same time was prepared to use this argument of modest achievement to dismiss any possible goal of price stability. This was particularly incongruous because up to then, monetary policy had never been clearly aimed at such a goal. So it was not clear that history was at all relevant.

A brief digression, foreshadowed by these comments. By and large, the Economic Council of Canada had proved to be a disappointment. From its start back in the early 1960s, it had been burdened with an unrealistic mandate that was never re-examined. The council was required by law to slog through the process of publishing each and every 12 months a review of "the medium and long-term prospects and problems of the economy" and also had decided to come up each time with medium-term performance goals. This had proved to be a real drag both for the council and for those of us (including me when I was chief of the Bank's Research Department) who had the disheartening task of wading through the successive long and mushy volumes. The council should have shown some spirit and bucked against its mandate.

While there would be, as one would expect from so much material, some genuine insights from time to time, the overall added value from the exercise was less than grand. It tended to boil down to multiple pronouncements along the lines that Canada's economy would be in so much better shape if structural changes were made and if various parties learned to cooperate or coordinate more ("coordination" was the council's favourite word). This way, the council could always come up with optimistic targets (that others had to realize) whose speculatively conditional nature was generally lost on the media and parliamentarians. Overall, the council's pronouncements were an unflattering example of what you get when everything has to go through a committee (which the council was) that is charged with dispensing advice that is admittedly free, but where the advice-giver bears no responsibility for implementation.

It performed better when it took up a specific topic. One example was competition policy, where its report had made a real contribution to thinking and to policy. Surely the council would have done better overall if it had been invited, or had simply decided, to drop its dubious goal-setting role and focus more on economic efficiency questions—like the President's Council of Economic Advisors in Washington. Economic efficiency was certainly not an area that Ottawa was covering with any distinction through government departments. The Economic Council also differed from its Washington second cousin in its heavy reliance on permanent employees rather than on a continually changing but dynamic cast of economists from academia. The council was presumably set up to be something of an outside commentator. A more outside cast would have been less dependent on government in general and less awkwardly conscious of the "Ottawa" view.

In late October 1990, in a media conference after a speech in Moncton, I was somewhat taken aback to be asked whether "you or your officials from the Bank of Canada discussed with Mr. Wilson or with officials from his department the possibility of setting a public target for inflation that is just above zero." My response, all the time wondering where they got this information, was the following:

> I can't go into discussions with the Department of Finance at all, at any point, on anything. What I can tell you is that there has been some work done on such a concept at the Bank. We do work on all kinds of concepts of a monetary policy nature. That is certainly not the only thing we work on. But we are always looking at possibilities, we are always trying to improve.

In fact, discussions with Michael Wilson and his officials had already started, and the Bank's research staff had been doing very serious work on how to present and manage inflation targets.

Details of the to-and-fro of those discussions must, respectfully, remain closed, but it seems appropriate now to register that the initiative for introducing targets came not from the Bank but from the Department of Finance. Above and beyond the fact that I know that Michael Wilson thought that the Bank would be receptive to the general idea, I can only conjecture about the motivation.

Perhaps the considerations put forward by the Economic Council had been an element. But surely another, more pressing, one was that the Goods and Services Tax (GST) was going to be unleashed at the beginning of 1991. That meant a substantial one-shot boost to consumer price inflation, and potentially much more if second-round (i.e., compensating, for example through cost-of-living clauses) wage and price increases developed as a result. Union leaders were already calling for 7 per cent increases in wages merely to cover the 7 per cent GST, although the direct tax impact on consumer prices overall was "only" about 1.5 per cent, because many items, such as household food for example, would not be taxed and there would also be favourable price effects from the simultaneous removal of the manufacturers' sales tax and the telecommunication services tax. At the same time, the Bank of Canada had already gone to some pains to make clear that it would not be financing any second-round inflation effects. The Bank's stiff stand had implications for interest rates and the budget deficit if such effects did occur. Inflation targets might conceivably help to head those interest-rate implications off.

Shortly after, another element was added to the brew. When the budget was tabled in February 1991, the government announced, somewhat in the image of the earlier 6 and 5 program, that it would be severely limiting federal government pay increases. This limit proved to be to zero and 3 per cent increases for the next two years. As in the case of 6 and 5, this wage decision again turned out to be contagious. Provincial governments, except for the new NDP government under Premier Bob Rae in Ontario, quickly followed suit. And with a delay, but with mounting fiscal problems, Ontario fell fractiously into line as well—with "Rae Days," or obligatory leave without pay, and so forth. Eventually, the federal limits were extended out in time; the zero and 3 became zero, 3, zero, and zero. And those zeroes were even extended for two years more by the Liberal government that arrived in 1993, making for a full six-year program of severe public service pay restraint.

As I saw it, these controls, unlike the situation for 6 and 5, had as much to do with government interest in holding down its spending as they did with furthering inflation reduction. The wage numbers were certainly far more rigorous than might have been implied by the inflation reduction targets themselves, and meant important cuts in real public sector wages—depending of course on how much inflation actually occurred. The Bank did not have any hand in governmental wage controls. It only learned of them right before the budget speech.

Looking at the Bank's situation more broadly, should it have pressed earlier for inflation targets rather than being on the receiving end of an initiative from the Department of Finance? Indeed, could the Bank not have announced targets by itself?

In my view, a unilateral move on the Bank's part would have been a bridge too far—in a broad political sense. Without entering into the details, it can be reasonably argued that inflation targets, in the way that they have to be implemented, are not so very different from, for example, monetary aggregate targets (although when monetary targets were introduced in the 1970s, while discussed with the government and situated very much in the context of the broad objectives of the Anti-Inflation Program, they had been announced directly and solely by the Bank of Canada). But it seemed to me that inflation targets were very different from targets phrased in terms of "money" in the impression they left as to the extent of the Bank's monetary scope and powers. Inflation targets did seem much broader in economic reach, though Bank of Canada targets for total dollar spending in the economy—something that economists also argue for from time to time—would have been perceived as broader still. All the same, once inflation targets had been proposed by the minister, I was happy to discuss the possibilities and see whether we could make better progress by introducing them. In any event, it was clear in the discussions with Finance that the Bank would be taking full responsibility for hitting the targets. In other words, monetary policy would be applied directly and unequivocally to them.

But to come back to the journalists' line of questioning, we did not favour just any targets. After all, the whole tenor of monetary policy, and in that sense the future of Canada's money, would come to depend on them. As regards the initial goals, an important feature was that while the targets were being introduced in early 1991, we made sure that the first formal objective, an inflation rate of 3 per cent, was to be met only by the end of 1992, almost two years later. This reflected the fact that with regard to what monetary policy could be expected to do, the major effects on inflation would show themselves only with an appreciable lag. It was particularly important from the standpoint of policy credibility to hit that first milestone, and we wanted enough time to be able to do that.

The issue of targets still further out on the horizon proved a deal more contentious. What exactly were the targets leading to? In particular, when they ended, if they ended, where would this leave inflation policy? Accordingly, I attached great importance in the discussions to ensuring that the agreement would include some kind of commitment about price stability that went beyond words. Words alone were too easy to ignore. It seemed to me that if the Bank was going to place its bets on a set of broad price numbers, and in the process quite likely provoke a shift in its relationship with the government, those numbers had better be longer term in nature, and ones that were clearly moving in an anti-inflationary direction for that longer term. In this vein, while the medium-term objective was set to be an inflation rate of 2 per cent, to be reached by the end of 1995, the official announcement went on to observe that:

Thereafter the objective would be further reductions in inflation until price stability is achieved. A good deal of work has already been done in Canada on what stability in the broad level of prices means operationally. This work suggests a rate of increase in consumer prices that is clearly below 2 per cent. However, a more precise definition is not being specified now—in the event that further evidence and analysis relevant to this matter become available in the next few years. A target path after 1995 also remains to be fixed, but again pending new evidence, the aim would be to continue to make steady progress.

This important provision regarding longer-term strategy was as far as matters could reasonably be pressed at the time. But long-term strategy or, more accurately, even the need for it remained an issue. Developments in December 1993, set in train by a new government at what it saw as an opportune moment and discussed in Chapter 10, would drive this home.

Two final comments on the 1991 agreement.

In practice, deviations from the inflation numbers targeted (bearing in mind that there is a one-percentage point margin on either side) have been negligible. But that was hardly to be assumed at the start, and considerable thought was given to the possibility of adverse inflation shocks that would have abrupt effects on the price level, such as further major increases in indirect taxes or large increases in oil prices. These shocks would probably not be quickly reversible. And with any large ones, where both Finance and the Bank allowed that we would know a large enough one when we saw it, it was agreed that the announced objective would be to at least push overall inflation back on target by the time the next, lower, target number came up—then basically at 18-month intervals. This implied that inflation shock bygones would be considered bygones, at least, as in the case of the GST, as regards their first-round effects. It was also settled that the particular trajectory back to the target path would in any case need to be agreed with the Department of Finance.

Second, it is worth recalling that in the fall of 1991, when Finance put forward the post-Meech Lake, pre-Charlottetown proposals on the Bank's mandate and increased provincial involvement, the agreed inflation targets, together with the provisions regarding eventual price stability, were already up and running. Put another way, our Ottawa colleagues probably took comfort from the fact that the targets and the surrounding provisions for consultation with Finance at each new step were already in place. So the proposed revisions that foresaw increased provincial involvement in the Bank of Canada's operations were likely to be less radical in terms of squeezing the scope for federal control than they might have appeared at first sight.

Initial Results: 1991 to 1993

Judging by what happened to prices, these initial targets for reducing inflation were a resounding success. In early 1991, when the GST was introduced, inflation was running year-over-year at close to 7 per cent. One year later, when the direct GST effect had dropped out, consumer prices were up less than 2 per cent. Excluding the volatile food and energy components, they were up about 3 per cent. With the federal government's direct controls, public sector wage increases of course slowed drastically, but so did those in the private sector. The economy began to grow again, although not fast enough initially to reduce unemployment, which peaked at about 11.5 per cent in late 1992. Inflation continued low throughout the three years to the end of 1993, with consumer prices averaging about 2 per cent. This was far better than before, especially considering that the shock from the GST missile had been well and truly dodged.

Monetary policy had already been turned onto a gradual easing path in 1990—after the political uncertainties surrounding the failure of Meech Lake were, in a narrow sense at least, behind the country—and this easing continued in the years 1991 through 1993. The only exception was the latter part of 1992, when a number of developments—some external (a spillover from exchange rate turmoil in

Europe) and some internal (notably, the defeat of the Charlottetown referendum proposal)—put substantial downward pressure on the exchange rate and induced a rise in short-term rates. This backup was encouraged at times by the Bank's own liquidity tightening operations. We encouraged it because the Bank wanted to ensure that the monetary confidence that was returning, and the lower interest rates that would be generated, were not set back by impatient action. We would, in effect, allow interest rates to decline as market confidence improved, but not try to force the pace through bursts of central bank liquidity creation.

This point is worth expanding. The memory of the tactical monetary policy setback of early 1990 was still there and still very relevant, because we were trying to encourage market interest rates to come down at the same time as the exchange rate was declining. This is a double dose of monetary easing that is far easier to prescribe than to achieve, since holders of Canadian dollars are in effect being "asked" to keep holding those dollars at declining interest rates even as the external, or exchange, value of their holdings is falling as well. Obviously, this double dose—loss in external value and in yield—needs to be managed rather cautiously. Above all, it would not be useful to trumpet the fact that the exchange value of the Canadian dollar would be going down.

Frequent debates were held within the Bank over the pace of easing that could be sustained, and the subject naturally came up with Finance as well, where Don Mazankowski had taken over as minister in 1991. He knew that I had a bias for steadiness and sustainability over speed. In any event, the overall result was a major drop in both interest rates and the exchange rate, and by any count, a substantial easing in monetary conditions.

When the inflation reduction targets were introduced back in February 1991, short-term rates were over 11 per cent and the Canadian dollar was about US 87 cents. By early 1994, at the end of my term and after some interesting discussions with Paul Martin, the new government's minister of finance, short-term interest rates were down to under 4 per cent, interest differentials over the United States had narrowed hugely, and the Canadian dollar had fallen to about US 76 cents. Clearly, the whole monetary tone had changed, and this was already showing up in a much more rapid advance in spending and output in the economy.

But to step back in time a little, the situation of mid-1993, with an election on the horizon, provoked yet another "Statement by Economists," that managed to amass some 60 signatures. This statement had a decidedly labour flavour to it, as did the signatories, several of whom were trade union officials. The following passage focuses on monetary policy:

> Many of our current problems are the result of a destructive economic policy agenda. The policy of "zero inflation" officially adopted by the Bank of Canada and federal government led to unnecessarily high short term interest rates and an overvalued Canadian dollar from 1988. This massively compounded the difficult problems faced by Canadian industry following the implementation of the Canada–US Free Trade Agreement, leading to the loss of almost 1 in 5 jobs in the manufacturing sector and many more jobs in related service industries.

As a modest contribution to truth in advertising, I will just note that over my term of office, the inflation record was not nearly as stellar as this statement pretends. The annual inflation rate averaged some 4 per cent annually, ranging between 1 and 7 per cent and peaking in 1991. This means that the Canadian consumer's dollar lost close to 30 per cent of its value over just those seven years—but apparently not enough of a loss for these economists. My successor, Gordon Thiessen, certainly had a far better record than this. That being said, I plan to take the opportunity later to explore some trade union views about what monetary policy should be, as opposed to the emphasis above on what it should *not* be.

Aside from these kinds of epistles, most people had by then come to agree that there was still one challenge looming for financial management and the economy—the fiscal deficit. This had been a nagging problem since the early 1980s, but had not been successfully addressed. Indeed, some went so far as to argue that the deficit was not a fiscal problem but rather a monetary one. For example, Professors Pierre Fortin and Lars Osberg, in their book *Unnecessary Debts*, cite Ottawa economist Michael McCracken (billing him, in the hyperbolical tone common throughout the book, as "Canada's foremost private sector economic forecaster") as demonstrating that "the increase in the debt-to-GDP ratio in the nineties is entirely due to the interest rate policy followed by the Bank of Canada." With such tendentiously melodramatic views as these around, which surely were shared by the 60 signatories to the statement, it is useful next, before bringing the monetary policy account up to date, to look more closely at what happened on the fiscal–monetary interaction front, how it happened, and what it implied.

CHAPTER 9

Fiscal and Monetary Policy: Together and Apart

In the interplay between fiscal (taxing, spending, and deficits—especially deficits) and monetary policies, many specific issues have arisen over the years. So this is difficult, slippery terrain that needs to be negotiated point by point. But let me start with one generalization. Always lurking behind the specifics—as, for example, the just-cited book of Professors Fortin and Osberg makes clear—have been broader questions of philosophies, or understanding, of economic management. Those questions, naturally enough, are thrown into greatest relief when the economy is not doing well. Then, narrow issues become pawns in a deeper business.

To make the general point more directly (and to a degree personally, but not, I am sure, uniquely in this world), if you have a central bank that is in some sense independent, it is almost inevitably going to be at some stage a disappointment to a fiscal authority. Some, looking at the ways bad monetary policy has been triggered around the world, would say that this is exactly why a central bank should be independent. In this spirit, Louis Rasminsky more than once insisted that the underlying rationale for independence was to provide some separation of the power to create money from the power to spend it.

Others would argue that this independence means a lack of coordination in economic policy that needs to be put right, but generally not, it seems, through changing fiscal policy. In this spirit, Carleton University (in Ottawa) economics professor Thomas Rymes, in his evidence before the Manley committee, presenting what he asserted was a "Keynesian" as opposed to a "new classical" view, was moved to ask rhetorically: "Why don't we go to the final stage of the evolution of central banks and simply say that they are an instrument of government policy and have them as a department of monetary affairs?" Of course, if the goal really is sublime fiscal–monetary coordination, and if one shares the touching faith displayed by Professor Rymes in the ability of wise, far-sighted, policy-makers to fine-tune their actions cooperatively in the interests of optimum economic performance, one might wish to consider making the money printing shop not even so much as a separate government department, but a subsection of one that already exists—say, the Department of Finance, in Canada's case.

Where should an account of the terrain begin? It isn't feasible or necessary to cover Canada's whole history of fiscal–monetary interactions. Such complex matters as those that arose when James Coyne was governor and Donald Fleming was minister of finance (in particular the massive and contentious effort in 1958, the "Conversion Loan episode," to lengthen considerably government debt maturities and ease the tasks of both debt and monetary management) are beyond the scope of this book. But even if the past three decades might not yield anything quite as high on the Richter scale as what happened then, they nonetheless provide plenty of compelling material. Certainly, the relative roles to be filled by fiscal and monetary policies have been debated hotly from the 1970s on.

With the Canadian economy suffering in the 1970s from both higher inflation and slower growth, fiscal policy was, like monetary policy, understandably subjected to steady pressure to do something (assuming that it really could) about growth. At that time, in most people's eyes this meant spending more money and increasing deficits rather than standing still or cutting taxes. Matters became still more contentious in the 1980s, as debt levels began to rise to perilous heights and the sensitivity of fiscal deficits to interest rate levels became a political as well as economic issue. Predictably, the situation gave rise to increasingly acid complaints, from within Ottawa as well as outside, about monetary policy—especially one that dared to be manifestly and unapologetically anti-inflationary. The more anti-inflationary the policy was seen to be, the more the complaints. This is an old story told many times around the world, and no one, least of all anyone at the Bank of Canada, should have been surprised to see it unfold.

Against this background, the underlying issue that played out in the fiscal–monetary tug of war of the late 1980s and early 1990s was the extent to which monetary policy would buckle or the degree to which budgetary policy would be able to improve its ways. Fiscal policy did improve, but only after pressure (described later in this chapter) came from down Mexico way. This was financial globalization at work. Some might regard that international influence as a terrible thing. Others would bear in mind that it finally got government to do what by any reasonable yardstick should have been done in the national interest much earlier.

Inflation Taxes

Government budgetary positions can get a short-run benefit from inflation in various ways. Economics textbooks emphasize the traditional "inflation tax" generated by the central government's sovereign ability to issue non-interest-bearing money in the form of currency—with the revenue showing up in the increased profits of the central bank, which are then transferred to the government. But probably more important in Canada is the fact that we have had a steeply progressive tax system that generally has not been indexed to counteract the distortions from inflation.

Income taxes rise as prices rise, but unless tax brackets are indexed, contributors' tax payments rise *faster* than inflation. This "bracket creep" effect was particularly apparent in Canada with the dramatic acceleration in inflation that occurred in the early 1970s. It was an important contributor to the sharp surge in revenues beyond budget expectations. Simon Reisman, then deputy minister of finance, used to tell how ministers would be keen to spend this extra money, allegedly so as to fulfill the budget deficit plan, but without much heed as to whether extra spending was really needed. This piece of the problem was plugged, in part at Simon Reisman's initiative, by the indexing of income tax brackets in 1974. But not without protest. One heard quite often the complaint that introducing tax bracket indexing meant that government now could not afford to finance its vital expenditures, as inflation pushed up their cost. Indexing—was it a "new classical" plot? Of course, this kind of argument did not make sense, because even with indexing, government revenues would still climb along with inflation, as would government outlays. The difference was that the tax take would no longer necessarily climb *faster* than inflation. But why should it?

A decade or so later, however, the indexing situation became a sight trickier to handle. The federal government's decision in 1986 to index tax brackets only for inflation above 3 per cent annually meant, looked at simply, that revenue would be below its maximum possible if inflation was held below 3 per cent.

This state of affairs led one academic, Professor David Johnson, to wonder publicly and at length in 1990 in *Canadian Public Policy* whether the Bank and Finance were talking to each other, since we seemed to have different views as to how much inflation was desirable. The Bank, as he saw it, was on the lower side—Professor Johnson said we were at "zero." Finance would presumably, because of these indexing arrangements, want at least 3 per cent. Naturally, this potential divergence in inflation objectives, whatever might have been the Bank's target, had not escaped our attention, but we had decided that it was a fiscal detail, even if an unfortunate one. The Bank was also of the view that a detail like this should not be seen as determining the fundamental course of monetary policy. Finance did not try to persuade us otherwise. Professor Johnson's thesis was different. He thought that:

> The Bank should explicitly acknowledge the policy domi-
> nance of the Minister of Finance and inform the public
> that Parliament has chosen to raise tax rates and reduce
> transfers through partial indexation and a low but positive
> rate of inflation. The Bank should operate monetary policy
> to accommodate a low but positive rate of inflation over
> the medium term.

It seemed to me that this suggested scenario was stretching matters a bit. If Parliament in its wisdom really intended to use inflation
systematically to increase revenue, it should be transparent about
what it was up to with this inflation tax and not leave the explaining to the Bank of Canada. Then everybody—including Parliament,
the Bank of Canada, and sundry savers and investors—could wrestle with the consequences. All the same, there is no denying that
this kind of revenue-raising consideration might have coloured
Finance views in favour of higher inflation numbers when practical
inflation targeting issues were joined with the Bank in late 1990.

Tax bracket indexation was made complete again in 2000.
What was particularly interesting about this move was its context.
Inflation had been relatively low for some time—generally below 2
per cent—but the resulting upward creep in the tax take due to the
absence of indexation until 3 per cent inflation had been noticed
and had become an increasingly common cause for complaint. The
moral I draw from this is that people do pay attention to the cumu-
latively negative effects that even relatively low rates of inflation
can have on real incomes.

Disappointments from Monetary Policy

All the same, tax bracket indexation was not the heart of the monetary–fiscal debate. What was central was the conviction that by
fighting inflation, monetary policy was keeping interest rates up,
keeping the economy down, and in effect driving the budget into

deficit. Obviously, according to this story, a more inflationary monetary policy would have made a lot of good difference.

This is another tale told at many times in many places. Its basic problem is that what might work in the short run—some monetary easing to grease the budget's wheels—does not work when you look further out. Then, with inflation moving higher, interest rates will be higher, not lower. And these days, with heightened premonitions about inflation, this "long run" turns up sooner than it used to—and certainly before we all have died off. Furthermore, and more broadly still, either monetary policy is committed to producing a less inflationary outcome in the economy's best interest, or it is not. If it is committed, it should pursue that goal steadily, not intermittently. I must say that I thought it was committed.

In my term of office, the ever-smouldering politics of the issue had a brief public flare-up in hearings before the House Committee on Finance—hearings on the national debt. These were held in mid-1993 and, perhaps not by coincidence, just before the federal election in October. One striking part of those hearings was the attempt of the Official Opposition, led on this occasion by Herb Gray and Diane Marleau, to argue that the Department of Finance, when it published sensitivity tables showing the effects of various changes in economic and financial assumptions on the fiscal deficit (in particular, the effects of "a sustained 100 basis points decline in all interest rates") was making a point that was substantive rather than merely arithmetical in regard to economic and financial outcomes.

Clearly their intent, in implying that interest rates could be placed anywhere that the authorities wanted, was to drive a wedge between Finance and the Bank. This was evident in the strong interest that the opposition showed in having me back to debate the issues with David Dodge, then deputy minister of finance (why didn't they ask for the minister himself?), even though there was hardly anything substantive to debate, at least as regards the particular points that the committee was interested in talking about. With the decline in inflation, interest rates had already come down a long way, but obviously there could never be enough of this, especially just before an election.

The prime piece of evidence that the opposition put to the Bank at the hearings was not the sensitivity analysis prepared by Finance, but a study just put out by Wharton Economic Forecasting Associates, the Canadian branch of a US-based economic consulting group, entitled "Has Monetary Policy Been Too Tight?" This study—in essence a counter-factual (i.e., "what if?") simulation from Wharton's large computer model of the Canadian economy—purported to show that an easier monetary (i.e., lower interest rate) policy for the late 1980s and early 1990s would have generated a far smaller deficit. I first read the piece in *Canadian Business Economics*. But I was also sent a copy of a customized British Columbia version with a covering note by the then relatively obscure (but now much more reportable) provincial minister of finance, Glen Clark.

This simulation was taken up avidly, not just in Parliament but also outside. This itself was not surprising, given what it purported to demonstrate—through the use of computers and econometrics, no less. What *was* surprising was that such flimsy material, computer-based or not, was seen as fit to be published. Its own results showed that by 1991, inflation was on a strongly rising path and running at 8 per cent, compared with the 5.5 per cent that was actually achieved. But never mind. According to Wharton's rules for the simulation, short-term interest rates were somehow going to be pushed down, in Canada anyway, from 7.5 per cent in 1991 to 5.5 per cent for 1992.

Anyone who knows anything about the kinds of calculations done by savers and investors would realize that these kinds of results pose huge questions of financial feasibility and consistency that the Wharton model did not even begin to address. But not addressing them is just not good enough for serious policy discussion, no matter how fancy the econometric model. Indeed, it is telling that one reason the model could not deal with those issues in any realistic manner was because it was incapable of explaining the behaviour of the Canadian dollar exchange rate. The behaviour of the currency was bound to have a huge impact, especially in the strained financial circumstances that the model was being asked to envisage, and that impact would not have been pleasant. As is well known, Canada's currency tended to the weak side for much of the 1990s, but the impact from Wharton-type policies would have made the weakness actually realized look like strength.

Besides the holes in terms of technical and financial market believability, a deeper credibility question was also apparent. The way the simulation was set up assumed that the whole budget process (e.g., decisions about tax rates and program spending) would have developed in exactly the same way whether monetary policy was "easier" or not. This assumption, implying that fiscal policy decisions over a number of years would be made in isolation from the economic and financial environment, was heroically unrealistic. In fact, historical experience tells us that government spending has tended to fill the financing space available at any given time. That was why Finance argued for the indexation of tax brackets in the 1970s, for example.

The implications of the worsening deficit-debt problem had already been clearly and starkly put forward by the Progressive Conservative government in 1985 in a Finance background paper entitled "Reducing the Deficit and Controlling the National Debt." As is well known, timely vigorous action was not taken. Apparently, the media told us, the reason why action was not taken was concern about the electoral damage that would come from curbing government transfers to individuals—particularly pensions. If they were reduced, then "Goodbye Charlie Brown" was the forceful message, piped shrilly by a little old lady to the startled but certainly attentive Prime Minister Mulroney while walking near Parliament one day, and reprised avidly by the media.

Nevertheless, any attempt to curb government spending would have to go the transfer route because transfers, rather than the purchase of goods and services, make up the bulk of the federal government's outlays. Fiscally speaking, the federal government is not so much an employer as a gigantic cheque-writing machine. The political issue that faced the government was which of its many transfer cheques were going to be sliced—those for provinces, at least in the first instance, or those directly to individuals. When substantial action was finally taken, in 1995, it was the provinces that took the first download. Naturally, individuals eventually had to take it, either from provincial governments directly or later when provincial governments passed on what they could to their municipalities, and so forth. As Don Mazankowski used to emphasize in a similar context, there is in the end only one taxpayer.

I did not press at the mid-1993 hearings the matter of possible alternative, stronger, fiscal policies to the ones actually pursued. I did not wish to leave the impression that by appealing for stronger fiscal policy, I might not be standing firm on monetary policy. Not surprisingly, but for quite different reasons, neither did any of the committee members seek to discuss what fiscal policy should do differently—too much of a hot chestnut for a pre-election campaign.

For me, the June 1993 hearings were the last of many appearances before the Finance Committee, where Mr. Gray and Ms. Marleau were fairly recent arrivals. They were the last in a longish line of Liberal finance critics, beginning with Roy MacLaren back in 1987. It seemed, in the way each participant went about criticizing and opposing, that this line registered the full range of the Liberal Party's ideological rainbow—starting, appropriately, with Mr. MacLaren at one end of the spectrum and finishing with Mr. Gray at the other. Indeed, Mr. Gray generally gave the impression of being to the left of some of the committee members from the NDP. One interesting feature, given the rapid turnover of Liberal finance critics, was that Paul Martin was never a member of our small but ever-changing encounter group. At that time, the story was that he did not wish to be minister of finance. But did Herb Gray or Diane Marleau?

Challenges from Fiscal Policy

Up to now, my focus has been on the effects of an anti-inflationary monetary policy on the fiscal position. How about movement going the other way? Here I shall not linger greatly on more personal manifestations such as "Don't bite the hand that feeds you," muttered emotionally by a very senior Finance bureaucrat after a difficult meeting. This particular monetary-to-fiscal-to-monetary sequence must be regarded as an aberration, but it did make me wonder what might be put in play—perhaps the prospects for my salary, which had to be approved by the government, and in ways that remained mysteriously uncertain to the Bank, including, apparently, to its directors. Those ways could no doubt get still more uncertain, although the 1991 federal government wage freeze did clarify matters considerably.

A more generally interesting and important issue was the view that there could be some trade-off whereby monetary policy would bring down interest rates in return for fiscal tightening. Indeed, I had the impression that there had been attempts to "sell" fiscal tightening to the federal Cabinet on this basis. The basic policy problem with this way of looking at matters was, as I discussed earlier, that it was not broad enough. It was basically correct insofar as, all else being equal, a dose of fiscal tightening should lead to monetary easing in terms of interest rates and, no doubt, the exchange rate. That is fairly standard economics. The real question, and difficulty, lay in moving from this understanding to the more controversial assumption that interest rates would actually go down from wherever they were. Quite possibly they might go up—even if by less than they might have before. That possibility had to be allowed for because the Bank's target was inflation, not interest rates. And inflation, rather than falling, might still be rising—as it clearly was in the late 1980s. This meant that I was always cautious about supplying fiscal advice, even privately, because there would inevitably be a hook—namely, what would monetary policy do to help? And that, as I have just indicated, was a very slippery path for the Bank.

One particular aspect of the fiscal–monetary complexity was the Bank's attitude to the new value-added tax, the GST. Our feelings were decidedly mixed. On the one hand, anyone who cared to look seriously would realize that there was a crying need to replace the manufacturers' excise tax. In terms of its design, it was a bad tax, and furthermore its base was eroding rapidly. On the other hand, the GST, at least as finally orchestrated, would give a real jolt to inflation. I was also mindful that the income tax cuts that had initially been proposed to parallel the GST, and which would have provided a helpful policy offset, had been dealt away in an earlier budget, no doubt for sound political (i.e., electoral) reasons. My answer was to recognize, and be prepared to accommodate, the inevitable one-shot boost to prices, but also to make clear well in advance that monetary policy would not be financing any second-round inflation spillovers. The aim was to ensure that the boost to inflation would indeed be only one shot. This approach, as pointed out earlier, was subsequently incorporated into the design of the inflation reduction targets generally.

One channel by which fiscal pressures could have affected monetary policy was the financial market impact arising from the sheer weight of debt issues. In Canada, the Bank's status as the government's fiscal agent makes very clear its responsibility to see to it that the government's debt is sold at the lowest cost available. But even if a central bank were not the fiscal agent, it probably would still feel a responsibility to try to provide the liquidity for favourable money and bond market conditions during periods when new issues are being launched onto the market. In my tenure at the Bank, new bond issues were launched very frequently and there was always a large weekly treasury bill tender to fuss about. I still recall the gulps, especially in the senior echelons of the Securities Department, when in 1980, the Government of Canada put forward its first billion-dollar issue. The Securities Department always worried a lot over how on earth the last dollars of a new issue—or in this case, the last couple of hundred million or so—could be sold at decent prices.

All the same, these debt issues proved easier for the market to absorb than some in the Bank had feared. I think that this was not so much because of any unusual effort on the Bank's part to see to it that the initial market conditions for any issue were favourable. Rather, it was because—and this is worth emphasizing—notwithstanding the vastly increased supply of government paper, Canada's monetary policy was still viewed by bond purchasers as one that made holding the nation's bonds worthwhile. In short, bond buyers still must have had reasonable confidence that they would not get hosed through an inflationary monetary policy. We certainly tried to make sure that the international bond rating agencies appreciated this when their representatives came calling.

It was difficult, however, to reconcile the arguments they gave when they explained how they arrived at Canada's top sovereign debt rating. On the one hand, the agencies set great store by the undeniable fact that the sovereign, the Government of Canada, in the end controlled the money printing press. That meant that in a technical sense, the debt in national currency could always be serviced if the government had a mind to. For default risk, the particular risk that was being rated, it did not really matter what the rate of inflation, the rate of interest, or the rate of currency exchange might be. The crucial point was that domestic currency could always be printed to make the necessary debt-service payments. This is why Government of Canada debt was invariably the highest-ranking debt in the country. By this printing press criterion, the only reason for pushing a sovereign country down from the top grade would be in the very unlikely event that the sovereign authority would decide that it was really cheaper to default—taking into account all the economic, financial, and political considerations—than it would be to print more debt-service money.

On the other hand, the rating agencies also explicitly gave Canada credit for the fact that its central bank appeared to have a strongly anti-inflationary monetary policy. But that of course meant, in contradiction to the printing press view, that the amount of money created was likely to be constrained and, in particular, not so greatly influenced by government debt-servicing needs. Our main debt-management interlocutor in Finance, Nicholas Le Pan (now Superintendent of Financial Institutions), could readily appreciate the problems that we saw in the split logic of rating agencies. But Nick and I understandably agreed that since either argument favoured a high rating for Canada, it was far wiser not to draw the incongruity to their attention. Let sleeping contradictions lie if they save you money.

Another fiscal–monetary issue that surfaced, in a more vexatious way, was differences of view over the appropriate term structure of the debt. There was a period in the early 1990s when

Finance officials were more than a little keen on compressing further a debt maturity schedule that had already become mighty short. By then, the average term to maturity (the average period by which all the different issues of debt had to be paid off or refinanced) for marketable debt had come down to only four years, from close to seven years a decade before. The complex rationale for going shorter still was twofold. In the first place, Finance argued that the Bank's monetary policy would, when its boat came in, bring about lower interest rates across the whole maturity spectrum. So if the debt was by then even more short-term, this would generate considerable budgetary savings. Furthermore, the debt maturity could then be lengthened at much less interest cost. Secondly, there were near-term savings as well, since the interest yield curve was generally upward sloping. That is, longer-term rates were normally higher than shorter-term ones, in this way compensating for the greater risk involved in holding longer-term assets. Given this reality, Finance saw considerable merit in exploiting the positive yield curve and borrowing overwhelmingly at short term.

The Bank saw serious problems with this way of looking at debt management. We felt it was too activist by far and posed a serious conflict between the Bank's monetary policy responsibilities and its assigned role as federal government debt agent. Taking Finance's positive yield-curve argument to its logical conclusion implied that all the debt would finish up with a maturity as short as one day. But if government debt turned over at anything close to this rate, the task of running monetary policy would become impossible. The Bank would be on a debt refinancing treadmill. So where would Finance stop? Those concerns needed to be addressed and thrashed out. This was the only instance in my direct dealings with Finance officials when I felt it might have been necessary to go and raise the matter we were discussing with their boss, the minister. When I told them this, they backed down and started discussing the issues.

It seems that in more recent years, the view in Finance as to appropriate maturity structures for the debt has, happily, been closer to that of the Bank's—that is, don't make interest rate or liquidity bets but try to get the debt maturities distributed rather evenly over time. This change of heart was provoked by seeing how short-term interest rates could spiral up at a time of financial crisis. The close call of the 1995 Quebec referendum on sovereignty, and the resulting prospect of shattered financial markets, wonderfully concentrated minds in Ottawa regarding prudent debt management. It's again an ill wind... The average term to maturity now is back close to seven years.

One final point on fiscal agent matters. Since the Bank had to absorb directly the regular expenses of debt management, the issuer, Finance, tended to pay little attention to the fact that some kinds of debt were much more expensive to manage than others. This was particularly relevant for Canada Savings Bonds, a retail-type instrument with all the attendant marketing costs involved in its distribution. In the end, the government's accounts would have to absorb those costs, because heavier debt management outlays by the Bank meant fewer profits to turn over to the Receiver General each year. But this meant that the Bank's expenditure budget in this important area was uncontrollable. Try explaining that to the media when they came calling regarding our expenses.

I will add here, in case these comments on encounters involving Finance have been misunderstood, that such exchanges were all part of a vigorous day's work. Differences of view were bound to arise, but throughout my career at the Bank, dealings with Finance counterparts from ministers down were invariably conducted on extremely professional and principled lines. It was a demanding business, but I always felt that each party had a lot of respect for the other's integrity and seriousness. And each party felt doubly obliged to do its homework, with the result that meetings were always to the point and of high intellectual and policy quality. Admittedly, Finance was not averse to occasionally trying on a "good cop, bad cop" routine, but the person customarily cast as Mr. Bad Cop had to make good arguments as well—perhaps even better ones.

Dealings with Provinces

When the provinces were in a "fed-bashing" mode, as was generally the case, fallout from this activity invariably landed on the Bank of Canada. My predecessor, Gerald Bouey, was often asked by the minister of finance to attend federal–provincial meetings. Some of these, particularly the one held with first ministers in miserable circumstances in December 1980—even the weather was awful—were truly electric. At that time, letting the dollar fall was being popularly touted as a remedy for the nation's economic problems, and Governor Bouey was being pressed on the matter. One of the premiers asked him what would happen to provincial debt payments if the exchange rate could somehow be pushed down by 10 per cent. Bearing in mind that provincial debt was largely in foreign currencies, Mr. Bouey noted that those payments would go up by 10 per cent. This stopped the charge for depreciation in its tracks.

For whatever reason, I was never asked as governor to attend such an event, although I knew that provincial counterparts to the federal side had more than once expressed interest in seeing the Bank there. In fact, as the reader may recall, one of the dishes offered up by the federal government in 1991 in its menu for more provincial involvement in the Bank of Canada's affairs had been the governor's regular attendance at federal–provincial meetings. But all I ever needed was an invitation from the minister of finance.

Whatever the pros and cons of a governor turning up at federal–provincial tax and spending reunions, this did not deter me from paying calls on individual provincial ministers of finance when feasible. This was generally in connection with a visit to their city for a speech, and such calls were usually not much more than courtesy—the exchange of a few bits of information, a thank you, and goodbye. But in the case of Ontario, the exchanges became a degree or two more intense.

Clearly, the NDP government that was elected in 1990 was having trouble with its finances, notwithstanding Ontario's remarkable creativity in developing new instruments for raising funds. Admittedly, it had inherited a bad budgetary scene from the previous Liberal government, which had tried hard to spend its way to re-election. When the NDP came in, the only way sense could be made of Ontario's fiscal position was by assuming that the economy would persist in an inflationary boom while interest rates would nevertheless be pushed down. This eventuality was not in the cards, least of all in the hand that the Bank was playing from. But not to be deterred, with the arrival of an economic slowdown that turned into a recession, the NDP government aimed at spending its way out. While there were no great choices in this situation, this one not only was bound to fail, it would turn an already poor provincial financial situation into one that was close to disastrous.

"Close to disastrous" is not too strong a term. In the early 1990s, as its debt tripled, the province had its rating cut three times by Standard and Poors—from AAA to AA-—and the spread for its longer-term debt over the federal government's rose to a full percentage point. This margin may not seem like a lot, but it was extremely unusual for Canada, particularly since markets tend to assume that a province's debt is guaranteed, in fact if not legally, by the federal government. This was also barely below the spread charged to Quebec, which had to deal with basic political question marks as well as its own major budgetary problems.

But that was not all. The Ontario government was reportedly getting strong advice from its more militant backers on the labour side—led by Bob White, then head of the Canadian Auto Workers—to go for broke, in more senses than one. Mr. White has since protested that this advice, i.e., to default on the debt, was aimed at Saskatchewan, not Ontario. This seems a distinction without much of a difference, except that Saskatchewan's debt was much smaller. Defaulting on debt service was a step with awesome implications, not only economic but also political, that could have brought grief to all levels of government in Canada, not to speak of the economy in general.

These same issues had been comprehensively agonized over before, back in the mid-1930s, when many provinces, above all those in the West, found themselves in desperate financial straits. Alberta, in part apparently because of the influence of its then Social Credit ideology, partially defaulted on its debt in 1936 and was not able to restore its credit until 1945. But other provinces managed, one way or another, to scrape through without defaulting. In Saskatchewan's case, scraping through required at one stage a direct loan from the Bank of Canada to meet a pressing maturity.

The extent to which provincial defaults would have a general Canadian impact had been a subject of particularly acute debate in Ottawa throughout the 1930s. Quite a few argued, as Robert Bryce noted in his history of the Finance Department, that a "federal refusal to bolster the flagging credit of such provinces [in particular, Manitoba and Saskatchewan] would be viewed by the financial world as an exercise in sound financial judgment and economizing," thus enhancing the Dominion's credit. However, others, including Governor Graham Towers, had prevailed. They feared that further provincial defaults, coming so soon after Alberta's, would trigger a chain of debt repudiations by municipalities, school districts, and even private enterprises throughout Western Canada, and that no one, including the federal government, would be spared from the ensuing bad financial and economic reaction.

Turning back to the Ontario debt dilemma, I should add that it is erroneous to think of debt holders as plutocrats, as so many commentators do. Some of the major debt holders who would have been hit by a default were pension funds. More cautious fellow NDP governments in other provinces (such as Saskatchewan) would also have been caught up in the wreckage—a kind of friendly fire catastrophe. But in the end, the Ontario NDP decided to bear down on its financial problems through its "Social Contract" incomes policy, even if this meant alienating support among its dug-in trade union leadership wing. That segment of the party was all for making its point by marching over the cliff regardless.

In this stirring period, I had meetings with Floyd Laughren, Ontario minister of finance (at my request) and with Premier Bob Rae (at his request). I saw those meetings as a chance to present monetary policy and to discuss it if necessary, and in each case I did a bit of both. It was more of a presentation with Mr. Rae and his colleagues and more of a debate in the office of Mr. Laughren, with a young aide present who obviously had a radically different view as to how the Canadian economic system should be managed in general, and demonstrably no time for anti-inflationary monetary policy in particular. To what extent his views had real currency throughout the Ontario government is difficult to say, because while the youngster did most of the talking on the Ontario side, the minister and deputy minister said very little.

Cornered

By way of wrap-up here, I want to skip ahead to focus on the circumstances of a federal fiscal event that occurred after I left office but that in a sense supplies closure to the kinds of issues I have been discussing in this chapter. This was the important deficit cutting budget of February 1995. My purpose is not to discuss what happened in that budget, but to trace some crucial links to earlier developments—in particular, how the budget approach was precipitated by events that Minister of Finance Paul Martin could not control. Those events were monetary in nature, the harsh reality of saver and investor confidence and financial market arithmetic.

The Bank and Finance had worked hard for years to sustain confidence in Canada's finances. It was magnificent to see the remarkable lengths of punishing long-distance travel to which Finance officials would go after each budget to spread what they portrayed as a good message in international financial capitals. But despite such personal heroics, flurries of loss of confidence were, unfortunately, still not unknown. Notable in recent years had been the one in 1990, when the Bank abruptly attempted to alter its interest rate track, and that in late 1992 after European exchange rate turmoil and after the failure of the Charlottetown constitutional referendum. But the financial crisis that broke out in late 1994 and early 1995 was far more severe. Admittedly, developments on the international side played a triggering role—namely, a further rise in US interest rates in response to inflation pressures and turmoil in Mexico on account of its public debt crisis and botched devaluation. Still, these external events only served to expose more fully the already fragile nature of the federal government's deficit and debt position. While the new government had been in office since October 1993, it had yet to take any significant steps to improve its situation. Perhaps it hoped that time, chance, and low interest rates— not necessarily in that order of precedence—would bail it out.

The Bank of Canada was trying hard to keep interest rates down, but there were limits to what it could achieve in the face of a rise in US rates. Let me be more precise. Those limits were ultimately determined not by the Bank, but by the preferences of holders of Canadian debt—in particular, by their willingness to hold on to that debt as the supply mounted, US rates rose, and the currency declined. The Bank's job in this context was to try to figure out what would, at lowest cost, give debt holders comfort. The best it could do was to try to ensure that confidence in the monetary policy framework did not go out the window too. Still, in this situation the biggest risk was that at some stage, holders would start projecting further exchange rate decline and head for the exits—in the process pushing the exchange rate down more, and also driving up further the interest costs for Canadian debt. The resulting phenomenon of higher market interest rates *and* a falling currency, as one market feeds on and intensifies the problems in the other, is the hallmark of a confidence crisis.

With mounting uncertainty as to how the government would deal with its deficit and debt, this vicious circle of lower exchange rate and higher interest rates is exactly what began to hit the Canadian market in spades from the last days of 1994. So the jig was finally up as regards any thoughts the government might have had of getting lower interest rates, and thereby a lower deficit, merely by pressing for easy money and a weaker Canadian dollar. By this extreme stage there was, as Margaret Thatcher would have said, "no alternative" to taking steps to drastically curb federal cheque writing. And this for once was really true for a government that valued its future—financial or otherwise. Both tax room, as much for political as economic reasons, and debt room, as financial markets were making abundantly clear, were to all practical intents used up. What steps were taken next in Ottawa is fiscal and political—not monetary—history.

CHAPTER 10

A New
Monetary Policy?

Before the 1993 Election

Attacking monetary policy was a prominent feature in the Liberal opposition's early approach to the 1993 federal election campaign. Not that we had been without forewarnings. For some years opposition politicians, whether Liberals or New Democrats, had been taking the unusual step of turning up at the Bank's spring press briefing for its annual report. Their purpose was to condemn the policy in front of the assembled scribes and camera crews, and get on the six o'clock news into the bargain.

A systematic foretaste had also been forthcoming in the aggressive approach taken by opposition representatives in the June Finance Committee hearings. This, according to some media commentary, pointed to the likelihood that a Liberal victory would mean Herb Gray might be the next minister of finance. Given his lines of attack, I did wonder if what he would or even could try to do in office could bear much resemblance to the views he expressed at mid-year. But as the October election date drew closer, a mist descended. Monetary policy issues—in particular, the actual choices to be made—seemed to become more of a hot potato than a campaign weapon.

The declared authoritative source for the monetary policy ground that was to be staked out by the Liberal Party going into the October election was its Red Book, more formally entitled "Creating

Opportunity: The Liberal Plan for Canada." Before it was finally released in mid-September, the press chattered greatly about its likely contents, indicating that monetary policy would be figuring in a prominent way. All this was especially intriguing if you were in the Bank of Canada and not in the habit of being a prime exhibit at an election. But then the tone changed. Close to the publication date, the word was that monetary policy issues would be downplayed. What a difference it can make if you think you will actually have to answer for what you say or print.

When "Creating Opportunity" did appear, it certainly seemed as if something must have tripped up its prose on the way to the printing house. The references to monetary policy start robustly enough. On the second page of the "Economic Framework" section, "the Conservatives' single-minded fight against inflation" is condemned. But when the readers look for backup to this forthright declaration in terms of an alternative policy (for example, as a simple point, would there now be more inflation, or a "balanced"—i.e., ambiguous—fight against inflation?), the pickings are slim indeed. Admittedly, the document did devote four full pages to a section entitled "Fiscal and Monetary Policy." But determined readers only get to monetary policy at the very bottom of the last of these four pages, and they do not get much then for their patience. All that is stated is simply that:

> The Liberal two-track policy of economic growth and fiscal responsibility will make possible a monetary policy that produces lower real interest rates and keeps inflation low, so that we can be competitive with our main trading partners.

Was this a joke? I don't think that anyone with a decent understanding of monetary policy matters could have made this up if they tried. But let me see if I can inject some meaning into it anyway. First, we have to set aside the multiple ambiguities in "so that we can be competitive with our main trading partners" as being too difficult to fathom—unless it meant fixing the exchange rate, which was hardly plausible in this context. Then, the only reasonable plain-language interpretation of such a bundle of words is something like the following: *An irresponsible fiscal policy and a lack of growth have stopped monetary policy from producing low interest rates, and this irresponsibility is going to be put right.* Now Mr. Wilson or Mr. Mazankowski, for example, might justifiably have had problems with *this* single-minded view of things. Furthermore, it was far from being the line that the opposition had been taking in Parliament. And in fact, interest rates were already way down. They would also, ironically, go distinctly higher again for quite some time in 1994 and 1995. But whatever the statement's dubious qualities in terms of accuracy or balance, or its absolute lack of consistency with the party line at the June hearings, it could hardly be seen as a rejection of monetary policy or, more specifically, the objectives that the Bank of Canada had been pursuing.

Some, still perhaps harking back to June, might nevertheless have strained to see in the reference to interest rates a call as to what monetary policy should now do differently. That is to say, to their way of thinking, and even though interest rates were now lower, monetary policy should somehow make it still easier to finance the fiscal deficit. But even laying the interest rate reference at the door of monetary policy is effectively countered by a statement earlier in the document that one of the "five major problems facing the Canadian economy" was "high *long-term* real interest rates" (my emphasis). Even the most died-in-the-wool believer in the ability of central banks to orchestrate the whole spectrum of interest rates would have to allow that the Bank's influence over long-term rates, and especially *real* long-term rates, is far more tenuous than any influence it might happen to have over, say, interest rates in the short-term money market.

I am probably in danger of having too much fun getting my gums into material that is newspaper-thin. On the evidence, one has to conclude that these few phrases were hastily cobbled together, possibly by a committee. They are most likely the frayed and essentially unserious remnants of an earlier, more extensive (if not necessarily more serious), monetary policy piece. This is not so surprising, especially if it had been concluded upon further reflection that monetary policy had after all been doing the right thing.

Otherwise, why not be clear on what was wrong and what was going to be done? Too difficult to expect? Well, the document could be very clear about its plans when it wanted to be—when, for example, it stated that "a Liberal government will replace the GST" and would also "renegotiate both the FTA and NAFTA." More recently, attention has been focused, and not without considerable provocation from governmental actions, on the Red Book's clear commitment to establishing an independent ethics counsellor who would, crucially, report to Parliament rather than to the prime minister. Of course, none of these steps was taken, but that is not the point I am aiming to make, or at least it is only part of the point.

The deeper issue that such episodes pose is not what a particular government said and did or did not do, but rather in what context political commitments—sensible or not and however specific—can be realistically taken as having lasting value. More particularly, if a sense of commitment and the assurance that comes with it do matter (as they certainly do in national monetary affairs), how does a government supply them? Obviously, not through pre-election promises, not through mere written statements, and not even by having a central bank. I will be expanding further at the end of this book on the kinds of challenges that all this represents.

What Happened After

The Liberals' confusion regarding what to say about monetary policy before the election carried over into uncertainty over what to do when it was won. Rumours swirled, and the media became increasingly thrilled. I stayed calm, having long since taken the view that it would be best to sit back, observe the show, and see what was pushed on stage before responding. One thing I said nothing about was my future in central banking. While my seven-year term of office was due to expire at the end of January 1994, I was never asked whether I wanted to continue, although my silence on the matter was probably (and reasonably) taken by both the Bank's board and the incoming government as evidence that I might be prepared to stay.

For anyone thinking I might stay, collateral evidence was to be found in the fact that in the fall of 1993 I had accepted the chairmanship of the committee of G-10 central bank governors, which met regularly in Basel, Switzerland, succeeding Jacques de Larosière, who was moving at fairly short notice from the Banque de France to head the crisis-ridden European Bank for Reconstruction and Development. My central bank counterparts were aware that I might not be around in a few months, recognizing the political ramifications around the question of my possible reappointment.

The Bank's outside directors had the statutory responsibility of deciding who to nominate. That is, they had to put forward a name for the approval of the minister of finance. But this approval has never been automatic, even on less controversial occasions. Indeed, according to past directors, disagreements on appointments had arisen between the minister and the Bank board even when the two sides had the same political colouration—not that political colouration seemed to matter that much in the way most directors worked and saw their fundamental fiduciary responsibilities. Of course, I was not privy to what was happening in the fall of 1993 in the potentially complex nomination/approval process in which the directors and the minister had to engage. The only time I learned that Bank directors had been to see the minister was when I read about it in the newspapers. What they proposed or discussed I never knew, and it was not my business to know.

What was my business were the terms under which I might, if asked, consider a second term. I had already decided in my own mind that I would accept reappointment only under the right policy conditions, and it remained to be seen what, if any, conditions the new government might want to lay down.

These matters finally came to a head in mid-December. I was then told, in the first instance by a top Department of Finance emissary, that in exchange for my reappointment the government wanted agreement on a modification of the inflation targets. The crucial area was the statement made back in 1991 as part of the original joint announcement (spelled out and discussed in Chapter 8) to the effect that the eventual goal was "price stability" and that this meant a rate of inflation clearly below 2 per cent. In further discussion, the minister was adamant that this provision had to go, leaving the end point at 1 to 3 per cent. I told him that this was unacceptable. I did propose as an alternative a target end range of .5 to 2.5 per cent, which yielded a midpoint "clearly below 2 per cent," as a specified working definition of price stability for the indefinite future, but this was rejected out of hand. So we agreed to disagree, and my term was effectively over. If the board were to nominate me, or in fact had nominated me, the government would not approve the nomination. I also told the minister that it was up to him to let Fred Hyndman, the director from Prince Edward Island and chair of the board's special committee on appointments, know what had happened so that the board could settle on what to do next. I did not discuss the matter with Mr. Hyndman or the board.

I decided in December 1993 that it would be best if I made no public comment at that time. Nor will I now discuss the intimacies of my confessionals with Mr. Martin (there were three meetings, but only the third one really counted) or try to explain on the government's behalf why it was so determined to have this provision dropped. For one thing, it was not explained to me, though I suspected from the questions asked around the issue that it had something to do with financing the budget deficit. But what I feel I can comment upon at this time is why the provision was important to me as a matter of principle, and what was at stake more generally.

There were two related reasons why I did not go along. First, I retained the view that it was far better in terms of the strategy of inflation targeting, and the corresponding ability of monetary policy to deliver monetary confidence, to have a longer-run goal, and naturally one that was as strong and credible as was reasonably possible. Second, there had been nothing in the behaviour of inflation and the economy since 1991 that suggested that the kind of long-run goal contemplated in the original inflation target agreement had become unrealizable and therefore not credible. So why should I agree to change at that time? The fact that the minister wanted the change did not seem by itself a good enough reason.

Accentuate the positive. One of the generally more perceptive observers of Canadian monetary performance, Professor David Laidler, has expressed the view that what happened in December 1993 was the "reaffirmation" of "a slightly modified version of the 1991 targets." Insofar as the general inflation target apparatus was retained by the new government, his view is correct. At that point in the government's life, it certainly would have been a foolish step to discard the framework in its entirety. However, his suggestion that the alteration was slight is, for the reasons I have indicated, on shakier ground. Furthermore, in the same way as I considered the modification unacceptable, the government evidently saw it as one that was so important that it absolutely had to get it, even though any change that generated uncertainty had the potential for significant costs in terms of increased interest charges, given the very large size of the national debt.

But what to say? For that, I refer the reader back to the end of Chapter 1 and the strong opening sentences of the December 1993 joint Bank of Canada–Government of Canada announcement on inflation targets that are quoted there. The challenge with that announcement is how to reconcile the resolute opening declaration on monetary policy purposes (in effect a preamble) with the weakened specifics that follow. One way is simply to view the opening sentences as mere spin and the actual numbers as the substance. Another way, admittedly strained but altogether more positive, is to accept on faith the position in the 1993 statement that "more experience in operating under these conditions ... with inflation as low as it is now ... would be helpful before an appropriate longer term objective is determined." But a weakness in this position is that it was not, in fact, necessary in terms of the existing target timetable to make any changes at all in late 1993.

In January 1998, the targets were extended again and once more pitched at 1 to 3 per cent—through the year 2001. At the time of the extension, it was reiterated that "it would be helpful to have a longer period of time in which the economy demonstrated more fully its ability to perform well under conditions of low inflation before determining the appropriate long-run target consistent with price stability." The targets were extended again in 2001, once more at 1 to 3 per cent but for a longer period than before.

Meanwhile, the economy had gotten stronger while inflation had been clearly below 2 per cent more often than not, notwithstanding periodic surges in energy prices and the need to absorb in domestic costs a major decline in the currency. Furthermore, any revenue-raising argument for more inflation based on partial indexing of tax brackets was recently taken off the table as well. Quite what experience was being waited for is unclear. And why it is unclear remains unclear as well.

What Price Transparency?

What do these events tell us about political limits to real transparency in regard to monetary policy? The way the changeover was managed hinged directly on the minister's responsibility to approve any appointment by the Bank's board of a governor or senior deputy governor. But if my term had not been expiring so soon, another mechanism could have come into play—namely, the power of the minister to issue to the Bank a directive on policy. This was discussed at length in Chapter 2, and the only point to be made here is that it might have been a problem for Mr. Martin to use a directive because he would also, by law, have had to render his reasons explicit. In December 1993, making reasons explicit, even simply by describing what changes were being made in the inflation targets, was apparently not thought either desirable or required, even though the changes were clearly considered essential.

There is a complicated relationship between policies, personalities and, again, the matter of transparency. For some time, John Crow as an individual had been the subject of fairly intense media focus. Much of this, no doubt, reflected the inevitable human, and therefore media, interest in the concrete. The more substantive issues relating to the pros and cons of a particular kind of policy are, after all, rather general. In this spirit, anyone who thinks it is relevant to know my father's occupation at my birth or to explore

details of my childhood, schooling, marital status, religious affilia-
tion, and so forth, can find bits of interpretation in a lengthy inves-
tigative report published in the *Globe and Mail* in September 1990.
Controversy about policy almost always gets translated into views
about the person seen as most directly responsible. This is part of
the charm of being governor of the Bank of Canada or of being any
public person.

But it also seemed that there was another, more subtle line in
the persistent focus of monetary policy critics. To the extent that
they could identify the policy as being that of an individual, and
therefore by implication peculiar (in both senses of the term), the
greater their chances of discounting it without having to argue the
ideas or principles involved. The problem with this approach is
that it runs counter to the public interest in facilitating, not ham-
pering, coherent discussion of policy alternatives. And the political
presentation of monetary policy alternatives in the fall of 1993 was
far from coherent, if indeed there was any presentation at all.

Still, this does not mean that a personal angle will not succeed.
Against this background, a new government was able to avoid
spelling out what, if anything, was new about its monetary policy—helped, it must be allowed, by a general inability or unwillingness to see nonsensical statements about that policy (in particular,
those gracing the Red Book) for what they were. Indeed, in this situation it was quite easy for the government to cast the policy in
different ways, depending on the speaker and the audience. It
could even indicate, for anyone who wanted to believe it, that the
change of governor had nothing to do with policy, notwithstanding the fact that it had been blasting what had been done for the
previous six years. After all, the Bank continued to be "independent," didn't it?

From Inflation To?

By early 1994, a great deal of the ground had been laid for a better
monetary and economic performance. But that progress had been
obscured by daubs of political brushwork as the new government
set about preserving face. The official line, at least as articulated by

Finance Minister Paul Martin to the media, seemed to come down to the following: It is important to keep inflation down because it was very costly to the economy to reduce it in the first place and we don't want to go through that again.

This was a mixed message. As such, its virtue, and perhaps its purpose, was that it could be read in different ways. It did have its constructive aspects, acknowledging not only the general good sense of keeping inflation down, but also that there was some kind of governmental commitment to this end. This was underlined in the decision to stay with inflation targets, however unenthusiastic Ottawa felt about it at the time. But any commitment has not gone further than this. The sentiments framed in the robust opening sentences of the 1993 inflation targets agreement were subsequently allowed to fade into dark background. The official mantra has become "low inflation," not "price stability." Both these terms are more rhetorical than scientific, but "low inflation" is clearly weaker. And if there is any sense of commitment, it has not been allowed to extend as far as re-examining the Bank of Canada's mandate in the interests of reinforcing long-term confidence in Canada's money.

Another problematic point is that the official position, because it emphasizes the transitional costs of moving to a better monetary performance, leaves a strong suggestion that if inflation were to rise again—whether through miscalculation or bad luck—not much of an effort would be exerted to bring it down. This inaction would be consistent with the salvo in the Red Book against any attack on inflation that is "single-minded." Fortunately, the adverse inflation scenario has not yet been tested seriously. But by the law of averages, it will be, especially since current policy is focused on ensuring that there is some inflation.

What I have just said may arguably constitute too theoretical and therefore too cautious a view. This is because experience is an invaluable teacher. The economy has done rather well overall, with an inflation record that once seemed to many beyond Canada's capacity to achieve and hence ill advised for the Bank of Canada to seek. This should have had a constructive impact on public perceptions and expectations for what policy should do in the future. It may also eventually have an impact on perceptions in government, even though the inevitable official tendency in these matters is to raise standards only when it is absolutely driven to. The problem with this kind of "just in time" approach is that taking action only when you absolutely have to act has no more policy value than that—when you have no choice but to act. It is unlikely to be the best time from the standpoint of good long-term policy results, especially when building confidence rather than excitedly fighting crises is what is really needed.

In the rest of this chapter, I want to offer some reflections on particular aspects of the course of Canadian monetary policy: the costs of getting inflation down; the alternatives on offer; the path of transition to something better; the value of good price performance; the significance of inflation targets; and the need for balance. These are complex questions, not easily simplified, that require a reader's concentration. But they are important.

Costs

Because it is so often distorted or ignored, the point needs to be made (see also, for example, Professor Peter Howitt's piece in *Where We Go from Here*) that the costs of getting inflation down in terms of subpar economic performance, or even recession, are transitional. That is to say, they do not persist. This, of course, does not mean that they are unimportant. Rather, it means that any such costs have to be set against something that has longer-term economic value. That "something" is providing a monetary standard (and what flows from that standard in an economy based upon it) in which citizens justifiably have confidence. Furthermore, once the transitional costs have been dealt with, as they largely have been in Canada, they are out of the picture.

In this same context of transition, we can also usefully debate such issues as whether it would have been better to have had, for example, more and earlier fiscal strengthening; a more aggressive start to monetary policy anti-inflation efforts in 1987–90; earlier inflation reduction targets; or more anti-inflationary resolution all round in the 1970s. Although such questions are now water under the bridge, trying to answer them may still tell us something that would be helpful in future circumstances.

Looking back over the whole process of inflation reduction, it is worth bearing in mind that it took many years. Perhaps it took too long, and maybe it would have been possible to shift inflation earlier. This can be debated. But the more common charge levied against monetary policy has not been procrastination, but rather that the inflation reduction process was draconian—too much, too fast. I like to think that there was some determination shown. But considering the rather stately pace at which inflation came down, my impression is that those who raise this charge really think that inflation should not have been reduced at all—that the effort made was not worth it because the benefits are scarce. This is the crucial issue. But before getting directly into it, I want to spend a moment looking at the matter from a slightly different angle.

Alternatives

What were the alternatives on offer? It never seemed to me that anything at all convincing was put forward. Critics overwhelmingly limited themselves to carping about what was being done, and when they had something more to say, it was a vague gesture in the direction of price controls—and certainly not wage controls if they were in the labour movement, although it has been shown time and time again that wage controls are the only controls that are really likely to work.

At about the time that I became governor, monetary policy was in a broad way hanging on to the exchange rate, in the sense of not letting it depreciate too far too fast. Beyond this, perhaps critics thought that it was desirable to stabilize inflation, if one could, at wherever it was at. I recall one Canadian economics professor telling me in the early 1980s that a reasonable goal for the Bank would be to try to hold inflation "where it was at"—then about 10 per cent. One problem with this kind of approach, which might sound comfortingly plausible on the surface, is that where inflation is "at" is a very shaky notion. Inflation could shift and be "at" somewhere else. So what rate of inflation would we be arguing for? Did he, or we, want an inflation target of 10 per cent? Was that a good number for the Canadian economy? Did it not matter very much?

Another approach could have been to have a policy of trying to secure an inflation rate that matched that of the United States. For much of our history from the early 1970s, that would certainly have been better than what we managed to achieve. Twinning with the United States on inflation certainly seemed to interest Mr. Chrétien when he began campaigning in early 1993, at least in the sense that he wondered out loud why we needed to do better on inflation than the Americans. (I am presuming here that he did not want us to return to doing worse.) If matching whatever the United States might do was indeed the desired objective, the most policy-effective way to get it would have been to fix the US–Canadian dollar exchange rate, even though his apparent political preference was to have our currency depreciate. Of course, there is in principle no harm in doing better on inflation than the United States, but that should not be the objective of our policy. Our proper goal should be to do well on inflation for our own economic sake. The United States can, and will, take care of itself.

Yet another approach might best be termed populist. A good example was the views held by an association styling itself the Bank of Canada for Canadians Coalition. This body, a kind of temporary (I believe) interest group comprised of a mix of business people and academics, had been formed in the early 1990s with the apparent purpose of ensuring that I was not reappointed. It also seems to have had at the back of its mind some alternative policy, although that, unfortunately (but in my experience, not surprisingly), was less clear. The following paragraph, taken from its open letter to the prime minister after his 1993 election victory, should indicate how clear it was not:

If you wish to create jobs and contain the deficit, you need to have the Bank of Canada working for you, as it did for your Liberal predecessors from 1939 to mid-1970s. Inflation need not result from an accommodating monetary policy. There are many other more effective and less damaging tools for dealing with inflation than high real interest rates.

What this says in essence, in the absence of any specification and analysis of these "many other tools," is that in the interests of good economic performance, monetary policy should finance the rate of inflation that turns up. The coalition also seemed to think (though this is admittedly less than totally clear) that the inflation financed this way would be low. Needless to say, as history has shown before and since, this is a blind alley. That is why I hesitate to call it an alternative policy. But the coalition group was presumably serious and seemed to think it would have political impact. Perhaps it did. And perhaps it also saw comfort for its views in the obscure desires regarding monetary policy that can be teased out of the 1993 Red Book.

This pretty much exhausts the list of monetary policy alternatives to what the Bank of Canada actually tried to do when I was there—that is, move the Canadian monetary experience in the direction of price stability as a worthy long-term objective, and put on the table the question of what "price stability" could mean.

Transition

With the path of inflation reduction being rather gradual, the inflation habit was slow to change. But as it did, difficult withdrawal symptoms showed up in important policy and economic areas. One related to the ability of government to manage deficits, and another concerned the ability of business to take a harder look at costs in the light of declining inflation. My colleagues and I were certainly aware that one risk that monetary policy ran was that even though its long-run objectives were the right ones, the effort of getting there could prove too stressful for the inflation-induced expectations, and inflationary ways of going about things, that were by then in place. This meant that if monetary policy stood its ground, there could be some kind of crisis. (Recall, for example, the encouragement to Ontario—or was it Saskatchewan?—to default.) Monetary policy and the Bank of Canada would get overwhelmed by the crisis, and nothing would have been achieved except a demonstration of failure—not a pretty sight to contemplate.

Turning first to government deficits, I have already discussed at length in the preceding chapter the Siamese-twin relationship between monetary and fiscal policies and the complications that this can involve. So here I can be relatively brief.

It was already apparent in the mid-1980s that the fiscal transition away from inflation could be a real problem. In my Hanson lecture, I had made explicit reference to what I termed the "disagreeable arithmetic" that could arise. This was a glancing homage to the well-known "Some Unpleasant Monetarist Arithmetic" paper by American professors Thomas Sargent and Neil Wallace that first highlighted the way government debt problems could overwhelm even the best-intentioned monetary policy. The reference to disagreeable arithmetic was specifically intended to call attention to the sharp rise in government debt and debt service burdens, both federal and provincial, that had already taken place, and the adverse implications of these burdens for confidence in monetary policy. If fiscal policy could not make the adjustment from an inflationary environment, it would be game over and a totally different business—disaster mitigation. But fiscal policy itself, whether in the particularly hair-raising case of Ontario or at the federal level, did in the end get a grip on its situation. Whether this was because of or in spite of monetary policy I will leave to others closer to fiscal decision making to debate. Still, I should add in defence of monetary policy that some provinces, notably Alberta and Saskatchewan, had recognized the problem earlier than the federal government or Ontario, and had already begun to tackle their deficit situations, each in their own way.

The other transition issue that stood out was the exchange rate and its effect on business decisions. The Bank was very conscious that the Canadian dollar should be allowed to rise if necessary. Given the excessive focus on dampening the rise in the currency in the early 1970s, we were certainly not prepared to suggest that there was any preordained monetary policy limit to how far it could go. As I had pointed out in my Hanson lecture, "the pursuit of short-term exchange rate stability cannot be pushed so far that it jeopardizes the good domestic price performance that is the objective of monetary policy." The reader is entitled to take my word for it that this is pretty strong central bankerese for the basic point that as far as monetary policy was concerned, the exchange rate would not be stopped from going up simply because it was going up. In other words, we were not running a low Canadian dollar policy.

As the Canadian dollar appreciated in the late 1980s, those in the export industries certainly let the Bank of Canada know it. The Canadian Manufacturers' Association and the Canadian Pulp and Paper Association were particularly vocal in their concerns. Thomas d'Aquino, president of the Business Council on National Issues, a gathering of heads of large Canadian corporations (now titled the Canadian Council of Chief Executives), told me later that the council had held particularly vigorous debates on this issue. In the end, it was basically supportive because enough people there had an appreciation of the monetary policy strategy, including the fact that what monetary policy was trying to bring about was not, of course, a high (or low, for that matter) Canadian dollar as a matter of policy. The exchange rate was simply not a target for what the Bank did.

However, this point was difficult to get across more generally. Any detailed discussion of the currency's behaviour by the Bank was bound to generate the suspicion that we were not only targeting it but also trying to talk or drive it down. But such a suspicion would attract speculators fast and would also be bad for interest rates, as expectations of a declining currency began to be factored into calculations of expected returns in Canadian funds.

One exchange rate angle that was pressed by commentators of all stripes, including some in government, was that since Canada in the late 1980s and early 1990s was adjusting to North American free trade, this was not the time for monetary policy to be trying to bring inflation down and, in the process, push up the currency. The reasoning was that a cheap Canadian dollar would help a lot, boosting selling prospects just as Canadian companies were restructuring toward the US market. I had sympathy with this argument because of the undoubted importance of freeing up Canadian trade. But I could not see how we could both have a properly credible monetary policy and arrange the value of the Canadian dollar in this way.

One consideration favouring a higher dollar from a domestic standpoint was that its rise would send a particularly clear message to business that it needed to control domestic costs better than before—otherwise it would lose export markets. This was particularly to the point because a widespread tendency in the past, in both the public and private sectors, had been to see a weaker currency as the escape hatch from a poor performance on inflation, and therefore the reason why we should have a currency that floated—down, that is. But a declining dollar had a tendency to perpetuate itself in a cycle of inflation, depreciation, greater inflation, and so on—a dead end. This time the cycle, if any, was going to be different, as also would be the ending. When business decisions, after a difficult passage, became less inflationary in the early 1990s, the exchange rate also came down—but without the Bank talking about it.

Value

There seems to be a more general appreciation these days of the broad economic benefits of a climate approaching price stability. Along with much lower interest rates than used to prevail, there is also perhaps a better understanding that these rates do not come out of thin air. Simply put, they have to be earned through good, sustained monetary performance. Not recognizing this was the basic problem, for instance, with the way Herb Gray and Diane Marleau approached interest rates, and what the Bank could do about them, at the parliamentary hearings in mid-1993. Another, less visible but equally important, element is that a more assured monetary policy regime encourages forward planning and longer horizons, making future values more secure and reducing the costs of investment. More generally, confidence in the future value of money should make the economy more efficient and productive by allowing markets to work better.

As all this has become apparent, the axis of debate about Canadian monetary policy should be shifting too. The argument should be not whether policy should actually seek inflation, but rather how much our inflation can and should be reduced on a sustainable basis. But even though the case for more solid performance on the inflation front has been enhanced by what has happened in the past decade, it is doubtful on the evidence whether government will be prepared to help move things any further in this direction, and government seems to have an increasingly peremptory say in what happens with monetary policy. The latest agreement on inflation targets, issued in May 2001, confirms this.

Any desire to use policy to prop or push inflation up will find support from two sets of economic arguments. One has to do with attitudes toward wage rates, and the other has to do with limits to low interest rates. This is not the place to discuss these arguments in great detail. The interested reader can find plenty of literature on them, especially the one relating to wages. But since they do get repeated, I want to situate them in a Canadian context, even at the risk of some heavier going.

As regards the general argument from wages, it hinges on the proposition that what really matters to the employee is the money, or nominal, wage rather than that same wage adjusted for inflation—the real wage. This means that whether for "fairness" reasons or other factors, there will be strong reluctance to impose cuts in money wages and strong resistance to accepting them, however low the rate of price inflation, and even if prices are declining. Such a money wage "floor" becomes a general economic inefficiency when inflation gets low enough. That is to say, the variations in real wages across different categories of workers will be less than they should be for a well-functioning labour market, and this can push up the rate of unemployment. So the upshot is—to maximize jobs, we need some inflation so as to get the right industrial dispersion of real wages. This argument also implies that at too low a rate of inflation, real wages in the economy will turn out on average to be too high.

There has been much debate among specialists as to how widespread any such wage floor phenomenon is, and also, given the wide variety of employment and wage payment practices in the modern economy, what practical importance it may have in adversely affecting general economic performance. One thing to bear in mind is that supposed wage floors are far from being the only relevant factor in how flexible labour markets are, or in how the whole economy performs in an inflation-free environment. Another large area, for example, is the unfavourable economic impact of the interaction of inflation with taxes. This issue, involving various aspects of the tax system, goes well beyond the matter of whether tax brackets are indexed.

In any event, two Canadian aspects of this wage debate—one institutional and one more general—merit attention. As regards the institutional side, bear in mind that the virtue of inflation with respect to any wage floors is that it improves employment by making cuts in real wages more palatable. Simply put, the argument goes, with inflation employees simply don't notice that their earnings have gone down.

But that is not at all how the Canadian labour movement, which has been a clear fan of inflation, sees the process. Its vision is quite the reverse. According to the thinking of the Canadian Labour Congress, as expressed by its president Bob White in a letter to *The Economist* in 1996, with a "stronger pro-growth monetary policy...employers would, in tight labour markets, be forced to invest more in worker skills and in innovation." No description is provided of the monetary policy or inflation path required to fit this bill. But a moment's thought makes clear that monetary policy, in order to finance "tight labour markets," would in effect be required to supply whatever inflation was necessary as firms were pressed to displace increasingly expensive workers (with their real wage being pushed up through tight labour demand) by investing in labour-saving equipment. This inflation-driven investment would, according to this view, be the main source of increases in labour productivity and, hopefully, real wages.

But there is no reason to think that any maintained rate of inflation, however high, would actually achieve what Mr. White was apparently seeking. What we would need instead would be price inflation (and monetary accommodation of that inflation) that kept it consistently ahead of wage expectations in order to dampen the effect on profits of the upward push of real wages. Otherwise, how would employers justify the hiring of additional workers? This situation is explosive—a recipe not merely for inflation but for hyperinflation. Furthermore, it is a story essentially about wage acceleration under tight demand, rather than one about how to get real wage cuts through inflation. It also calls to mind the prescient critique in 1936 of another eminent Canadian-born economist, Jacob Viner. In phrasing that matches the ironic vividness of Keynes himself, Viner noted in his classic review of the *General Theory* in the *Quarterly Journal of Economics* that:

> In a world organized in accordance with Keynes' specifications there would be a constant race between the printing press and the business agents of the trade unions, with the problem of unemployment largely solved if the printing press could maintain a constant lead....

I should add that such a "printing press" policy would not in fact solve any problems of unemployment either. Since it would produce ever-accelerating inflation, any market-based economic system on which it was inflicted would first deteriorate and then collapse into barter trade under the pressures of hyperinflation. This destructive process would not create jobs, net, and only peculiar ones, gross.

While the two pro-inflation arguments outlined above are in fact very different, both are typically thought of as Keynesian in nature. The first relies principally on money illusion (simply put, the inability to adjust for inflation in one's thinking), and the second relies on maintaining inflationary aggregate demand but nonetheless continual surprises to the upside in the amount of inflation that turns up. To what extent Keynes himself would have endorsed either of these views is debatable. I do not think that he would have had any time at all for the one based on continual inflation surprises to stay ahead.

A more general consideration for the wage debate has to do with the role of the exchange rate in all this. The rigid money wage argument sketched above pays no attention to the effect of exchange rate changes, perhaps because it was developed in the United States. But given exchange rate flexibility and a large international goods and services sector, which Canada certainly has since 40 per cent of its output is exported, there can also be rather a lot of flexibility in Canadian wages in real terms when they are measured against the price in Canadian dollars of international goods and services. This Canadian reality detracts greatly from any possible relevance of a wage floor argument that is framed in purely domestic (i.e., US) terms—particularly because Canada can, demonstrably, turn in a good price performance while retaining an exchange rate that is flexible.

As regards the effect from the fact that interest rates cannot, effectively, go below zero, a similar exchange rate consideration applies. In this case, the pro-inflation argument is that at very low inflation, the economy can be hampered by the inability of monetary policy in an economic recession to drive down real interest rates far enough because nominal rates have effectively a zero floor. So far so bad, and Japan is often cited as an example of the perils in this regard.

But again, this argument does not give any weight to the effect of monetary policy through the exchange rate—in this particular case, through exchange rate depreciation. Here Canada, as a relatively small open economy, enjoys a significant advantage over Japan, for example. That country's deflation problems, following from the asset-price bubble and subsequent policy immobility, could have been alleviated through focusing on the exchange rate—something well within the Bank of Japan's money-printing capabilities. But the sensitivity of the United States to the yen/US dollar relationship is very high and gets easily linked with bilateral trade issues. Japan also has to worry about the reactions of its Asian trading partners.

All in all, the case for good Canadian economic performance through price stability stands up to these counters on behalf of a policy of sustained, or even accelerating, inflation rather well. Hounds bark. They scrap over whether the objective of inflationary policies is to push the real wage up or to hold it down. But the caravan continues on anyway.

Targets

Inflation targets may well help countries attain good economic performance, but more time and exposure will also improve our knowledge in this area. Certainly, Canada's inflation performance has been better since targets were instituted in 1991. This in itself suggests that such targetry has had a good effect. The quantitative economic modelling work that has been done is also consistent with a direct contribution from targeting, not just in Canada but elsewhere. In addition, inflation has stayed closer to target than the range of uncertainty that could be derived from the Bank of Canada's models of the inflation process (at least, those models available when I was there) would have given one any right to expect.

However, one difficulty with these calculations regarding the contribution of targets is that over the relevant period, inflation performance almost everywhere in the industrial world has been better than expected—including in particular the United States, which has no inflation targets. At the same time, it seems the Federal Reserve has been focusing more clearly on inflation than it used to. Indeed, it has been argued—as does, for example, Harvard economics professor Gregory Mankiw in an assessment of US monetary policy in the past decade—that the Federal Reserve has "covert inflation targets." But quite why its targets are or should be covert, or whether covert targets have the same general properties as officially announced ones, he does not make fully clear.

It seems evident that official targets will help a great deal in communication. They certainly make clear what the focus of monetary action is and should be. That is a considerable plus when one is trying to do policy. They may also help in generating constructive expectations in the marketplace, especially of course when they are "good" targets. So at the risk of repetition, let me again suggest that targets that are structured so as to generate prospects of good price performance over a sustained longer run are better than those that do not. The Canadians who now decide these things are prepared to go a half step in this direction—as of May 2001, they are using longer targets (ones with a more extended time horizon than before), although not stronger ones. Perhaps strength will follow.

Balance

This stock-taking would not be complete without re-emphasizing that a monetary focus on price stability does not mean, and never has meant, setting aside the real economy. Above and beyond the fact that a solid base of confidence in the future value of money is fundamental to the way a market economy performs, there is also ample space for monetary policy to react to cyclical disturbances. It is simply fallacious to suggest otherwise. The fallacy is the implicit and unjustifiable assumption lying at the back of much commentary that monetary policy actions should be pressed in only one direction—that is, the kind of directional bias that Jacob Viner was drawing attention to.

The truth is that actions have to be balanced. In other words, while monetary policy under a price stability framework is perfectly capable of acting as required to sustain demand, output, and employment, it should by the same token deal promptly with emerging excessive inflation. And if inflation for whatever reason does get off target, it should also be clear from the arrangements that good monetary performance will be restored. How can this be assured? Thinking about this seems to move us beyond inflation targets themselves to the nature and basis of the economic policy institutions that guide them and guide monetary policy. I have already reviewed back at the start the institutional arrangements we have in Canada for managing our money and the questions surrounding them. In my final chapter, I will revisit those questions more broadly—both in terms of what monetary policy *can* do and, equally importantly, what it *should* aim to do.

CHAPTER 11

ଚର

Financial
Futures

Monetary Policy's Grasp

What if a central bank pressed its buzzer but no one came? Looking at the parade of financial and/or technological innovations
that could loosen a central bank's leverage on the financial system,
theoreticians have with some regularity been speculating about a
likely fade-out of monetary policy into impotence. But not so fast
and not so sure.

If it were fast and sure, we would be there already, since this
parade started many decades ago when chequing deposits issued by
commercial banks began to be more widely used to finance transactions than the banknotes that were increasingly the preserve of a
central bank. (In fact, the movement beyond central bank money
started well before the Bank of Canada, and before monetary policy as we think of it today was even dreamt of.) But banknotes
became less and less significant for monetary policy and commercial banks' liquidity needs more and more important, so the shift
proved irrelevant. On the Bank's own account, when it announced
some 15 years ago that it was eliminating positive statutory cash
reserve requirements for chartered banks, some attentive souls worried that it had given up the policy ghost. With the requirements
gone, how was it going to stop bank deposits from multiplying
indefinitely? To make a long and rather technical story short, the
record shows that it could and did.

Still, financial change has accelerated greatly in recent years, with the proliferation of non-bank financial institutions; the increased blurring of the distinctions between banks and non-bank institutions; the creation of a wide range of transferable accounts beyond simple chequing deposits; the widespread use of credit cards; the increasing use of debit cards; the explosive growth of financial derivatives; and the advent of e-money, smart cards, electronic purses, and so on. Not surprisingly, interest in whether these changes might make a real difference to what monetary policy can do has accelerated alongside.

Despite all these innovations, the ability of the central bank to control the supply of liquidity to financial institutions through its day-to-day operations remains crucial and effective, and that power does not need positive reserve requirements to make it work. Because the Bank controls liquidity, it also controls the overnight rate charged for short-term funds trading in the Canadian money market. That has not altered, even if the financial superstructure has changed quite a lot and will no doubt change further. In this vein, the Bank felt confident enough to assert—back in 1987 when it issued a discussion paper on how it would implement monetary policy in the absence of requirements for chartered banks to hold positive reserve balances at the central bank—that in a world without such reserves, it "would expect to have virtually the same degree of influence on interest rates as it currently has."

Even so, the skeptic can reasonably ask how much influence that is. While control of banking liquidity may provide a monetary policy lever, is that lever very long? In 1991, we issued another notice concerning monetary policy in this reserve-free situation. There, we observed more precisely and cautiously than before that the zero reserve requirement system would permit the Bank "to exercise a degree of influence over *very short-term rates* [my emphasis] similar to that under the current system." This description of our leverage clearly claimed an influence over the very shortest-term rates—in Canada, money market overnight rates, which are similar to the Federal funds rate in the United States. What it did not assert was that this took us very far in influencing financial and economic behaviour generally. This choice of phrasing deliberately left a number of important questions open. How much influence do movements in overnight rates have over other, longer-term interest rates? How much influence do such rates have anyway on spending decisions in the economy? And if spending is affected, how much and when is inflation impacted as opposed to, say, employment?

Such questions, going as they do beyond monetary policy's initial impact into the way it is transmitted further in the economy, are and always will be complicated. They are bread and butter for economists at the Bank of Canada and mother's milk for many outside economists and the learned journals that cater to them. They often reach the media in simplified form, when journalists and investment commentators get excited about the possible effects of central bank actions on all kinds of things including, now, exuberance or the lack thereof in the stock market. Since the issues concerning how monetary policy works come in so many different forms, with potentially so many varied effects in the economy—effects that also depend significantly on the time periods over which one chooses to measure them—they are always hotly debated. Some of the debate focuses on their finer points and some stems from a more ideological position, as, for example, in the way the term "monetarist" came to be employed years ago more as an accusation than description. Woe unto those who thought that some measure of money and the pace of its expansion might have a place in thinking about the transmission of monetary policy actions or, even more dreadful, in considering the proper conduct of monetary policy in general!

Ideologically inspired or not, attempts by Canada and other countries to get mileage out of some version of "money" in gauging monetary policy have been strikingly unsuccessful. The European Central Bank is currently in the process of supplying yet another example of this lack of success.

More broadly, experience has demonstrated convincingly that it is extremely difficult to say anything simple but applicable in all circumstances about the details of how monetary policy actions get transmitted across the economy. In trying once again to make things helpfully simple, the Bank of Canada did for a while vigorously promote the notion of a monetary conditions index as a way of summarizing and publicizing the combined influence of both interest rate and exchange rate changes on the economy (discussed in Chapter 6). But this apparently neat concept proved in practice more slippery to understand or explain than the Bank had reckoned. The index is still around, but it has now been relegated to the chorus line.

All that being said, the evidence is abundant that one way or another—through varying impacts on interest rates, through the exchange rate, through "money," through "credit," or even, nowadays, through the stock market perhaps—Canadian monetary policy does have an impact on our financial markets and through them, on what happens in the economy. And this is so notwithstanding the fact that the Bank always has to manoeuvre with a sharp awareness of what other policies, both in Canada and outside, are up to and how other economies, above all the United States, are faring. On a slightly different plane, Milton Friedman famously described the lags in the effects of monetary policy as "long and variable." But this is not to deny that for any country, the effects are there and are important—just that one probably should not put great faith in policy fine-tuning. I perhaps need only observe, as a way of concluding this discussion of influence, that during my tenure there was a widespread conviction that the actions of the Bank of Canada were having an impact. I thought so as well.

But to be worth its while, the favourable impact on inflation and the investment for good economic performance that was achieved needed to endure. To get an effect that would be lasting, we needed to build up public understanding and confidence in what the central bank was up to, and belief that a policy of monetary integrity would last. That involved more than transparency. It also involved consistency, a track record, and a plan. In short, it involved policy credibility and the ability to sustain it.

So my main concern was not to argue that Canadian monetary policy could or would be an agent of economic change—everyone could see that it was. Rather, most of what the Bank said or did was directed at a broader and more important question—namely, what monetary policy should be trying to achieve for the Canadian economy. Instead of focusing on means or technique, the emphasis was, surely more appropriately, on clarifying monetary policy ends and making progress toward them.

The Bank's Reach

What should those ends be? Because the popular tendency is to assign to monetary policy all kinds of properties and powers, implausible though those attributions might be, it matters a great deal to be clear about what that policy has a fair chance of achieving—in other words, back to where this book started.

"Sound money and plenty of it," as the folk saying goes.[1] Many and varied have been the ideas, judging by the Bank's incoming letter files, as to how it can best go about its money-creating business and how it should reconcile the opposing pressures to print lots of money and also sustain confidence in that money's purchasing value. Indeed, for many years Canada harboured a vigorous political movement, Social Credit, inspired in its initial stages by a disarmingly naive theory as to how prosperity could be achieved through printing money. Would that it were so easy. Fortunate it was, then, for me to be bracketed by a predecessor and a successor who came from around its heartland in Western Canada. They were prepared to field questions and complaints from the Social Credit camp that those of us not brought up in such a special climate found difficult to comprehend, let alone reply to. That is why I have not dealt with them in this book. More recently, former Liberal politician Paul Hellyer has been expounding his own set of monetary recipes, from his own political party, to anyone who would listen—again, not dealt with in this book. From this angle, views about a nation's monetary management and the institutions that underpin it must seem to many like a Tower of Babel, with

---

[1] I recall seeing this aphorism in a piece written by the late Douglas Purvis of Queen's University. There, he attributed it to "Anon."

people talking past each other and always unfinished business. So what's a central bank to do?

Anyone who has actually done monetary policy, including, I might add, Alan Greenspan, is bound to have a relatively restrained view as to the number of things it can achieve. Experienced central bankers are acutely conscious of the limited tools that they have, so they naturally regard their feasible objectives as limited as well—even if, as in the United States recently, members of the species have been seen as walking on water and clairvoyant to boot. It is no contradiction for them also to trust that this sunny view of their potency lasts. After all, it means that the economy is doing well, whatever in reality might be the central bank's contribution to that state of grace.

The Canadian economy has been doing quite well in recent years. With our exposure to US developments, it would be going too far to give Canadian monetary policy, or indeed any Canadian policy, a great deal of credit for this. Indeed, no one—not even official Canada boosters—has done so. But I must emphasize that the quality of our money is one contribution to our prosperity that we can do something about, and that it would not be too much to suggest that improved Canadian monetary confidence has been one part of a better story. After all, it is only through maintaining such confidence that domestic interest rates can be sustained at relatively low levels, notwithstanding what happens elsewhere. Happily, the truth of this has been well demonstrated in recent years as confidence in Canada's monetary performance has improved, and the risk margin by which Canadian interest rates have traditionally been above US interest rates has, to all practical intents, vanished, and even reversed on occasion.

Admittedly, even in purely Canadian terms, many will contend that the really noteworthy improvement on our financial front in the past decade has been not in monetary policy but in governments' fiscal performance. There, the big event was the 1995 Pauline conversion to slashing the federal deficit, even if this conversion was forced on the government through the unwillingness of investors to give it any further benefit of the doubt regarding financial policies and the deficit. Furthermore, with that drastic shift for the better, many fears that budgetary demands would overwhelm monetary policy intentions, however clear and good those intentions might be, were probably dissipated. That in turn helped monetary policy's credibility and reinforced lower interest rates.

Still, taking strong budgetary action earlier—years earlier even—would obviously have been even better. For one thing, fiscal medicine applied then, though still unpopular and no doubt heavily criticized by the political opposition, would not have had to be so strong.

However, more foresighted action is probably too much to expect of our political decision-making process. The almost inevitable tendency to wait until a crisis is actually upon us is a problem that has made the picture of fiscal–monetary coordination—so popular in textbooks—so questionable in practice. But an independent Bank of Canada should be capable of foresighted action, so that at least one leg of national financial integrity has a chance of being preserved, whatever shortcomings arise on the fiscal side. Indeed, if a measure of central bank independence matters, it must be for such reasons. Other kinds of reasons are not nearly as compelling.

In other words, stressing the importance of fiscal corrections, however late in the day they turn out to be, does not let monetary policy off the hook for its own responsibilities. The fact that fiscal policies tend to be late to the party, or go off in different directions (we now have 11 such policies in Canada when you take account of the mounting budgetary weight of our increasingly individualized provinces), is no reason for believing that monetary policy should be judged by the same relaxed standard. At the same time, having the independence to do the right monetary thing also implies having a clear, commonly accepted, set of monetary principles.

How far have we progressed in that direction? How much further might we go? Nowadays, what Ottawa puts in the official shop window are the inflation targets that have, in one form or another, been in existence for over a decade. Having helped to inaugurate them back in 1991, I can readily appreciate their virtues. They supply transparency and focus regarding monetary policy goals. They do it in a dimension where monetary policy can hope to accomplish something of lasting value. They might also provide what Gerald Bouey was keenly looking for back in the troubled and uncertain times of the early 1980s—something that would qualify as "a place to stand." The fact that they have been kept going for more than 10 years—through exchange crises, energy price surges, and political change—is testimony to their resilience. And one can conjure with the possibility that our apparent ability to get unemployment down further now than in the 1980s without triggering more inflation may be a consequence of the presence and persistence of the inflation targets and the resulting buildup in confidence about the future (or lack of it) of inflation. They perhaps helped Governor Dodge to say without provoking outrage, as he did in June 2002, that "with the domestic economy showing strong momentum, the Bank will take whatever action is necessary to keep inflation near its 2 per cent target over the medium term."

But again, not so fast. Despite the emphasis now placed on them, inflation targets are more technique than substance, and we should not fall into the trap of assuming that any inflation target is bound to be a good one. The drop in inflation and the improved trade-off between inflation and unemployment seem to have occurred everywhere, inflation targets or not. What has been more prevalent than such targets is something more fundamental: monetary commitment to getting inflation down and keeping it down, in North America since the early 1980s at least.

Is there now commitment? In this vein, in my December 1993 bilateral discussions with Mr. Martin I suggested, as one constructive alternative to simply abandoning the long-run inflation goal, that we could swap targets for a clearer statement of longer-run principles. But I got no response. At the moment, we have more of the opposite: the targets without the principles. It would be better to have both.

Where does this leave us? Early in 2001, in commenting upon the appointment of a new Bank of Canada governor, *The Economist* magazine made reference, naturally enough, to those inflation targets. In particular, it noted that the existing band of 1 to 3 per cent had been "set by Mr. Dodge's predecessors." This is hardly the case. Formally, the targets are set by agreement with the minister of finance. So on that basis, it could just as easily have said that the band had been set by Mr. Martin and his predecessors, and that would also have been truer to the core reality.

That is to say, decisions relating to inflation targets are now effectively in the hands of the federal government, even if it chooses not to advertise the fact. It established this in no uncertain terms in late 1993. In that sense, the situation in Canada is not so very different from that of the United Kingdom (with which one expects *The Economist* to be more familiar), where the Chancellor of the Exchequer hands down the targets. One difference though is that our process is less transparent than theirs. Because it is less transparent, it muddies responsibility for monetary policy. This muddiness is not necessarily unintentional.

While inflation is a tax, even if not an explicit one, there is no need to go so far as to say that sovereign governments have a positive determination to live off inflation. But on the evidence, given the pressures of special interests and the short-run incentives that a government faces (including perhaps in our case providing now for a prime ministerial "political legacy"), this is surely the direction of cumulative bias to be concerned about. From that standpoint at least, it is a salutary discipline for the federal government to accept the constraint of having to set inflation targets publicly and explain them in detail. In other words, it is better than the government having untrammelled control of monetary policy power—that is, inflation power—with no targets at all.

That is the way that the target process seems to have helped in the United Kingdom. There, even though the government had a particularly shaky history of monetary management to live down, giving the Bank of England the authoritative independence actually to formulate monetary policy was never a political option. What the Bank of England did get was the independence to decide on the specific monetary policy actions to take so as to meet targets given to it by the chancellor. But this instrument independence, discussed in Chapter 2, is arguably not so much independence as simply a form of technical subcontracting to a specialized agency. It only becomes interesting as independence if you go a step further and assume that the reason for doing this is because the government would not have the fortitude to aim policy actions at its own declared targets. In that case, the arrangements for the Bank of England represent a particular kind of policy discipline—that is, allotting to the central bank the responsibility for bringing inflation back down to the targets when it drifts away, because the government is tempted to let it keep on drifting, at least on the upside. When we go that far, however, the question that presents itself is why one thinks that government will still have the fortitude to take its targets seriously when they come under pressure. These are political science questions, and challenging ones at that, which I will leave to the professionals in that field.

We have in Canada, to all practical intents, moved to that politically oriented model and the questions to which it gives rise. With the changes that have taken place via the implementation of inflation targets, policy formulation has moved inexorably toward the federal government's control. The Bank may write as much as it wants about inflation, inflation dynamics, and price stability, but as the inflation target renewal exercise demonstrates, it is the government's political decision, not the Bank's voluminous research, or even the actual better-than-target performance over the past decade, that calls the shots for the inflation that is in our future. At the same time, Ottawa chooses not to spell this out. After all, to present the relationship as it really is would eliminate the ability for the government to disclaim responsibility when convenient.

A situation where government is in the driver's seat for setting targets implies that with periodic elections and changing governments, it makes no real sense to talk of longer-run targets. It also makes little sense to talk of, or think about, price stability rather than inflation. In our case, and consistent with this situation, the longer-run provisions of the initial 1991 inflation target agreement—and also any clear references to what that term of political economy art, "price stability," might actually mean—were eliminated by the new government when it came into office in 1993. Recently, the final, lingering, vague references to price stability also got the chop.

More broadly than this, and even ignoring the fact that governments have been well known to promise one thing and do something else (the 1993 Red Book provides some egregious, still-breathing examples), one government cannot bind another. This rules out a lot of credibility from the start. In any case, given the ease with which we have managed to generate inflation in the past, there is something absurdist about having a policy whose avowed purpose is to see to it that the nation's money will be losing its value year in, year out—especially when doing this at a steady rate is promoted as a means of instilling monetary confidence.

What would not be absurd would be to revisit the Bank of Canada's mandate, in this particular instance with a mind to improving its say as regards determining inflation (or should one then say "price stability"?) targets. In that vein, the combination of a mandate grounded in price stability (the government already found the words for this in 1993), together with an open process of agreement on the targets—but where the Bank has, unlike the British case, to sign off on the consistency of the targets with price stability (and so face up to what "price stability" can mean)—would be a formula with some robustness to it.

I do not regard such a development as at all likely. But what just might incline the government to take a deeper view is a late-blooming concern about Canada's monetary credibility on the international side. This was, after all, a consideration that played a decisive role in the drastic fiscal shift for the better that took place in early 1995, through the second Liberal budget.

Ottawa has recently been absorbing the broad lesson that it is a bad idea to have a policy of promoting currency decline. So this lesson, and the desirability of acting on it, may well become more accepted in the future—given the reputation for depreciation and a bias toward depreciation that we have accumulated in recent years. In the mid-1990s, it was arguable that given the drastic turnaround in the federal government's fiscal stance—from ballooning deficits to debt reduction—there was a place for a monetary policy that was easy to the point of pushing the currency down, so long as that policy might stay credible in regard to inflation. This is what it tried to do, borrowing on the monetary credibility achieved earlier and augmented later by the government's own fiscal efforts. Such a need is not there now, and this could also be helpful in firming up Ottawa support for a sturdier monetary policy framework.

More deeply than this, the federal government should by now be catching on to the fact that in our globalized world, national currencies survive less by governmental fiat and more on their merits. And what Canada's recent "dollarization" mini-debate has underlined is that the most enduringly solid feature that a national money can have is to maintain its purchasing value, since this will encourage citizens to hold it. Of the two reasonably convincing ways of doing this—by irrevocably fixing to someone else's currency or by following a policy of domestic monetary integrity—the latter is the more immediately attractive, both economically and politically, if we have the stuff to do it. Our friends in Argentina and Ecuador, for example, chose to try the other route. But we do not have to, at least not yet. So one part of any currency debate (something that looks to be an abiding feature of the Canadian scene) should be whether an independent central bank is needed to provide substance and credibility to a Canadian dollar, whether viewed from within our boundaries or from the outside.

All things considered and despite the limitations, it might conceivably be a good thing for the government to have taken direct responsibility for what happens monetarily, as long as it becomes open about what it has taken on and about the implications. What is lost in central bank "independence" might be gained in monetary involvement from the political arm that is transparent, even if this involvement does not amount to commitment. But what this shift will require to be really convincing is more forthrightness from government as to what it sees as the nation's basic monetary goals, how it plans to live up to them, and correspondingly less hiding behind the Bank of Canada's skirts. This will mean discarding the polite fiction that the Bank has any real say over, and therefore responsibility for, monetary policy formulation—however convenient that story may be for the government and however flattering the Bank of Canada may find it. And if the Government of Canada cannot hack it from a monetary point of view, it could always then dollarize and turn policy over to the Federal Reserve, or redefine the Bank of Canada's role in the way I have just outlined earlier in this section—and for the better.

In the end, countries get the institutions they deserve and the monetary standard they deserve. At about the time I was leaving the Bank, Peter Cook, the long-enduring economic columnist of the *Globe and Mail*, wrote a piece in which he characterized the Bank as "Ottawa's one serious institution." By this, he presumably meant an entity that was not given to chasing after or covering up the latest political shift—or to promising things it would not deliver. He was probably exaggerating; I can think of at least a couple of other Ottawa bodies that ought to fit his bill. Even so, what this kind of thought does point toward is a serious policy responsibility and credibility that has existed in the nation's central bank, that needs more general scrutiny than it has received until now, and that should not be abandoned lightly—certainly not without a better discussion of what is honestly available to take its place.

BIBLIOGRAPHY

ᎾᎨ

List of cited works and documents

Chapter 1: A Question of Purpose

Bank of Canada Act, R.C., C.B.-2, S.1. Preamble.

Bouey, Gerald K., "Monetary Policy—Finding a Place to Stand," 1982 Per Jacobsson Lecture, Toronto, September (Washington: Per Jacobsson Foundation, 1982).

Bryce, Robert B., *Maturing in Hard Times: Canada's Department of Finance Through the Great Depression* (Kingston and Montreal: McGill-Queen's University Press, 1986).

Commission on Money and Credit, *Money and Credit: Their Influence on Jobs, Prices, and Growth* (Englewood Cliffs., N.J.: Prentice-Hall, 1961).

Crow, John W., "The Work of Canadian Monetary Policy," Eric John Hanson Memorial Lecture Series, University of Alberta, January 1988.

Fullerton, Douglas H., *Graham Towers and His Times* (Toronto: McClelland and Stewart, 1986).

Government of Canada, *Canadian Federalism and Economic Union: Partnership for Prosperity* (Ottawa, September 1991).

Greenspan, Alan, "Discussion," *The Future of Central Banking: Tercentenary Symposium of the Bank of England* (Cambridge: Cambridge University Press, 1994).

House of Commons Standing Committee on Finance, Subcommittee on the Bank of Canada, *The Mandate and Governance of the Bank of Canada* (Ottawa, 1992).

Leman, Beaudry, *Memorandum of Dissent*, Report of the Royal Commission on Banking and Currency in Canada (Ottawa, 1933).

Mundell, Robert A., "De la surévaluation du dollar canadien," *Actualité Economique* (March 1991).

Un Québec libre de ses choix, Report of the Constitutional Committee of the Liberal Party of Quebec, January 1991 (mimeo, Bank of Canada library).

Report of the Committee on the Working of the Monetary System (Radcliffe Report) (London, 1959).

Report of the Royal Commission on Banking and Finance (the Porter Commission) (Ottawa, 1964).

"Statement of the Government of Canada and the Bank of Canada on Monetary Policy Objectives," Department of Finance news release, December 22, 1993.

Watts, George S., *The Bank of Canada: Origins and Early History* (Ottawa: Carleton University Press, 1993).

Chapter 2: Putting the Bank in Its Place

Bank of Canada, *Annual Report of the Governor for the Year 1961* (Ottawa, March 1962).

Bank of Canada Act, Section 14.

Blinder, Alan S., "The Federal Reserve in the Nation's Service," Address given at Princeton University, April 26, 1996 (mimeo, Bank of Canada library).

Bryce, Robert B., *Maturing in Hard Times: Canada's Department of Finance Through the Great Depression* (Kingston and Montreal: McGill-Queen's University Press, 1986).

De Long, J. Bradford, "America's Only Peacetime Inflation: The 1970s," *National Bureau of Economic Research, Historical Paper 84* (May 1996).

Fischer, Stanley, "Central Bank Independence Revisited," *American Economics Association Papers and Proceedings* (May 1995).

—, "Modern Central Banking," *The Future of Central Banking: Tercentenary Symposium of the Bank of England* (Cambridge: Cambridge University Press, 1994).

Fortin, Pierre, "The Great Canadian Slump," *The Canadian Journal of Economics* (Vol. 29, No. 4, November 1996).

Fullerton, Douglas H., *Graham Towers and His Times* (Toronto: McClelland and Stewart, 1986).

House of Commons Standing Committee on Finance, Subcommittee on the Bank of Canada, *The Mandate and Governance of the Bank of Canada* (Ottawa, 1992).

Rasminsky, Louis, Letter to the Editor, *Toronto Globe and Mail*, October 3, 1975.

Report of the Royal Commission on Banking and Finance (Porter Commission) (Ottawa, 1964).

Toronto Globe and Mail, March 20, 2001.

Chapter 4: Financial Stability: Doing What a Central Bank Can

Estey, Willard Z., *Report of the Inquiry into the Collapse of the CCB and the Northland Bank* (Ottawa: August 1986).

Kaufman, Henry, "Structural Changes in the Financial Markets: Economic and Policy Significance," Federal Reserve Bank of Kansas City, *Economic Review* (Vol. 79, No. 2, Second Quarter 1994).

Meyer, Laurence H., "An Agenda for Bank Supervision and Regulation" (Board of Governors, Federal Reserve: Washington, D.C.), September 27, 1999.

Chapter 6: Exchange Rate Matters

Crow, John W., "How the Exchange Rate Fits In," *Bank of Canada Review* (September 1992).

Chapter 7: Monetary Policy in the 1970s and 1980s

Bank of Canada, *Annual Report of the Governor for the Year 1989* (Ottawa, March 1990).

Barber, Clarence L., and John C. P. McCallum, *Unemployment and Inflation: The Canadian Experience* (Toronto: James Lorimer & Co., 1980).

Bouey, Gerald K., "Recent Monetary Developments," Remarks to the Business Outlook Conference of the Conference Board of Canada, Toronto, October 11, 1973 (mimeo, Bank of Canada library).

—, Remarks to the 46th Annual Meeting of the Canadian Chamber of Commerce, Saskatoon, September 22, 1975 (mimeo, Bank of Canada library).

Burns, Arthur F., "The Anguish of Central Banking," 1979 Per Jacobsson Lecture, Belgrade, Yugoslavia, September 1979 (Washington: Per Jacobsson Foundation).

Canadian Conference of Catholic Bishops, Ethical Reflections on the Economic Crisis, Ottawa, January 5, 1983 (mimeo, Bank of Canada library).

Crow, John W., "The Bank of Canada and Its Objectives," *Bank of Canada Review* (April 1987).

Department of Finance, Budget Speech delivered by the Honourable John N. Turner, Ottawa: February 19, 1973 (mimeo, Bank of Canada library).

Donner, Arthur W., and Douglas D. Peters, *The Monetarist Counter-Revolution: A Critique of Canadian Monetary Policy 1975–79*, (Toronto: James Lorimer & Co., 1979).

Economic Council of Canada, *Sixth Annual Review: Perspectives 1975* (Ottawa, 1969).

Friedman, Milton, and Anna Jacobson Schwartz, *The Great Contraction: 1929-1933* (Princeton: Princeton University Press, 1965).

Gordon, H. Scott, *The Economists Versus the Bank of Canada* (Toronto: Ryerson Press, 1961).

Laidler, David E. W., and William B. Robson, *The Great Canadian Disinflation: The Economics and Politics of Monetary Policy in Canada, 1988–93* (Toronto: C.D. Howe Institute, 1993).

Muirhead, Bruce, *Against the Odds: The Public Life and Times of Louis Rasminsky* (Toronto: University of Toronto Press, 1999).

The Royal Bank of Canada, Monthly Letter, July 1930 (mimeo, Royal Bank library).

Statement by Canadian Economists, October 21, 1982 (mimeo, Bank of Canada library).

Chapter 8: Creating Inflation Targets

Crow, John W., Press conference on the occasion of a speech to the Greater Moncton Chamber of Commerce, October 24, 1990 (mimeo, Bank of Canada library).

—, "Targeting Monetary Policy," *Bank of Canada Review* (December 1989).

Economic Council of Canada, *Transitions for the 90s: Twenty-Seventh Annual Review* (Ottawa: 1990).

Osberg, Lars, and Pierre Fortin, editors, *Unnecessary Debts* (Toronto: James Lorimer & Co., 1996).

Statement by economists re May 15th rally, "Reclaim Our Future: Make It Work," May 1993 (mimeo, Bank of Canada library).

"Targets for Reducing Inflation," *Bank of Canada Review* (March 1991).

Chapter 9: Fiscal and Monetary Policy: Together and Apart

Bryce, Robert B., *Maturing in Hard Times: Canada's Department of Finance Through the Great Depression* (Kingston and Montreal: McGill-Queen's University Press, 1986).

Department of Finance, "Reducing the Deficit and Controlling the National Debt" (Ottawa: November 1985).

House of Commons Standing Committee on Finance, Subcommittee on the Bank of Canada, Minutes of Proceedings and Evidence, 5:50, December 9, 1991.

Johnson, David R., "An Evaluation of the Bank of Canada Zero Inflation Target: Do Michael Wilson and John Crow Agree?" *Canadian Public Policy* (September 1990).

Rusk, James, "CLC Head Suggested Ontario Default. Rae's Memoirs Cite Fight with White." *Toronto Globe and Mail*, October 8, 1996.

Stokes, Ernie, "Has Monetary Policy Been Too Tight?" *Canadian Business Economics* (1:1, Fall 1992).

White, Bob, Letter to the Editor, *Toronto Globe and Mail*, October 10, 1996.

Chapter 10: A New Monetary Policy?

Bank of Canada for Canadians Coalition, open letter to Mr. Chrétien, November 1, 1993 (mimeo, Bank of Canada library).

Creating Opportunity: The Liberal Plan for Canada (Ottawa: The Liberal Party of Canada, September 1993).

Greenspon, Edward, and Harvey Enchin, "I Am Constant as the Northern Star," *Toronto Globe and Mail*, September 1, 1990.

"Joint Statement of the Government of Canada and the Bank of Canada on the Extension of the Inflation Control Targets," Department of Finance news release, February 24, 1998.

Laidler, David, "Editor's Introduction," in *Where We Go From Here: Inflation Targets in Canada's Monetary Policy Regime* (Toronto: C.D. Howe Institute, 1997).

Mankiw, N. Gregory, "U.S. Monetary Policy During the 1990s," National Bureau of Economic Research, Working Paper No. 8471, September 2001.

Sargent, Thomas J., and Neil Wallace, "Some Unpleasant Monetarist Arithmetic," Federal Reserve Bank of Minneapolis, *Quarterly Review*, Vol. 5, No. 3 (Fall 1981).

Viner, Jacob, "Mr. Keynes on the Causes of Unemployment," *Quarterly Journal of Economics* (Harvard University: November 1936).

C.D. Howe Institute, *Where We Go from Here: Inflation Targets in Canada's Monetary Policy Regime* (Toronto: 1997).

White, Bob, Letter to the Editor, *The Economist*, September 21, 1996.

Chapter 11: Financial Futures

Bank of Canada, "The Implementation of Monetary Policy in the Absence of Reserve Requirements," *Discussion Paper No. 1* (Ottawa: September 30, 1987).

Bank of Canada, "Notice Concerning the Implementation of Monetary Policy in a System with Zero Reserve Requirements," *Bank of Canada Review* (September 1991).

Cook, Peter, "Ottawa's One Serious Institution," *Toronto Globe and Mail*, January 6, 1994.

Dodge, David, "Trust, Transparency, and Financial Markets," Remarks to the Greater Halifax Partnership, Halifax, June 11, 2002 (Bank of Canada website).

"Dodging Downdrafts," *The Economist*, January 27, 2001.

INDEX

ᙡᙠ